IN THE VALE OF TRALEE

In the Vale of Tralee

The archaeology of the N22 Tralee Bypass

Edited by
Patricia Long, Paul O'Keeffe and Isabel Bennett

With contributions by
Louise Baker, Katharina Becker, Lyndsey Clark, Eoin Grogan,
James Hession, Stephen Hourihan, Patricia Long,
Enda O'Flaherty, Scott Timpany and Carmelita Troy

TII Heritage 9

First published in 2020 by
Transport Infrastructure Ireland
Parkgate Business Centre, Parkgate Street, Dublin 8, D08 DK10

Library of Congress Cataloguing-in-Publication Data are available for this book.
A CIP catalogue record for this book is available from the British Library.

Material from Ordnance Survey Ireland is reproduced with the permission of the Government of Ireland and Ordnance Survey Ireland under permit number EN0045220.

Paperback 978-1-911633-19-8
ePub 978-1-911633-20-4
ISSN 2009-8480
TII Heritage 9

Copy-editing: Wordwell Ltd
Cover design, typesetting and layout: Wordwell Ltd
Index: Geraldine Begley

Printed by: Graficas Castuera, Pamplona

Front and back cover — The N22 Tralee Bypass in Ballybeggan, with an early medieval ringfort (RMP KE029-124) in the foreground. Only four fields away a similar, but previously undocumented, ringfort at Ballinorig West 2 was discovered on the route of the bypass. View to south-west towards Tralee, and beyond to the Slieve Mish Mountains, Tralee Bay and the Dingle Peninsula (Laurence Dunne Archaeology).

Spine image — Early medieval glass bead recovered from a sink-hole at Knockawaddra West 2.

CONTENTS

FOREWORD

The N22 Tralee Bypass is the largest infrastructure investment in County Kerry in recent years. It amounts to a major and lasting change in the local landscape, with many benefits for the quality of life in the town and its hinterland. By connecting four of the five national routes that terminate in Tralee (N21, N22, N69 and N70), the new road provides a safer road network and reduces journey times between the town and other destinations. In removing unnecessary traffic from the town centre, the new road helps to preserve its character of place and its attractiveness as a destination. It includes 9 km of walkway/cycleway, in keeping with a new generation of roads designed for a greater variety of transport modes, and thus promotes personal health as well as transport efficiency and safety.

The Tralee Bypass project has also given us a greater understanding of the early history and prehistory of the area, informed by the archaeological investigations that were carried out along the route in advance of construction. The primary element of these investigations was a systematic programme of test excavations throughout the greenfield lands (86 ha) acquired for the project. Thirty-three previously unknown archaeological sites were discovered and excavated by Rubicon Heritage Ltd and Irish Archaeological Consultancy Ltd. The excavations produced evidence for c. 6,000 years of human occupation in the valley of the River Lee and its catchment area, representing all facets of life. Here we see people building homes and organising a productive landscape of field boundaries, grain stores and droveways. We also obtain glimpses of how this landscape was conceptualised in prehistory as a sacred place, where the ancestors and the gods were never far from daily life. In its volume and variety this evidence provides a deep foundation for future archaeological research in the area and is of lasting importance as a contribution to the heritage of County Kerry.

Of course, the full value of the archaeological investigations can only be realised when we make the results available to the public. This is why, in collaboration with Kerry County Council and other local authorities, dissemination is an integral part of our approach to archaeology on TII-funded projects. Within a year of completing the Tralee excavations in 2011, articles describing the key findings appeared in the *Journal of the Kerry Archaeological and Historical Society*. In 2014 a public seminar was organised in partnership with the Kerry County Museum in Tralee, where many of the artefacts recovered from the bypass excavations were put on temporary display. This book is the culmination of that process. It is an accessible and attractive publication and this is a credit to the authors, to the editors, Patricia Long, Paul O'Keeffe and Isabel Bennett, and to the designers, Nick Maxwell and his team at Wordwell Ltd. We offer them our warm congratulations and hope that you will enjoy their art and work.

Peter Walsh
Chief Executive
Transport Infrastructure Ireland

NOTE ON ACCESSING FINAL REPORTS AND SUPPORTING DATA

The final excavation reports for all of the archaeological sites excavated on the N22 Tralee Bypass have been published on-line in the TII Digital Heritage Collections hosted by the Digital Repository of Ireland (DRI). The reports can be accessed on the DRI website by searching for 'TII Digital Heritage Collections' in an internet search engine or by entering this link https://repository.dri.ie/catalog/v6936m966 into an internet browser. This will bring you to the TII Digital Heritage Collections homepage. The easiest way to download a specific excavation report is to enter the relevant excavation registration number listed in Table A (e.g. E4296) into the 'Search' box on the homepage. This will open a new window with an embedded image of the excavation report. Clicking on the embedded report image opens another window from which the report can be downloaded.

The geophysical survey reports for the project have also been published in the TII Digital Heritage Collections and can be accessed by entering their respective survey registration numbers in the 'Search' box on the homepage—R0277 (Harrison 2010) and 11R33 (Bonsall 2011).

An Excel spreadsheet of the radiocarbon dates obtained for all of the archaeological sites excavated on the project can be accessed by searching for 'A056_N22 Tralee Bypass Radiocarbon Dates' on the homepage.

Table A—List of final excavation reports available for download from the TII Digital Heritage Collections.

Site (excavation registration no.)	Site description	Excavation director (report author(s))
Ballindooganig 1 (E4296)	Late Neolithic/Copper Age burnt mounds	James Hession (Carmelita Troy)
Ballindooganig 2 (E4316)	Post-medieval limekiln	James Hession (Carmelita Troy and Lyndsey Clark)
Ballingowan 1 (E4288)	Multi-period site: Late Neolithic/Early Bronze Age double pit alignment; pit containing Beaker pottery; Bronze Age settlement areas, enclosure, cereal-drying kiln and droveway; Iron Age metal-working; early medieval building and cereal-drying kiln	Tony Bartlett (Colm Moloney)
Ballinorig South 1 & 2 (E4303 & E4304)	Late Neolithic/Copper Age trough and pits	James Hession (Carmelita Troy)
Ballinorig West 1 (E4307)	Multi-period burnt mounds: Late Neolithic/Copper Age; Early Bronze Age; Middle Bronze Age	James Hession (Lyndsey Clark)
Ballinorig West 2 (E4306)	Multi-period site: Neolithic and Bronze Age occupation; early medieval bivallate enclosure	James Hession (Lyndsey Clark)
Ballinorig West 3 (E4317)	Multi-period site: Early Bronze Age cremation burial; early medieval cereal-drying kiln	James Hession (Lyndsey Clark and Carmelita Troy)
Ballinorig West 4 (E4305)	Multi-period site: Bronze Age pit; Iron Age penannular ring-ditch, cremation burials and industrial activity; early medieval iron-smelting furnace and cereal-drying kilns; post-medieval limekiln	James Hession (Stephen Hourihan)
Ballynabrennagh Lower 1 (E4297)	Multi-period site: Middle Bronze Age round-house; Iron Age pits	Tony Bartlett (Stephen Hourihan)
Caherleheen 1 (E4309)	Late Neolithic burnt mound	Liam McKinstry (Stephen Hourihan)
Caherleheen 2 (E4310)	Non-archaeological	Tony Bartlett (Stephen Hourihan)

continued overleaf

Table A (continued)—List of final excavation reports available for download from the TII Digital Heritage Collections.

Site (excavation registration no.)	Site description	Excavation director (report author(s))
Camp 1 (E4311)	Multi-period site: Middle and Late Bronze Age burnt mounds; post-medieval brick clamps	Liam McKinstry (Stephen Hourihan)
Camp 2 (E4308)	Bronze Age burnt mound	Liam McKinstry (Stephen Hourihan)
Camp 4 (E4313)	Late Neolithic/Copper Age burnt mound	Liam McKinstry (Stephen Hourihan)
Camp 5 (E4318)	Multi-period site: Late Bronze Age burnt mound; post-medieval brick-production waste	Tony Bartlett (Stephen Hourihan)
Clashedmond 1 (E4289)	Multi-period site: Middle–Late Bronze Age pits and post-holes; enclosure; post-medieval townland boundary	Liam McKinstry (Carmelita Troy)
Dromavally 1 (E4314)	Post-medieval limekilns	Liam McKinstry (Stephen Hourihan and Lyndsey Clark)
Dromavally 2 (E4315)	Copper Age/Early Bronze Age burnt mound	Liam McKinstry (Stephen Hourihan)
Dromthacker 1 (E4298)	Early Bronze Age trough, pit and hearth	James Hession (Carmelita Troy)
Dromthacker 2 (E4299)	Early medieval hearth	James Hession (Carmelita Troy)
Gortbrack East 1 (E4300)	Early medieval charcoal-production pit	James Hession (Stephen Hourihan)
Gortbrack East 2 (E4301)	Burnt spread, pits, post-hole and stake-holes	James Hession (Stephen Hourihan)
Gortbrack East 3 (E4302)	Early Bronze Age burnt mound	James Hession (Stephen Hourihan)
Knockawaddra Middle 1 (E4294)	Multi-period site: Middle Bronze Age burnt mound; post-medieval limekiln	Tony Bartlett (Stephen Hourihan)
Knockawaddra Middle 2 (E4295)	Multi-period site: Middle–Late Bronze Age houses; early medieval building	Tony Bartlett (Stephen Hourihan and Lyndsey Clark)
Knockawaddra West 1 (E4293)	Middle–Late Bronze Age burnt mound	Tony Bartlett (Stephen Hourihan)
Knockawaddra West 2 (E4292)	Sink-hole containing cultural material: flint debitage; Middle Bronze Age burnt animal bone; iron slag; early medieval glass bead	Tony Bartlett (Stephen Hourihan)
Lismore 1 (E4290)	Post-medieval vernacular buildings and limekiln	Tony Bartlett (Carmelita Troy)
Lismore 2 (E4291)	Late Bronze Age burnt mound	Tony Bartlett (Carmelita Troy)
Manor East 1 (E4323)	Multi-period site: Early Neolithic house; Middle–Late Neolithic pits; Middle Bronze Age cremation burials; Late Bronze Age building; Iron Age pits and possible structure; early medieval pits and hearth	Liam McKinstry (Lyndsey Clark)
Manor East 2 (E4322)	Multi-period site: Neolithic pits; Iron Age pits, post-holes and stake-holes	Liam McKinstry (Stephen Hourihan)
Manor East 3 (E4321)	Non-archaeological	Liam McKinstry (Stephen Hourihan)
Manor East 4 (E4328)	Multi-period site: Early Neolithic pits; Early Bronze Age hearth; former stream channel containing late medieval wooden stakes	James Kyle (Shane Delaney)
Manor East 7 (E4330)	Three deposits (one of stone and two of stone and timber) forming crossing points over a former stream channel; one dated to the early medieval period	David Bayley (Shane Delaney)
Poulawaddra 1 (E4320)	Non-archaeological	Liam McKinstry (Carmelita Troy)
Poulawaddra 3 (E4319)	Non-archaeological	Liam McKinstry (Carmelita Troy)

ACKNOWLEDGEMENTS

The investigations described in this book were funded by the Irish government under the National Development Plan 2007–2013 and the Transport 21 programme and were commissioned by Kerry County Council on behalf of the National Roads Authority, now Transport Infrastructure Ireland (TII).

Ministerial directions were provided by the Department of Environment, Heritage and Local Government, represented by Mark Keegan of the National Monuments Service, in consultation with the National Museum of Ireland.

The Kerry National Road Design Office Engineers were Tracy Smith (Senior Executive Engineer), Declan O'Mahony (Resident Engineer) and James Sayers (Resident Engineer).

The TII Archaeologists were James Eogan (Senior Archaeologist), Sébastien Joubert (Project Archaeologist) and Paul O'Keeffe (Project Archaeologist). Thanks to Jerry O'Sullivan for reading and commenting on a draft version of this work.

The engineering consultant for the project was Halcrow Barry Ltd. The Halcrow Barry team consisted of Liam Prendiville (Project Manager), Ernie Crawford (Employer's Representative) and John Condon (Senior Resident Engineer). ASM Group acted as Project Supervisor for the Construction Stage for the archaeological investigations.

The Environmental Impact Statement (EIS) was prepared by Atkins. The Archaeology and Cultural Heritage chapter of the EIS was prepared by Sheila Lane and Associates.

Rubicon Heritage Services Ltd (formerly Headland Archaeology Ireland Ltd) carried out the archaeological excavations on the bypass route, except for excavations in two wetland areas. The project was managed for Rubicon by Senior Archaeologist Patricia Long, with logistical assistance from Stephen Hourihan and George Morgan, and health and safety co-ordination from James Gubbins. The excavation directors were James Hession, Tony Bartlett and Liam McKinstry, who were assisted by excavation supervisors Marie Bartlett, Ken Smith, Martin McGowan, Philip Kenny, Deirdre Walsh and John Olney and a team of over 50 excavation assistants. Architectural and site survey was overseen by Brian McDomhnaill and undertaken by Daniel Yates and Seamus O'Donovan. Geophysical survey was undertaken for Rubicon by Scott Harrison, with further survey carried out by James Bonsall of Earthsound Archaeological Geophysics. The illustrations for the project reports and for this book were prepared by Jonathan Millar, Hannah Simms and Sara Nylund. Damian Shiels reviewed excavation reports and drafts of this book. Also involved in the post-excavation stage were Carmelita Troy (post-excavation co-ordination), Lyndsey Clark, Stephen Hourihan and Colm Moloney (excavation report writing). Underwater surveys were carried out by Moore Marine Services Ltd. Aerial photography was carried out by Aerialphoto.ie. Plant was provided by Cronin Plant Hire Ltd of Currow.

Irish Archaeological Consultancy Ltd (IAC) carried out two excavations on the bypass route. The project was managed for IAC by Shane Delaney. The excavation directors were James Kyle and David Bayley, who were assisted by excavation supervisor Eoghan Barret and a team of eight excavation assistants.

Dan Noonan Archaeological Consultancy acted as archaeological advisers to the main contractor, BAM Civil Ltd, during the construction phase.

Artefact conservation was undertaken by Susannah Kelly. Specialist analyses were undertaken by Carmelita Troy, Claudia Tommasino Suárez, Damian Shiels, Maurice Hurley, Margaret Mannion, Cecily Cropper, Farina Sternke, Richard Unitt, Miriam Carroll, Katharina Becker, Barry Cosham, Niamh Doyle, Eoin Grogan, Helen Roche, Richard O'Brien, Ellen O Carroll, Abby Mynett, Laura Scott, Eileen Reilly,† Bettina Stefanini and Scott Timpany. Radiocarbon dating was carried out by the Scottish Universities Environmental Research Centre and the ^{14}CHRONO Centre (QUB).

Thanks to Michael Connolly, Kerry County Archaeologist, for supplying information and images during the course of the work. Kerry County Museum kindly provided a venue for a seminar on the results of the excavation in 2014. Thanks to James Herriott for use of his aerial photograph in Chapter 1. Thanks also to Fiachra Dunne of Laurence Dunne Archaeology who provided the aerial photograph used on the cover of this book. Laurence Dunne Archaeology also provided an image for Chapter 1.

1
INTRODUCTION

Patricia Long

Illus. 1.1—Aerial view of Tralee town and bay, view to west (John Herriott Aerial Photography).

Tralee is the largest town in County Kerry. It is situated at the confluence of the Big River and the River Lee, just at the neck of the Dingle Peninsula, where the Lee estuary begins to widen into Tralee Bay (Illus. 1.1). The urban area is medieval in origin, while the surrounding countryside has a rich and varied cultural heritage dating from prehistoric times. The construction of the N22 Tralee Bypass and the Tralee to Bealagrellagh Link Road provided a rare opportunity to explore this heritage through large-scale archaeological investigation, the results of which are presented in this volume (Illus. 1.2).

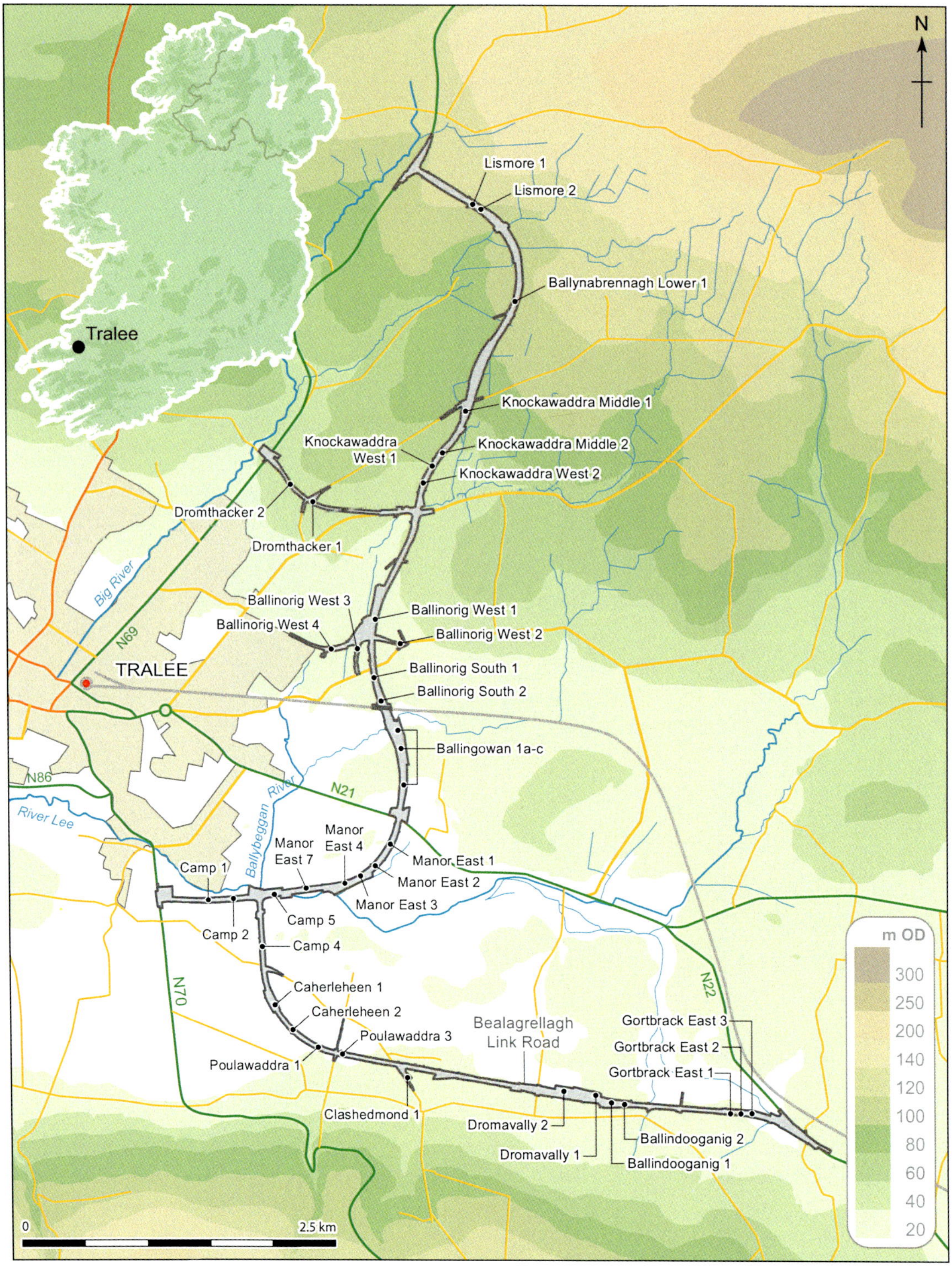

Illus. 1.2—Excavated archaeological sites on the N22 Tralee Bypass.

Project background

The N22 Tralee Bypass comprises 8 km of dual carriageway, extending southwards from its junction with the N69 Listowel Road in Lissatanvally as far as the townland of Camp, where it connects with the N70 Castlemaine Road. It also links national routes converging on the town from Limerick (N21) and Cork (N22) and provides improved access to the N86 Dingle Road. The Bealagrellagh Link Road is a single carriageway of some 5.5 km that provides an alternative access to Tralee for traffic coming from the south. In this volume the entire route, including the link road, is referred to simply as the Tralee Bypass.

Following route selection, an Environmental Impact Statement (EIS) was prepared by Atkins (2008) on behalf of Kerry County Council, and the proposed road development was subsequently approved by An Bord Pleanála (Ref. PL08.HA0016) in September 2009. Archaeological fieldwork was carried out in 2010 and 2011. Construction of the road by BAM Civil Ltd started in July 2011 and the route was officially opened by Jimmy Deenihan TD, Minister for Arts, Heritage and the Gaeltacht, in August 2013.

Archaeological investigations

The Archaeological and Cultural Heritage chapter of the EIS was prepared by Sheila Lane and Associates and provided an assessment of the preferred route and its impact on the receiving archaeological, architectural and cultural heritage environment. This concluded that the bypass would affect the setting and environs of five archaeological monuments that are listed on the Record of Monuments and Places (RMP)—an enclosure (KE029-292), a ring-barrow (KE029-258), a burnt mound (KE029-257), an enclosure, field system and field boundary (KE029-122) and an enclosure and field boundaries (KE029-160). The EIS also highlighted direct impacts on three architectural heritage features—a demesne wall (Ballybeggan and Ballinorig West), a forge and a pump bay (both in Dromthacker).

The EIS recommendations formed the basis of a programme of archaeological investigation undertaken by Headland Archaeology (Ireland) Ltd (now Rubicon Heritage Services Ltd) and Irish Archaeological Consultancy Ltd in advance of road construction. The investigations were carried out under Ministerial Directions issued by the Minister for the Environment, Heritage and Local Government, in consultation with the National Museum of Ireland, and in accordance with Section 14A (2) of the National Monuments Acts (1930–2004) (Ministerial Directions No. A056).

A programme of test excavations was conducted between August and September 2010 to determine the presence or otherwise of subsurface archaeological remains within the road footprint. Mechanical excavators, working under constant archaeological supervision, were used to open a regular array of test trenches throughout the lands acquired for the road (Illus. 1.3). Site-specific test trenching was carried out at the location of the five RMP sites listed in the EIS (Long 2010a–e). No remains associated with the RMP sites were identified except for a pit that may have been associated with an enclosure at Knockawaddra West. In addition, 15 areas (7.62 ha) were

Illus. 1.3—Archaeological test excavations, under constant archaeological supervision, were opened throughout the route of the N22 Tralee Bypass (Rubicon Heritage Services Ltd).

targeted for geophysical survey (Harrison 2010), while wade surveys to search for underwater features and objects were conducted at 10 locations where the new road crossed a river/stream, including the Ballybeggan and Lee river crossings (Kieran & Hayden 2010). Twenty-three townland boundaries crossed by the new road were also recorded, as were the three architectural heritage sites identified in the EIS and a stone culvert identified by test excavations (Bartlett et al. 2010). Deep riverine and peat deposits in the River Lee floodplain and adjacent to a stream in Gortbrack East were investigated via a series of test pits (ibid.).

The test excavations resulted in the discovery of 41 potential archaeological sites. Upon further investigation, it was determined that two of these were of no archaeological significance (Poulawaddra 2 and Camp 3); another two (Manor East 5 and 6) comprised only stray pieces of ancient wood and one—a post-medieval wall near Bealagrellagh Castle—could be preserved *in situ*. The remaining 36 sites were confirmed as being of possible archaeological significance. A further site at Camp 5 was subsequently revealed during additional test excavations (Joubert 2010), bringing to 37 the total number of sites recommended for excavation. Each site was named after the townland in which it was situated and, where there was more than one site in a particular townland, numbers were assigned according to the order in which the sites were found. Excavations at 35 sites were carried out by Headland Archaeology (Ireland) Ltd between January and April 2011.

Table 1.1—Archaeological sites excavated on the N22 Tralee Bypass, listed from north to south (abbreviations: Reg. No. = registration number, Mes = Mesolithic, Neo = Neolithic, LN = Late Neolithic, CU = Copper Age, Br = Bronze Age, IA = Iron Age, EM = early medieval, LM = late medieval, PM = post-medieval, Mod = modern).

Site name	Reg. No.	Mes/ Neo	Neo	LN/ CU	CU/ Br	Br	Br/ IA	Iron Age	IA/ EM	EM	LM	PM/ Mod
Lismore 1	E4290											■
Lismore 2	E4291					■						■
Ballynabrennagh Lower 1	E4297					■		■				■
Knockawaddra Middle 1	E4294					■						■
Knockawaddra Middle 2	E4295		■			■				■		■
Knockawaddra West 1	E4293					■						
Knockawaddra West 2	E4292					■				■		
Dromthacker 1	E4298					■						
Dromthacker 2	E4299									■		
Ballinorig West 1	E4307			■		■						
Ballinorig West 2	E4306		■			■				■		
Ballinorig West 3	E4317					■				■		
Ballinorig West 4	E4305					■		■	■	■		■
Ballinorig South 1	E4303			■								
Ballinorig South 2	E4304	No datable material										
Ballingowan 1	E4288		■		■	■	■	■		■		
Manor East 1	E4323	■	■			■	■	■		■		■
Manor East 2	E4322		■					■				
Manor East 4	E4328		■			■					■	
Manor East 7	E4330									■		
Camp 5	E4318					■	■					■
Camp 2	E4308					■						
Camp 1	E4311					■						■
Camp 4	E4313			■								
Caherleheen 1	E4309		■									
Clashedmond 1	E4289					■				■ ?		■
Dromavally 2	E4315				■							
Dromavally 1	E4314											■
Ballindooganig 1	E4296			■								
Ballindooganig 2	E4316											■
Gortbrack East 1	E4300									■		
Gortbrack East 2	E4301					■ ?						
Gortbrack East 3	E4302					■						

Two sites on the northern floodplain of the River Lee (Manor East 4 and 7) were excavated by Irish Archaeological Consultancy Ltd in April 2011. During the excavation phase, four of the sites were deemed to be non-archaeological in nature: Manor East 3 (E4321), Caherleheen 2 (E4310), Poulawaddra 1 (E4320) and Poulawaddra 3 (E4319). The excavated sites represent most periods of human life in the hinterland of Tralee, from early prehistory to modern times (Table 1.1).

During the post-excavation phase, a range of materials was examined by specialists, including environmental remains from soil samples (i.e. pollen spores, insects, plant remains, wood and wood charcoal), human and animal bone, metal-working debris, prehistoric pottery and chipped-stone tools, early medieval glass and stone objects, and post-medieval pottery, clay pipes, glass and brick. Artefact conservation was carried out on fragile items and those likely to deteriorate following excavation, such as the prehistoric burial urn fragments from Manor East 1 and various metal objects. Ninety-three radiocarbon dates were obtained from samples of charred plant remains and bone at the Scottish Universities Environmental Research Centre (SUERC) and the ^{14}CHRONO Centre at Queen's University Belfast (Appendix 1). Detailed results of the specialist analyses and radiocarbon dating are presented as appendices in the final excavation reports (as listed in Table A), which are available for download in PDF format from the TII Digital Heritage Collections (https://repository.dri.ie/catalog/v6936m966).

The total greenfield area of the road project was 86 ha. Thirty-three archaeological sites were identified and excavated, which is one site per 2.6 ha of the project area. The combined area of the excavated sites was 9.3 ha, or c. 11% of the greenfield land acquired. Of particular note was the density of archaeology, particularly prehistoric archaeology, detected in the townlands of Ballingowan and Manor East. Two very large sites (Ballingowan 1 and Manor East 1) extended for an almost continuous 1 km stretch of the route, with a further three sites (Manor East 2, 4 and 7) located nearby. These archaeological remains were situated on a south-facing valley slope, bounded to the south by the River Lee floodplain and to the north by a small stream. The landscape between the two watercourses is punctuated by outcropping limestone bedrock, with flatter, soil-rich areas in between. Larger, more pronounced outcrops of limestone (known as reefs) are present just outside the bypass route to the north-west. While the individual elements of these sites are noteworthy, it is the density and continuity of remains in this area that make it stand out from the rest of the project. By contrast, a much lower density of archaeology was uncovered on the higher ground at the northern end of the route (from the stream in Ballingowan to the N69 Listowel Road). Archaeological discoveries were relatively evenly distributed along the undulating ground that characterised the link road to Bealagrellagh. The excavated sites represented a broad spectrum of activity from the Late Mesolithic/Early Neolithic transition to the post-medieval period, though with a notable scarcity of later medieval sites.

Chronology

While ongoing research is constantly refining the dates for important transitions between archaeological periods, for the purposes of consistency the following chronological periods are

Period	Dates
Early Mesolithic	8000 BC–6700? BC
Late Mesolithic	6700? BC–4000? BC
Early Neolithic	4000? BC–3400 BC
Middle Neolithic	3400 BC–3000 BC
Late Neolithic	3000 BC–2400 BC
Copper Age	2400 BC–2200 BC
Early Bronze Age	2200 BC–1600 BC
Middle Bronze Age	1600 BC–1100 BC
Late Bronze Age	1100 BC–700 BC
Early Iron Age	700 BC–400 BC
Developed Iron Age	400 BC–1 BC/AD
Late Iron Age	1 BC/AD–AD 400
Early medieval	AD 400–c. AD 1169
Late medieval	c. AD 1169–AD 1540
Post-medieval	AD 1540–AD 1700

Table 1.2—Chronological divisions used throughout this volume.

used throughout this book (Table 1.2; after Eogan and Shee Twohig 2011).

The radiocarbon dates obtained for all sites along the route are presented in Appendix 1. Radiocarbon dates cited in the text are calendrical dates calibrated to two-sigma (95.4%) levels of confidence. All dates cited in the text are radiocarbon dates unless otherwise stated.

Physical environment

The new road is mostly located within the Lee Valley, a relatively flat, low-lying agricultural landscape nestled between the Stack's and Slieve Mish mountains. The northern portion of the route, between Lissatanvally and Knockawaddra, rises to c. 120 m OD (Ordnance Datum) where it skirts the foothills of the Stack's Mountains. Further south it soon falls to around 20 m OD as it descends to the valley floor and the River Lee floodplain. The land throughout is generally used for grass pasture with dispersed farmsteads. Parts of the Lee floodplain have been reclaimed and are also under pasture, with wetter areas supporting rough pasture.

On the northern half of the route, the land is well drained with occasional limestone outcropping (Illus. 1.4). Peat and alluvial deposits have formed in the seasonally waterlogged floodplain of the River Lee (which was much more extensive prior to channelling), while south of the river, along the link road, the land is undulating with occasional marshy pockets.

The majority of rock formations in and around Tralee are Lower Carboniferous (Dinantian) and Middle Carboniferous (Namurian) in origin (Atkins 2008, 122). The main formations underlying the route, from north to south, include black shales and sandstone (Namurian), unbedded pale grey limestone (Cracoean Reef), massive limestones (Waulsortian Formation) and dark grey limestone and black mudstone (Ballysteen Formation) (ibid.).

The predominant soil association present along the route comprises gleys and peaty gleys (ibid., 214) (Illus. 1.5). These are heavy soils with a limited use-range and are suited to grassland rather than tillage. Brown earths, grey-brown podzolics and gleys occur over two small sections of the route. This soil association occurs widely in limestone areas throughout the country and is suitable for a variety of farming activities owing to its depth, free drainage and good moisture-holding capacity (ibid.).

Illus. 1.4—Limestone outcropping at Ballingowan. Similar outcropping was encountered in Manor East. Rocky elevations were favoured for funerary and settlement sites in the prehistory of the Tralee area (Rubicon Heritage Services Ltd).

Archaeological background

Until the mid-1990s very little was known about prehistoric human activity in the Tralee area, but discoveries during development-led excavations since then have changed this picture radically. We now have evidence of human activity from at least 6,000 years ago in the Lee Valley.

Neolithic period

There is some evidence, such as the coastal settlement site at An Baile Uachtarach Theas (Ferriter's Cove; Woodman et al. 1999), that Mesolithic settlers did penetrate into south-west Ireland, but the earliest known sites in the immediate vicinity of the bypass date from the Neolithic period. These include a passage tomb at Ballycarty (KE038-074), less than 2 km to the east (Illus. 1.6), which forms part of a significant prehistoric complex situated on a limestone reef (Connolly 1999; 2008). The tomb was discovered and excavated in 1996, revealing the remains of an overlying cairn set within a circular stone enclosure and fronted by an unusual curved façade or court (Connolly 1999). It is the most westerly passage tomb known in Ireland and the only one so far identified in County Kerry. About 1 km to the west, at Ballyseedy, is an earthen embanked enclosure which is 50 m in diameter (KE038-093). Such large embanked enclosures are thought likely to be ceremonial sites of Late Neolithic or Early Bronze Age date (e.g. Waddell 2010, 173).

During a survey of the Lee Valley, Connolly (2008, 133) identified 283 monuments suggested to be prehistoric in date. While these monuments are likely to span the prehistoric period, a number of henges, embanked enclosures, cairns, burnt mounds and barrows are likely to be

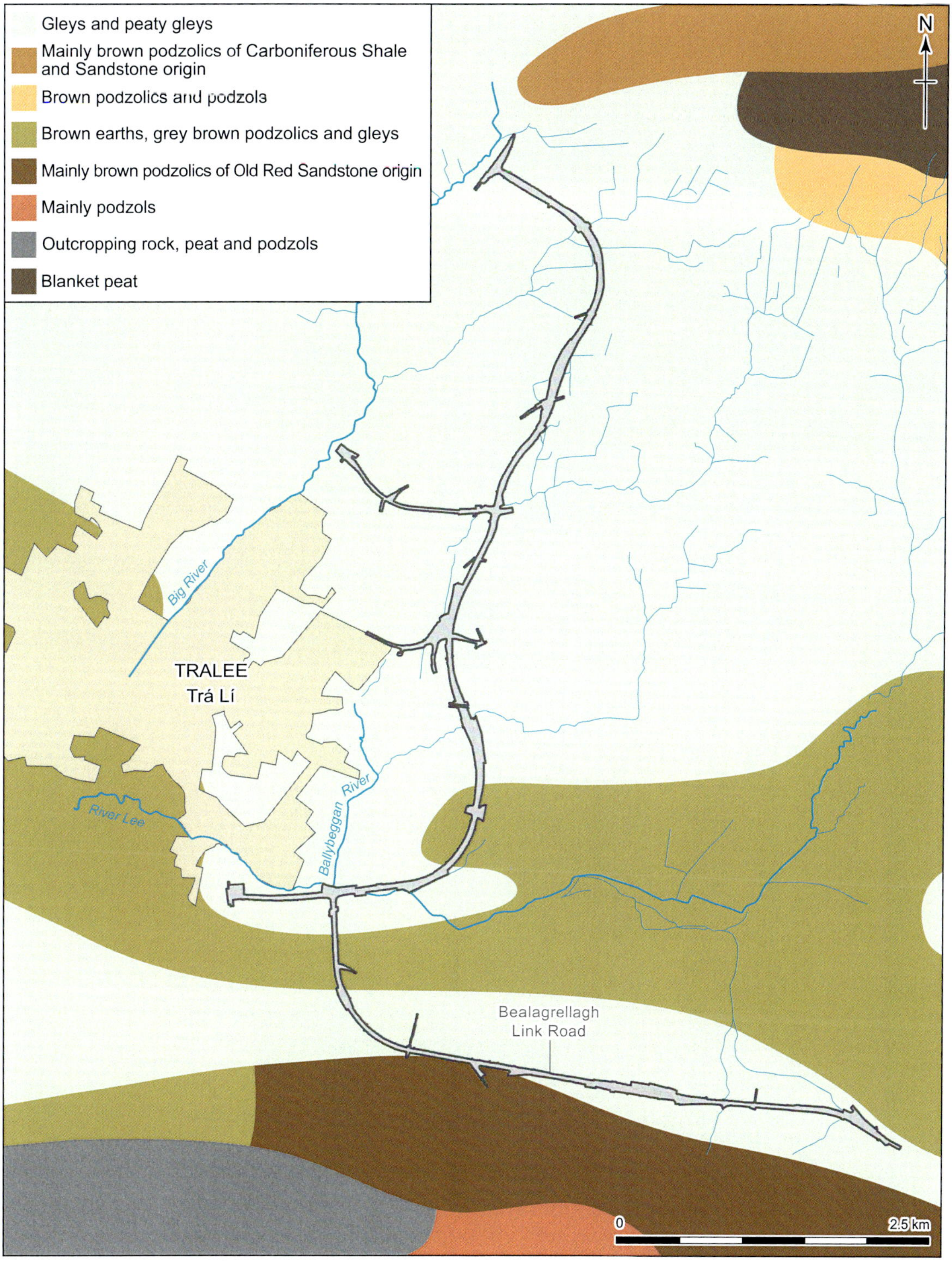

Illus. 1.5—Major soil types along the route of the new road (based on the National Soil Survey (NSS) General Soil Map of Ireland at 1:575,000).

Illus. 1.6—Aerial view of Ballycarty passage tomb complex (RMP KE038-074). This monument is less than 2 km east of the N22 Tralee Bypass (Michael Connolly, Kerry County Council).

Neolithic in date. Most of the sites are located to the south and within 2 km of the River Lee, with the greatest concentrations occurring in Ballycarty, Ballyseedy and Camp, at the point where the river bends to take its westward course to the sea. The presence of archaeological features on 80% of the limestone outcrops surveyed by Connolly indicates a preference for elevated positions within what is otherwise a relatively flat landscape (ibid.).

At Cloghers, just south of Tralee, an Early Neolithic rectangular house was excavated on the southern side of the River Lee (Kiely 2000), while further evidence of Neolithic settlement was discovered during various development-led excavations on the outskirts of the town at Mounthawk, Ballyvelly and Manor West (Dunne & Kiely 2005, 56; Dunne 1999; Dunne & Kiely 2005, 59). These sites are discussed further in Chapter 4.

Bronze Age

Burnt mounds are the most commonly discovered archaeological monuments in the country and are usually dated to the Bronze Age. There are 77 such sites known from the records of the Archaeological Survey of Ireland within 5 km of the bypass route. Other indications of possible Bronze Age activity in this area include eight standing stones, such as those in Camp (KE038-102) and Caherbreagh (KE029-263). Standing stones functioned as prehistoric burial markers, commemorative monuments and indicators of routeways or boundaries. There are 18 barrows and 11 ring-ditches (excluding KE029-258, which was investigated during the present project and found to be of no archaeological significance) recorded in the area, and some of these are likely to be Bronze Age burial monuments. There are also several undated cairns, mounds, earthworks and enclosures, at least some of which may represent prehistoric burial and/or settlement. Stray artefacts found over the years are a further indicator of Bronze Age activity. Some are likely to be the result of deliberate deposition of high-status or ceremonial objects, such as a hoard of six bronze horns from a bog in Clogherclemin, east of Tralee (Eogan 1983, 91).

In recent years, archaeological investigations prompted by the expansion of Tralee town have yielded numerous archaeological finds, many of which date from the prehistoric period. Several sites produced remains of domestic life, such as five prehistoric pits and a saddle quern and rubbing stone at Buntaloon (Dunne & Kiely 2005, 45). Bronze Age round-houses have been recorded at sites such as Cloghers (ibid.), Ballingowan (Dunne & Buckley 2010) and Killierisk (Lynch 2010). The burial practices of Bronze Age people have also been seen, with cremation burials at sites such as Ballingowan (Dunne & Buckley 2010) and a ring-barrow at Gortatlea/Flemby (Coyne 2002).

Iron Age

Evidence for the Iron Age in the Tralee area, although not plentiful, is being increasingly identified by development-led excavations. Perhaps most significantly, trial trenching at a bivallate hillfort in Knockanacuig/Lohercannan (KE029-112), on the south-west side of Tralee, has confirmed that it is Iron Age in date (Dunne & Bartlett 2009). Measuring 140 m by 135 m overall, this is likely to have been a high-status settlement enclosure. In the adjacent townland of Ballyvelly, a possible crematorium and associated burials were found to have had Iron Age phases of use (Dunne 1999). Some of the barrows, ring-ditches and other cairns and enclosures known in the area are also likely to represent burial monuments of Iron Age date.

Early medieval period

The early medieval period saw a significant increase in human settlement activity. The dominant archaeological site type of the period is the settlement enclosure known as a ringfort. Ringforts were small enclosed farmsteads, usually circular, and they are well represented within the broader environs of the new road, frequently occurring in clusters—e.g. the three ringforts within the same field in Ballinorig South (KE029-129–31). Given the density of such enclosures in the area, there is little doubt that there would have been a complex social landscape, and groups or pairs of ringforts would have been occupied by closely related families. It must be noted, however, that in the absence of dating evidence from the many unexcavated ringforts/enclosures it is impossible to say how many of these were in use at any one time. Moreover, some may simply have been cattle pounds and not homesteads.

Multivallate examples are also present, like that at Knockanush East (KE028-061), 7 km west of the bypass route (Illus. 1.7). Bivallate or multivallate ringforts—with two or more banks and

Illus. 1.7—Bivallate ringfort at Knockanush East (RMP KE028-061003), 6 km west of the N22 Tralee Bypass, view to south-east (Michael Connolly, Kerry County Council).

ditches—were of greater importance than those with a single enclosing element. These may have been higher-status settlements or more heavily defended cattle enclosures. Very few ringforts in the area have been fully excavated but a ringfort in Dromthacker (KE029-095), c. 150 m outside the road corridor, was excavated in 1997. It was found to contain two phases of occupation, including two round-houses (Cleary et al. 2008).

Alongside the settlement enclosures, Christianity also left its mark on the early medieval landscape of the Tralee area. Two ecclesiastical sites are known very close to the road corridor—a church, holy well and graveyard at Lismore (KE029-033), and a church, enclosure and burials at Ballynabrennagh Upper (KE029-042). More significant, however, is the small stone church at Ratass (KE029-157001), in the eastern suburbs of Tralee, which seems to have served as the diocesan centre of Kerry for a short period in the early 12th century (O'Keeffe 1998, 119). Although the church is believed to be 10th/11th-century in date, with later additions (Fanning 1977), the presence of an ogham stone and possible evidence for a large ecclesiastical enclosure are suggestive of earlier origins (Illus. 1.8; Connolly 2012, 172–8).

Including the Ratass example, there are 16 known ogham stones within 5 km of the new road. These are simple pillar stones bearing an inscription on one or more margins, usually

Illus. 1.8—This late sixth-century ogham stone (RMP KE029-157002) was used to build a tomb in Ratass Church in the 19th century. It was rediscovered during a clean-up of the church in 1975. The surviving inscription reads [A]NM SILLANN MAQ VATTILLOGG, which has been translated as 'name/inscription of Sílán son of Fáithloga(?)'[1] (National Monuments Service, Dept. of Culture, Heritage and the Gaeltacht).

including a name and sometimes a memorial message. Ogham is the earliest known written form of Irish and uses a system of notches and horizontal or diagonal lines to represent sounds in an early form of the language, as opposed to actual letters. Ogham stones were in use in Kerry between the fourth and eighth centuries. They would have fulfilled a variety of functions, both secular and religious, including marking burials and boundaries and asserting land ownership (Moore 2010).

Later medieval and post-medieval periods

The late medieval period in Ireland begins with the arrival of the Anglo-Normans in 1169. Castles, tower houses and moated earthwork sites are typical of this period and they were built and inhabited by both the Anglo-Normans and indigenous Irish lords.

In the immediate vicinity of the bypass, Bealagrellagh tower house (KE039-004) (Illus. 1.9) is thought to have been founded by the McElligotts. Other nearby tower houses include those at

[1] Ogham in 3D (https://ogham.celt.dias.ie/stone.php?lang=en&site=Ratass&stone=Ratass&stoneinfo=inscription, accessed May 2020).

Illus. 1.9—Remains of Bealagrellagh Castle (RMP KE039-004), a tower house of the McElligotts, view to east (Rubicon Heritage Services Ltd).

Ballybeggan (KE029-123) and Ballymullen (KE029-163), as well as the now-demolished tower house at Ballingowan (KE029-162).

The principal Anglo-Norman lords of Kerry were of the Geraldine family, descendants of Maurice FitzGerald, the first Earl of Desmond, who came to Ireland with the invasion of Henry II. Tralee town was founded by the one of the Geraldines, John of Shanid, in the 13th century (O'Carroll 2009, 5). Although situated on the Big River, which is now largely culverted, the town derives its name from the River Lee, as Trá Lí means 'the strand of the Lee' (Bradley et al. 1985, 94). John initially put in place the essential infrastructure of an Anglo-Norman town, namely a castle, a principal street (known as Burgess Street, possibly modern-day High Street) and a market-place adorned with a market cross (O'Carroll 2009, 5). The old core of the town was in the area now occupied by the southern half of Rock Street and Pembroke Street (Tralee Town Council 2003, 100). Although the town was often subject to flooding in winter, the presence of the river and the sea to the west was instrumental in its foundation and development. In 1243 a Dominican abbey was established by John of Shanid, and the Desmond survey of 1584 described how vessels of up to 5 tonnes could sail right up to its walls (O'Carroll 2009, 6). Parts of the walls of the abbey were uncovered during recent test excavations (Coyne 2011) (Illus. 1.10).

Illus. 1.10—Foundation remnants of the east range of the Dominican abbey (RMP KE029-119) endowed by John of Shanid (Fitzgerald) in 1243 and exposed during test excavation in the Abbey Carpark, view to north-east (Michael Connolly, Kerry County Council).

The great Castle of Tralee stood on what is now Denny Street. In the 19th century Archdeacon Rowan described it as 'a huge pile of blank walls without even a window' (O'Carroll 2009, 6). It was pulled down in 1826 to make way for the development of Denny Street (ibid.). The earliest evidence that Tralee had attained borough status dates from 1298, when it was noted that the burgesses of Tralee paid 100 shillings in rent annually (Bradley 1986, 37).

Throughout the Middle Ages, Tralee remained in the hands of the Geraldine Earls of Desmond. In 1580, the 15th Earl, Gerald FitzGerald, was forced to abandon Tralee during his failed rebellion against Queen Elizabeth I. Before he left, he burned the town, leaving all but the abbey razed. Crown forces then took control of the town and carried out a survey of Desmond's property, describing Tralee as a well-inhabited borough with a castle and edifices, all of which were ruined in the fire (Bradley et al. 1985, 96). In 1587, following the defeat of the Desmond Rebellion, Tralee was granted to Edward Denny. The Dennys slowly rebuilt the town in the early 17th century; it was besieged in 1641, however, by a large force of Confederate Catholics, who burned Sir Edward Denny's castle and over 100 houses. More destruction followed in 1652, when Cromwellian forces burned the Dominican abbey, and again in 1691, when the town and castle were burned, this time by Jacobite forces during the 'War of the Two Kings' (James II and William

Illus. 1.11—A 19th-century townhouse on the corner of Day Place and High Street, Tralee. Day Place was built by Justice Robert Day in 1795. It was primarily a residential street occupied by gentry, clergy and professionals and reflects the growing prosperity of Tralee in this period (Laurence Dunne Archaeology).

of Orange). A census of Ireland returned in 1659 showed a population of 277 for 'Traly Burrough' (Pender 1939, cited in Bradley et al. 1985).

Tralee was rebuilt in the 18th century and examples of grand townhouses from the period have survived on Denny Street, Castle Street and Day Place (Illus. 1.11). The 19th century brought further construction, including a fine courthouse. The town grew rapidly as an industrial and market town (Thomas 1992, 240). During the 1860s the Roman Catholic churches of St John's and Holy Cross were built. Today, Tralee is the county town and administrative centre of County Kerry.

The landscape surrounding the town underwent significant changes during the post-medieval period. The modernisation of the rural economy from the second half of the 18th century involved consolidation—the amalgamation of multiple smallholdings into much larger field units, where the small tenant farmers no longer had a place (McNamara 2011, 28). Many landlords embarked on an 'age of improvement' (ibid.) and agriculture became more commercial and mechanised. This resulted in the field systems demarcated by stone walls and hedgerows that we see in the modern landscape. The quality of the land was also improved through activities such as drainage and the spreading of lime.

In parallel with the developments in agriculture, by about 1860 Ireland had experienced something of a communications revolution through the construction of roads, canals and railways (Horner 2007, 22). Many of the roads built during this period form the basis of the existing modern road network.

2
EXCAVATION SUMMARIES

Lyndsey Clark and Stephen Hourihan

This chapter contains summary reports of eight of the most significant excavations conducted along the route of the bypass. They are presented in order from north to south, and by site name within each townland. In addition, details of 16 burnt mounds are summarised in a table at the end of this chapter. The final excavation reports for all of the archaeological sites excavated on the Tralee Bypass (as listed in Table A) can be accessed on the TII Digital Heritage Collections (https://repository.dri.ie/catalog/v6936m966).

Ballynabrennagh Lower 1: Bronze Age round-house and Iron Age pits[1]

This Bronze Age occupation site was on the south-facing slope of a pasture field. The northern boundary of the field formed the townland boundary between Ballynabrennagh Lower and Ballynabrennagh Upper. Excavation revealed a round-house of probable Middle Bronze Age date and a small cluster of Developed Iron Age pits and stake-holes (Illus. 2.1).

Round-house

The remains of a circular dwelling or 'round-house' (Structure 1) comprised a curvilinear slot-trench (003; 0.26 m wide by 0.17 m deep) that enclosed an area approximately 6 m in diameter. The slot-trench seemed to be only partly preserved owing to truncation by agricultural activity. A central hearth (1.43 m long by 0.82 m wide) of red oxidised silty clay was the only internal feature. No datable material was recovered from these features.

The reuse of the building was represented by a second curvilinear slot-trench (007; 0.28 m wide by 0.05 m) which truncated the earlier one. This was most likely a repair/improvement rather than the construction of a new house. The projected diameter would have been slightly larger than the original at 6.8 m. There was a post-hole at the northern end of the slot-trench, while a small pit (061) truncated the central hearth. The pit contained a sherd of pottery from a plain Middle Bronze Age domestic vessel, as well as small amounts of charred naked barley and emmer wheat. Alder charcoal from the pit was dated to the Late Neolithic/Copper Age (2471–2213 BC;

---

1 Ballynabrennagh Lower, Co. Kerry; barony: Trughanacmy; ITM 487490 617561; height 108 m OD; Excavation Reg. No. E4297; Ministerial Directions A056; Excavation Director: Tony Bartlett.

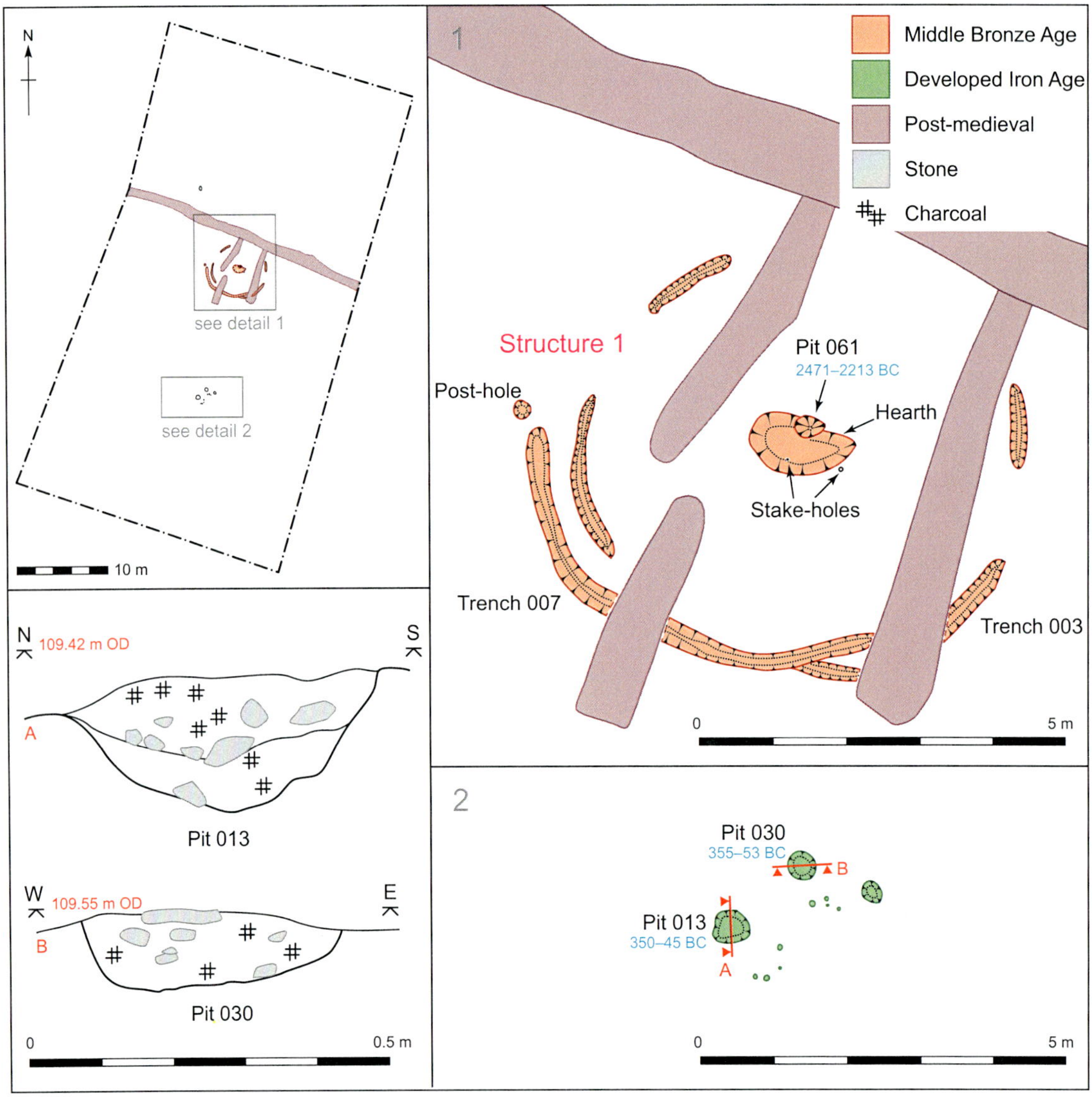

Illus. 2.1—Ballynabrennagh Lower 1. Bronze Age round-house and Iron Age pits.

SUERC-37259). Although it is possible that the date relates to the first phase of house construction, it is very unlikely that such a house would have been standing to be remodelled 600 years later. It seems reasonable, therefore, to discount the dated charcoal as residual material from an earlier episode on the site and to conclude that both phases of house construction date from the Middle Bronze Age. Two stake-holes were also identified to the south (cut into the pre-existing hearth) and south-east of the pit.

Developed Iron Age pits and stake-holes

A small cluster of features consisting of three subcircular pits (0.23–0.43 m in diameter by 0.10–0.18 m deep) and two groups of four stake-holes were located approximately 10 m south-west of the round-house. Although there was no obvious pattern to the stake-holes, it is possible that they were part of a light windbreak. Hazelnut shells from two possible waste pits (030 and 013) were dated to the Developed Iron Age (355–53 BC (SUERC-37258) and 350–45 BC (SUERC-37254)).

Post-medieval farming

A field drain and furrows of probable post-medieval date were also excavated, some of which truncated parts of the round-house. The furrows were 3 m apart, indicating spade-dug cultivation rather than ploughing.

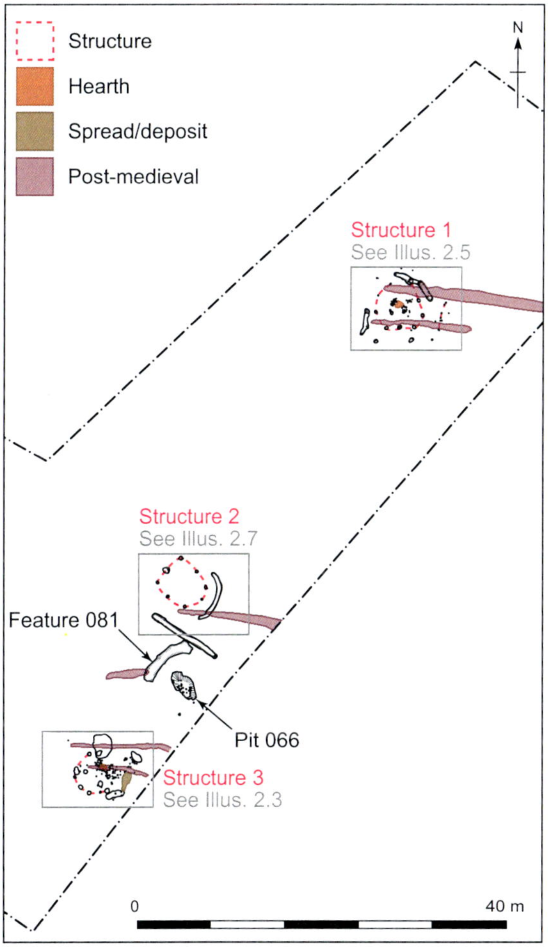

Illus. 2.2—Knockawaddra Middle 2. Bronze Age and early medieval buildings.

Knockawaddra Middle 2: two Bronze Age houses and an early medieval building[2]

This multi-period occupation site was located in a large, undulating, pasture field on the south-eastern side of a steep hill, overlooking a small stream. The western boundary of the field formed the townland boundary between Knockawaddra West and Knockawaddra Middle. Excavation revealed two Middle to Late Bronze Age houses (Structures 1 and 3) and an early medieval building (Structure 2) (Illus. 2.2).

Bronze Age houses

Structure 3 was the earliest and more southerly of the houses (Illus. 2.3). It was roughly circular in shape (c. 4.6 m in diameter), defined by seven post-holes/pits and possibly also by at least four stake-holes on its eastern side. There was no obvious entrance but the north-east side appears to have been open, though this may be the result of post-holes being cut away by a pit (076). The post-holes contained varying quantities of charcoal (mixture of oak and non-oak fragments), charred cereal grain (hulled barley and indeterminate cereals), burnt clay fragments and unidentifiable burnt bone. Internally, there was a

2 Knockawaddra Middle, Co. Kerry; barony: Trughanacmy; ITM 486913 616400; height 57 m OD; Excavation Reg. No. E4295; Ministerial Directions A056; Excavation Director: Tony Bartlett.

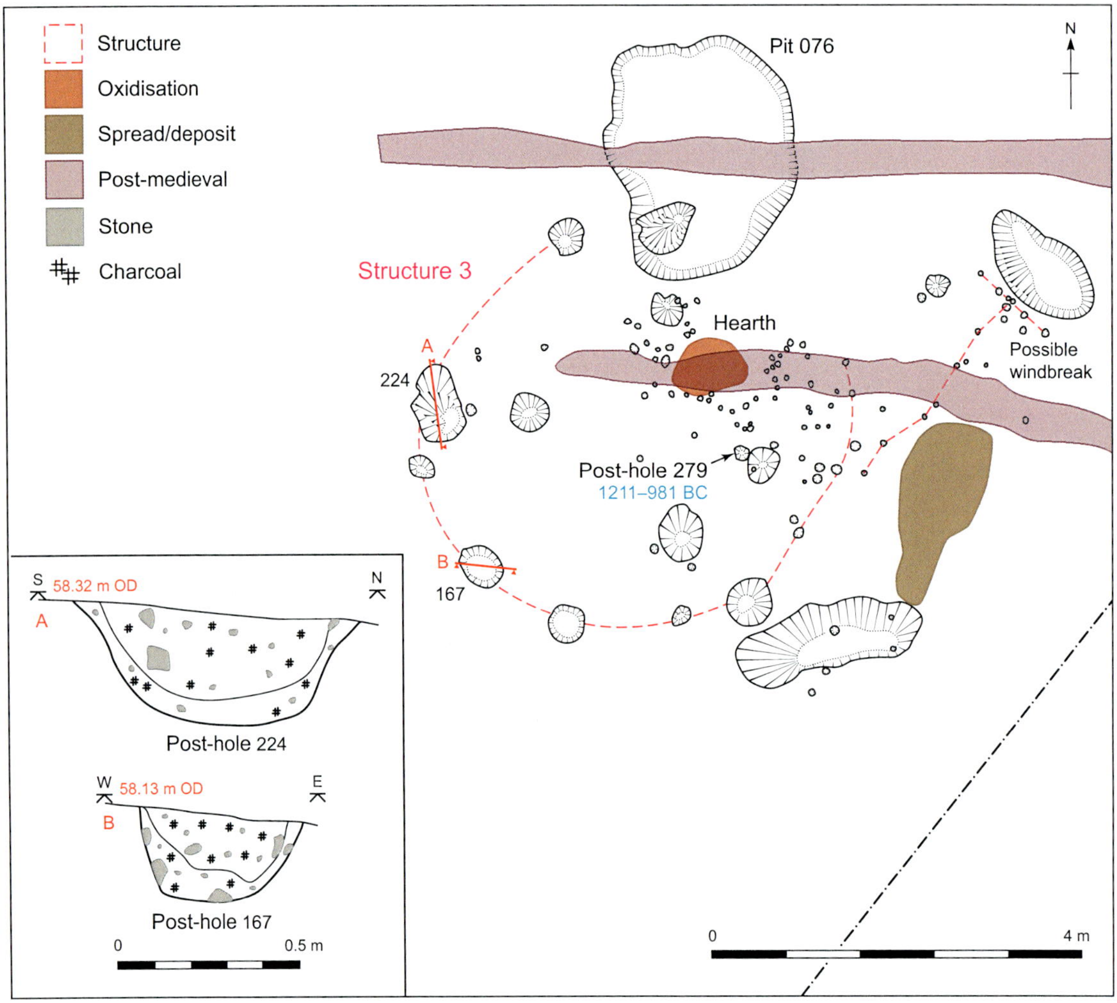

Illus. 2.3—Knockawaddra Middle 2. Bronze Age round-house (Structure 3) and associated features.

hearth, four large post-holes and numerous smaller post-holes and stake-holes. The four large post-holes formed a rectangular group and were probably for roof-support posts. Alder charcoal from one of the smaller post-holes (279) produced a date of 1211–981 BC (SUERC-37290).

Several large pits and post-holes of indeterminate function were recorded to the east of the house and contained varying amounts of charcoal, burnt clay and heat-shattered stones. An adjacent line of stake-holes may have formed a windbreak, perhaps shielding the entrance, while a heavily weathered, possibly limestone, polished stone axe was recovered from a large pit (076) immediately north of the house. This axe was unfinished and probably never used and is thought to be of Bronze Age date (Sternke 2012).

Approximately 10 m north-east of Structure 3, two badly corroded copper-alloy fragments, most likely representing the tip of a spearhead, were recovered from a stake-hole cut into the base

Illus. 2.4—Knockawaddra Middle 2. Fragment of a reworked rhyolite stone axe (E4295:001:001a) (Sara Nylund).

of a large pit (066) (see Chapter 5). A possible shale rubbing stone or pestle was recovered from an adjacent curvilinear feature (081), while a portion of a reworked Middle Neolithic rhyolite stone axe was recovered from topsoil (Illus. 2.4).

Structure 1 comprised nine post-holes. It was roughly subcircular and measured approximately 5.2 m (NNE/SSW) by 5 m (Illus. 2.5 and 2.6). The post-holes contained varying amounts of charcoal (oak and non-oak) and charred cereal grain (hulled barley), with one also producing a small fragment of chert debitage. Willow charcoal from one of the post-holes (030) returned a date of 1114–896 BC (SUERC-37288). The entrance was on the south-east side, where two small external post-holes appeared to form an elongated porch.

Internally, three clusters of stake-holes surrounded a central hearth, their positions suggesting that they supported a spit or perhaps some form of tripod used to suspend a cooking pot over the fire. The stake-holes contained charcoal (oak and non-oak) and very small quantities of charred cereal grain (hulled barley). External features included the remains of a possible drip-gully, identified on the north-east side of the structure, and several pits, post-holes and stake-holes that possibly acted as additional roof or wall supports. A possible windbreak comprising five stake-holes was located immediately north-east of the porch.

Structures 1 and 3 may have been occupied simultaneously, or at least within a short time of one another. The domestic nature of the houses is indicated by the presence of hearths in both, as well as charred cereal grains and burnt bone, all of which suggest that food was being prepared and/or consumed here.

Early medieval building

Structure 2 was located between the two Bronze Age houses and was initially presumed to be of similar date (Illus. 2.7). The radiocarbon dates and palaeoenvironmental assemblage from this build-

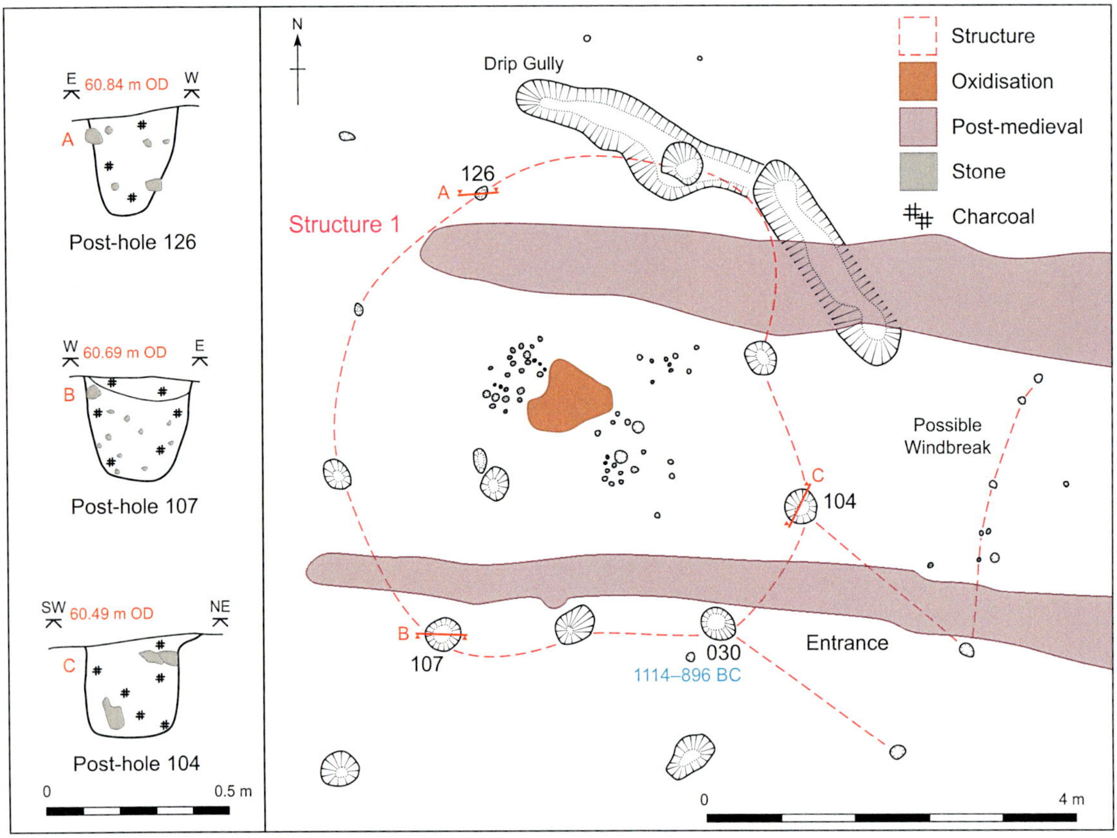

Illus. 2.5 (above)—Knockawaddra Middle 2. Bronze Age round-house (Structure 1) and associated features.

Illus. 2.6 (left)—Knockawaddra Middle 2. Post-excavation view of Bronze Age round-house (Structure 1) with entrance porch in foreground, view to north-west (Rubicon Heritage Services Ltd).

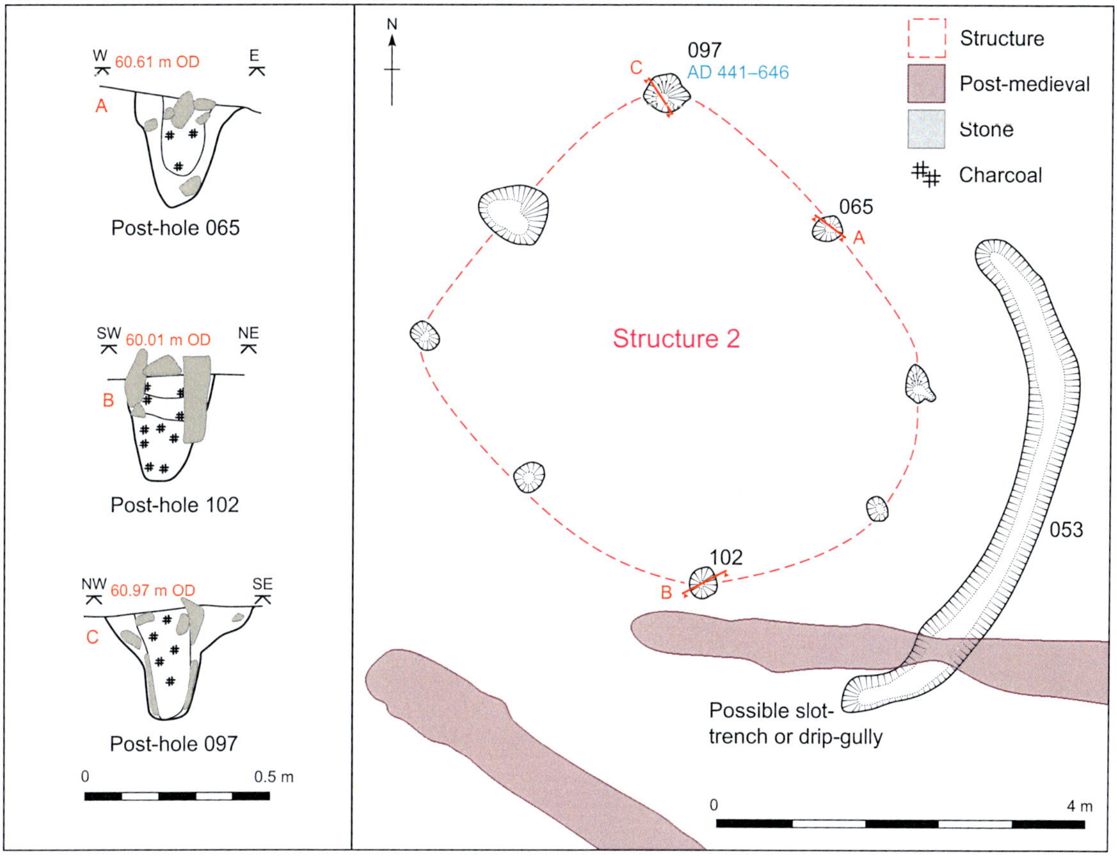

Illus. 2.7—Knockawaddra Middle 2. Early medieval building (Structure 2) and associated features.

ing revealed, however, that it was early medieval. It was defined by eight post-holes, between 1.2 m and 2 m apart, which formed a suboval building approximately 4.8 m NW/SE by 4 m wide. The post-holes contained charcoal (oak, hornbeam, willow, birch and hazel) and charred cereal grain. The grain included oats (22.3%) and hulled barley (32.3%), with lesser quantities of wheat (8.6%), including club-bread wheat and spelt wheat. These cereals are typical of early medieval assemblages. Hazel charcoal from one of the post-holes (097) returned a date of AD 441–646 (SUERC-37289). No internal features were identified. A curvilinear feature (053; 5.6 m long by 0.54 m wide by 0.16 m deep) to the south-east seemed to respect the curve of the house wall and possibly functioned as an external slot-trench or drip-gully.

The charred cereal grain, wild taxa (scentless mayweed, pale persicaria, sedges and bramble fruits) and hazelnut shell suggest that this was a domestic building, though the absence of a hearth casts doubt on whether it was actually a dwelling. Although its size and shape generally conform to those of previously excavated early medieval buildings, there are few examples of isolated, unenclosed buildings such as this in the archaeological record (O'Sullivan et al. 2010, 26).

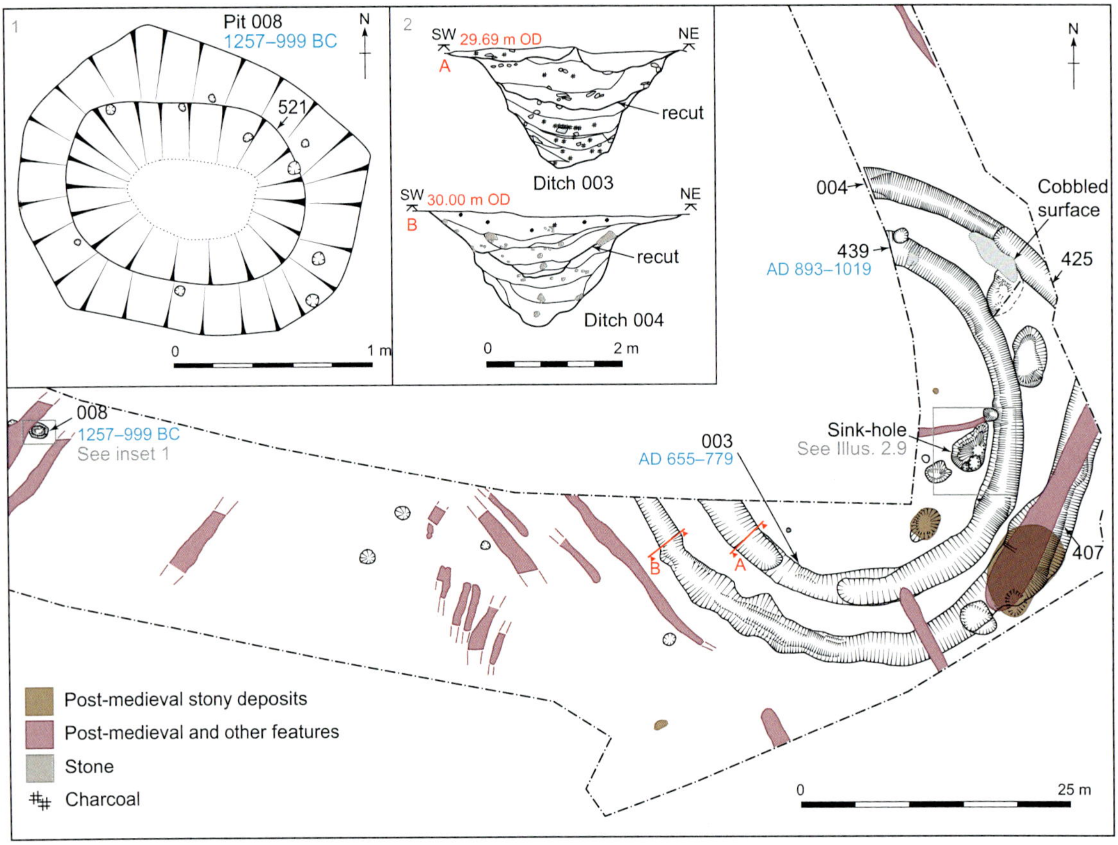

Illus. 2.8—Ballinorig West 2. Plan of all excavated features with (inset) sections of the ditches of the early medieval enclosure.

Ballinorig West 2: Neolithic and Bronze Age deposits, pit and stake-holes; early medieval bivallate enclosure[3]

This complex, multi-period site was located on a small rise in the north-east corner of a large pasture field that sloped gently from north to south. Prehistoric activity was represented by Neolithic and Bronze Age deposits, which had accumulated in a series of natural sink-holes, as well as by a Bronze Age pit and stake-holes. The most substantial element of the archaeological remains was an early medieval bivallate enclosure (Illus. 2.8).

Sink-hole deposits

An irregularly shaped sink-hole was located within the area enclosed by the inner ditch (003) of the early medieval enclosure (Illus. 2.9). It contained a range of prehistoric material, suggesting that it

3 Ballinorig West, Co. Kerry; barony: Trughanacmy; ITM 486554 614934; height 30 m OD; Excavation Reg. No. E4306; Ministerial Directions A056; Excavation Director: James Hession.

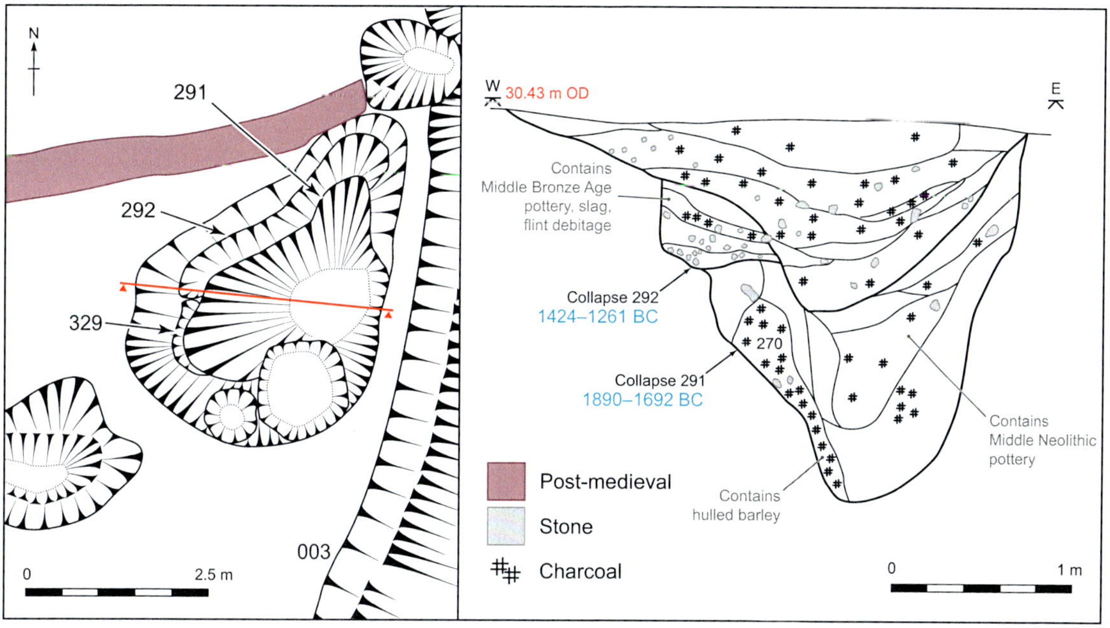

Illus. 2.9—Ballinorig West 2. Plan and section of sink-hole complex, with prehistoric deposits, located within the early medieval enclosure.

was used sporadically for the disposal of domestic waste from the Middle Neolithic until at least the Middle Bronze Age.

The sink-hole had collapsed in on itself on at least three occasions in the prehistoric period, resulting in its eventually extending to 4.9 m by 3.5 m by at least 2.8 m deep. The fills of the first or lower collapse (291) were quite mixed and contained varying quantities of charcoal, a single fragment of charred hazelnut shell and single grains of hulled barley and indeterminate cereals. Also present was one sherd of a Middle Neolithic globular bowl (E4306:264:001). Four further sherds (E4306:314:001–004, two of which refitted), representing a second bowl, and a flint hollow scraper (E4306:314:005) were recovered as residual finds from the adjacent early medieval enclosure ditch (003). Hazel charcoal from a lower fill of the sink-hole (270) returned an Early Bronze Age date of 1890–1692 BC (SUERC-37239).

Two further episodes of collapse and widening of the sink-hole (292 and 329) appear to have occurred in the Middle Bronze Age, judging by a date of 1424–1261 BC (SUERC-37241) obtained from hazel charcoal from one of the fills and the recovery of 357 sherds of pottery representing two plain Middle Bronze Age vessels (E4306:118:001–227 and E4306:336:001–130). A piece of flint debitage and a single fragment of ferrous slag were also retrieved. As no medieval finds were recovered from the sink-hole, it seems that it was not open when the enclosure was in use. There were, however, three further undated cavities at this location, and it is likely that they represent further episodes of collapse post-dating the Bronze Age.

Pit and stake-holes

A subcircular pit (008; 1.7 m long by 1.4 m wide by 0.47 m deep), with ten stake-holes cut into its base, was located at the western end of the site (Illus. 2.10). The stake-hole fills contained unidentified charcoal, while the overlying pit deposits contained heat-shattered stone and charcoal flecks. Alder charcoal from one of these deposits returned a date of 1257–999 BC (SUERC-37240). The pit was typical of a burnt mound trough, with the stake-holes indicating some form of wood lining that had either rotted away or was removed prior to the abandonment of the feature. There was no associated burnt mound in the immediate vicinity, though it is possible that one exists beyond the limits of the road footprint or had been removed from the present site by later tillage. This feature was truncated by a later, roughly circular pit (521; 1.10 m long by 1.06 m wide by 0.33 m deep) that was filled with similar material but was not dated.

Early medieval settlement enclosure

A previously unknown bivallate enclosure, defined by a pair of roughly concentric ditches, was discovered partly within the road footprint (Illus. 2.11). It was situated on a low rise in generally flat terrain, with good views to the east, south and west.

Illus. 2.10—Ballinorig West 2. Partly excavated fills of a Middle to Late Bronze Age pit and associated stake-holes, view to north (Rubicon Heritage Services Ltd).

Illus. 2.11—Ballinorig West 2. Aerial view of early medieval bivallate enclosure with a series of section trenches cut across the ditch fills (Aerialphoto.ie).

The inner ditch (003; 3.1 m wide by 1.9 m deep) was V-shaped in profile and enclosed an area c. 28 m in diameter. Its fills contained charcoal and cattle bone fragments. A sample of alder charcoal from one of the middle fills returned a date of AD 655–779 (SUERC-37238). Most deposits in the ditch seemed to be the result of natural silting, although one area along the south-western side may have been deliberately backfilled. The ditch was subsequently recut along its entire length, with an entrance causeway, 1.2 m wide, at its most southerly point.

The recut ditch (439; 2.9 m wide by 0.75 m deep) contained non-oak charcoal, single grains of oats, indeterminate cereal, wild taxa (docks/sorrels), a small quantity of blacksmithing waste and a burnt limestone rubbing stone. Two other limestone rubbing stones were recovered from topsoil. All three probably date from the Neolithic or Bronze Age. Hazel charcoal from one of the middle fills of the ditch returned a date of AD 893–1019 (SUERC-37242).

The outer enclosing ditch (004; 3.85 m wide by 1.7 m deep) was V-shaped in profile and enclosed an area c. 40 m in diameter. Its fills contained small quantities of non-oak charcoal, horse and cattle bone, as well as a piece of flint debitage of probable Neolithic or Early Bronze Age date. It was recut along its north-east and south-east sides by two ditches (425 and 407) which extended beyond the eastern limits of the excavation. Their fills contained fragments of cattle bone.

Although the outer ditch was not directly dated—attempts to obtain radiocarbon dates were unsuccessful—it was probably contemporary with the inner ditch, with the later recuts possibly representing a single episode of remodelling. No internal features contemporary with the occupation of the enclosure were identified. Nonetheless, the presence of charred cereal grain, animal bones and smithing waste indicates that it was probably a domestic enclosure and not, for instance, merely a cattle pound.

Stony spreads were laid over some of the infilled archaeological features in the post-medieval/early modern period, probably to level wet/sunken parts of the site. A 19th-century sickle blade and four unidentifiable iron objects were recovered from post-medieval/early modern features, including the cobbled surface.

Interpretation

While there were indications of Neolithic and Bronze Age activity at the site, there was no evidence of associated settlement from either period. Given the domestic nature of the ceramic assemblages, however, it is likely that such settlement did occur. Either the evidence for this lies beyond the footprint of the new road or the relevant features were slight and have been destroyed by later tillage.

By contrast, the bivallate enclosure provided clear evidence for early medieval settlement, though even here questions remain as to the precise dating and function of the site. Uncertainty surrounding the former arises from the fact that the dated material from both the original inner ditch and its later recut was obtained from middle fills. The actual digging of the ditches and recuts therefore most likely pre-dates the radiocarbon date ranges returned from their fills, though it is not known by how long. In any case, the primary ditches were probably cut in the seventh century or earlier, and the recut ditches between the ninth and 11th centuries.

Geophysical survey in the unexcavated portion of the enclosure did identify continuations of the ditches but they were poorly defined and no entrances could be discerned (Bonsall 2011).

Ballinorig West 3: Early Bronze Age cremation pit burial and early medieval cereal-drying kiln[4]

The site was in well-drained pasture that sloped gently from north to south, located between a ringfort (KE029-128) and a modern dwelling house.

Early Bronze Age cremation pit burial

The earliest activity identified on the site was the burial of cremated human remains, which had been placed in an inverted encrusted urn and interred in a small pit (086; 0.4 m long by 0.3 m wide) (Illus. 2.12). The burial had been damaged by ploughing and only fragments of the urn were present. All of the material (bone, pottery and soil matrix) was block-lifted by a conservator.

[4] Ballinorig West, Co. Kerry; barony: Trughanacmy; ITM 486231 614896; height 21 m OD; Excavation Reg. No. E4317; Ministerial Directions A056; Excavation Director: James Hession.

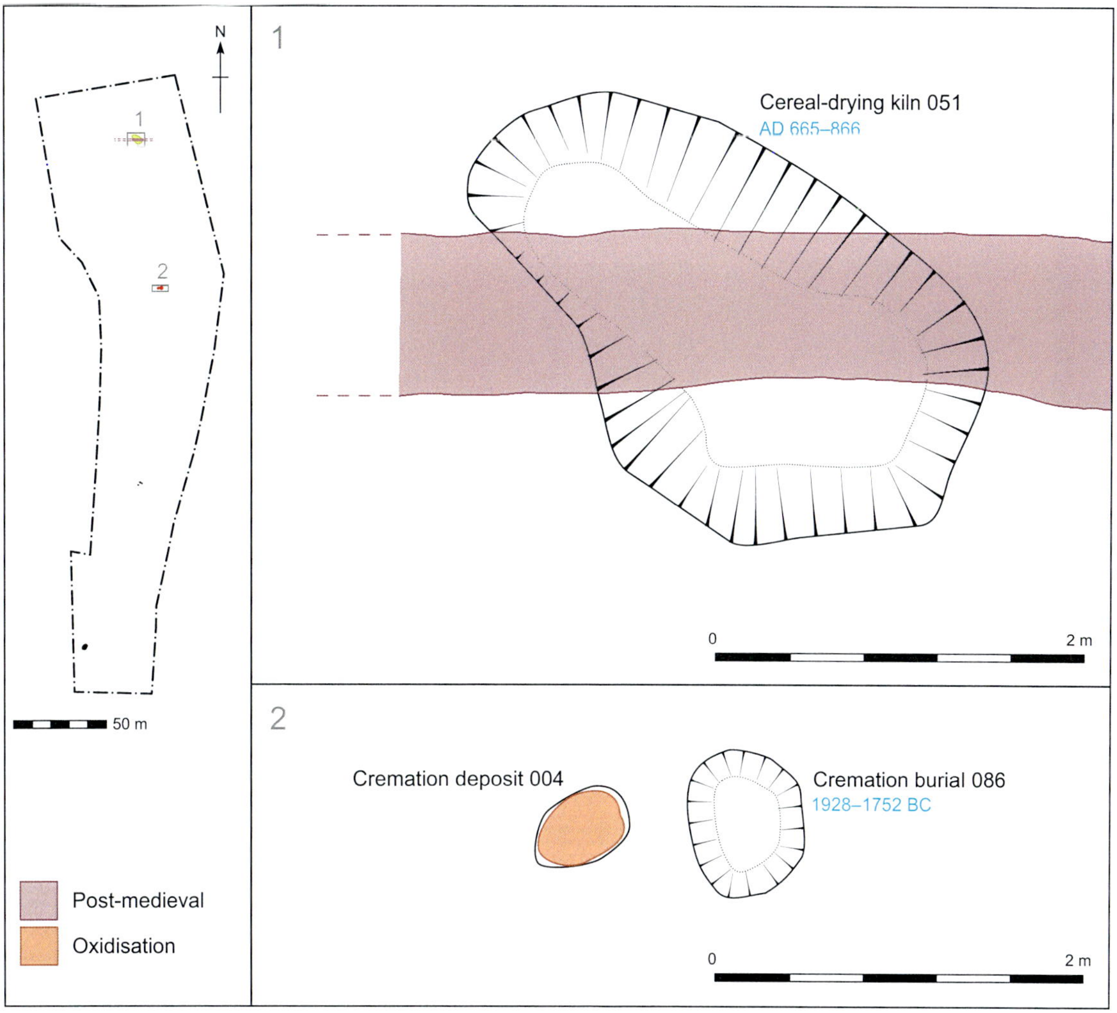

Illus. 2.12—Ballinorig West 3. Site plan with details of an Early Bronze Age cremation pit burial and early medieval cereal-drying kiln.

The surviving cremation deposit consisted of firmly compacted, mid-brown clayey silt, containing considerable amounts of oak charcoal and 519 g of cremated human bone. This was identified as the remains of an adult and a sub-adult. It is possible that these individuals were biologically related, although it is equally likely that they simply belonged to the same community and died around the same time. A sample of the cremated bone was dated to 1928–1752 BC (SUERC-37086). The ceramic assemblage comprises 57 sherds and 24 crumbs of prehistoric pottery, representing an Early Bronze Age encrusted urn (Illus. 2.13). Encrusted urns, while known in adjacent counties, have not previously been identified in County Kerry, making this a significant discovery (Roche & Grogan 2012e). Immediately west of the burial was a cremation deposit (004; 0.46 m by 0.37 m by 0.04 m deep) consisting of loosely compacted, mid-brown clayey silt with inclusions of oak and non-oak

Illus. 2.13—Ballinorig West 3. Surviving fragments (refitted) of an Early Bronze Age encrusted urn (E4317:003:001) from a cremation pit burial (086) (Sara Nylund).

charcoal, very occasional charred, indeterminate cereal grains and 1.6 g of cremated human bone. This material possibly represented drag or overspill from the plough-truncated urn burial. A fragment of quartz crystal debitage was also recovered from this deposit.

Early medieval cereal-drying kiln

The kiln was a large, pear-shaped pit (051) (3.4 m by 1.9 m by 0.6 m deep) containing five distinct deposits. The base exhibited a high degree of oxidisation (evidence of *in situ* burning), while the presence of alternating layers of charcoal-rich material, silt and oxidised deposits suggests multiple episodes of use. Both oak and non-oak charcoal was recovered, along with a large quantity of charred cereal grain and wild taxa, including hulled barley (the dominant cereal in the assemblage), oats, bread/club wheat, spelt wheat, rye, probable emmer wheat, indeterminate cereals, violet species and sedges. Oat grains from the basal fill produced a date of AD 665–866 (SUERC-37224). A fragment of quartz crystal debitage and a weathered siltstone rubbing stone were also recovered. These may be residual objects of prehistoric date.

Ballinorig West 4: Bronze Age pit; Iron Age penannular ring-ditch and industrial activity; early medieval iron-smelting furnace and cereal-drying kilns; post-medieval limekiln[5]

This multi-period funerary and industrial site was located in level, well-drained pasture, bordered by an unnamed tributary of the River Lee to the east and by a substantial limestone outcrop to the north-west. Two very large, infilled sink-holes were identified on the site but these did not contain archaeological material. Excavations revealed prehistoric ritual and industrial activity, as well as early medieval cereal kilns and a post-medieval limekiln (Illus. 2.14 and 2.15).

Illus. 2.14—Ballinorig West 4. Aerial view of site, with the Developed Iron Age ring-ditch visible at bottom (Aerialphoto.ie).

Late Bronze Age pit

An isolated pit (557; 0.47 m long by 0.38 m wide by 0.23 m deep) of unknown function was excavated in Area D. Alder charcoal from the fill returned a date of 1124–918 BC (SUERC-37253).

Early Iron Age waste pit

A small pit excavated in Area A (489; 0.56 m long by 0.55 m wide by 0.17 m deep) contained fragments of burnt bone—six of which were identified as sheep or goat—and charred,

---

5 Ballinorig West, Co. Kerry; barony: Trughanacmy; ITM 486044 614893; height 24 m OD; Excavation Reg. No. E4305; Ministerial Directions A056; Excavation Director: James Hession.

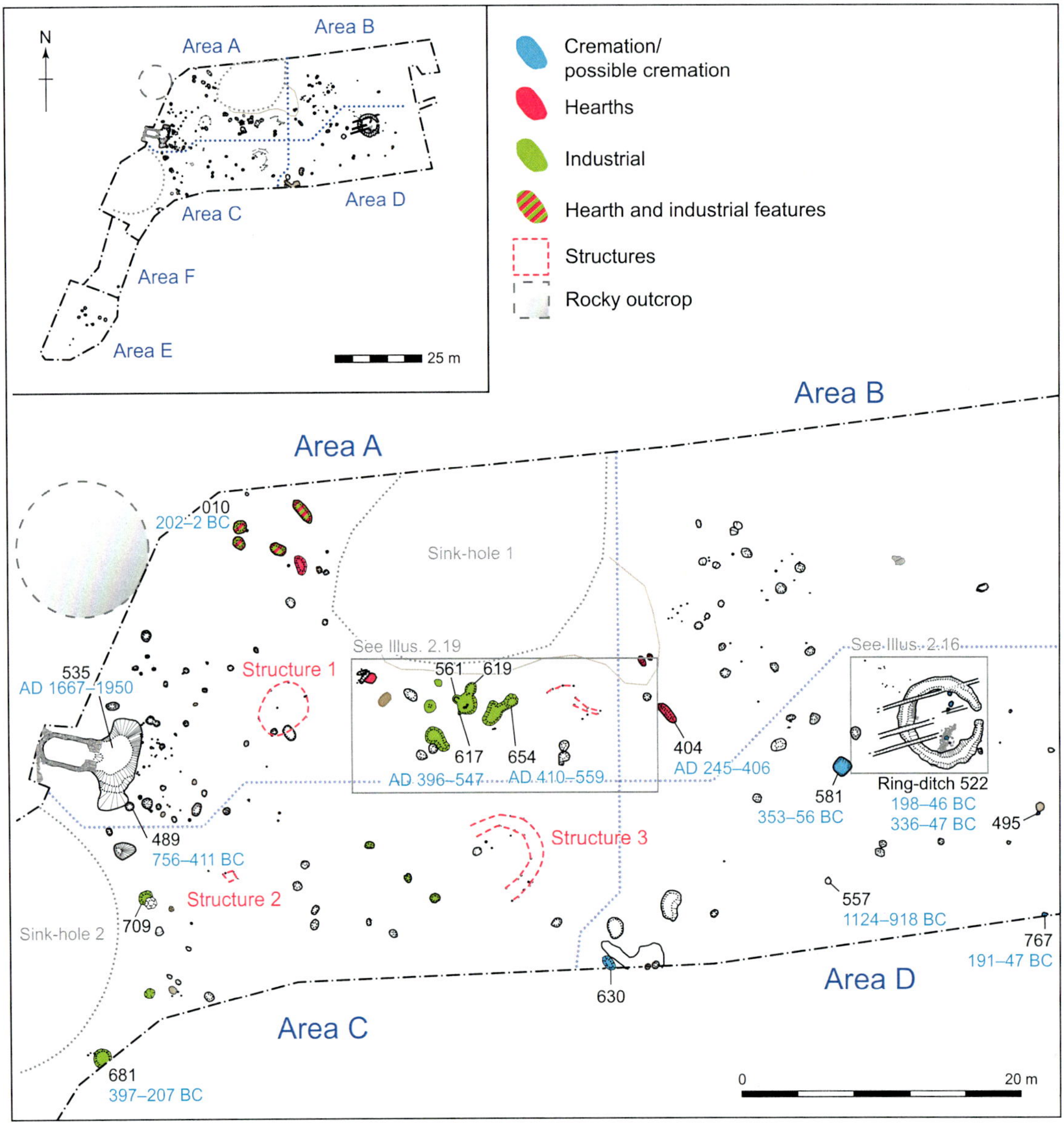

Illus. 2.15—Ballinorig West 4. This multi-period site had features of prehistoric and medieval date.

hulled barley grain (two-row variety), as well as flecks of hazel charcoal. The charcoal returned a date of 756–411 BC (SUERC-37248).

Developed Iron Age ring-ditch and cremation pit burials

A penannular ring-ditch (522) was identified in Area D (Illus. 2.16 and 2.17). It was situated on a slight, south-facing slope that was bordered to the north-west by a substantial limestone outcrop.

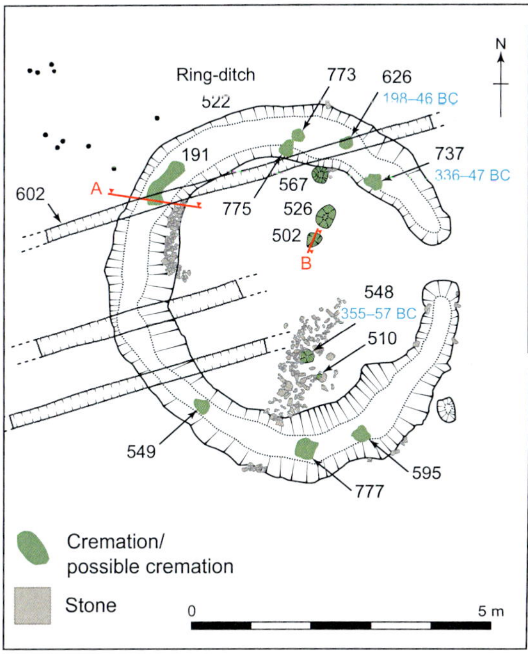

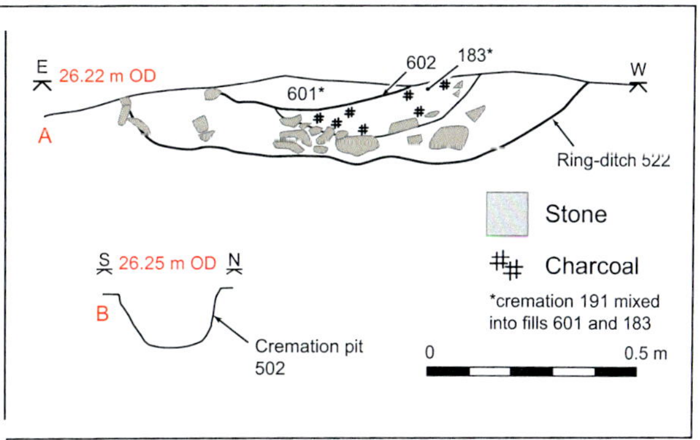

Illus. 2.16—Ballinorig West 4. Developed Iron Age ring-ditch and associated cremation pit burials. Plan of the excavated features (left) and sectional view of selected features (above).

Illus. 2.17—Ballinorig West 4. Aerial view of a Developed Iron Age ring-ditch (Aerialphoto.ie).

Illus. 2.18—Ballinorig West 4. Blue glass beads from a Developed Iron Age cremation pit burial (548) within the ring-ditch: E4305:187:001–004 (top) and E4305:538:001–002 (Rubicon Heritage Services Ltd).

The ditch (0.46 m wide by 0.17–0.41 m deep) enclosed an area 4.25 m north/south by 4.05 m, the interior of which was largely comprised of outcropping shale. The causewayed entrance (0.46 m wide) was located on the eastern side, facing towards the Stack's Mountains, and was possibly aligned with the rising sun.

The ditch was filled with several deposits that seemed to have been the result of natural silting but which contained concentrated deposits of cremated human bone. There were five cremation deposits within the upper ditch fills and three within the lower fills. In addition, scattered human bone was found mixed throughout the fills (183 and 523) (Table 2.1). No visible cuts were evident for these burial deposits and some had no clear edges. Only one of the deposits (626) was large enough to represent a full cremation; the rest are thought to be token burials. The ditch deposits produced a total of 2,453.8 g of human bone and returned two dates of 336–47 BC (deposit 737; SUERC-37090) and 198–46 BC (deposit 626; SUERC-37089). The ditch also contained a possibly used piece of limestone, as well as charcoal of oak, hazel, willow, apple-type (Pomoideae) and alder.

Five cremation pit burials were identified within the ring-ditch interior. Of these, two were cut into the shale outcrop. Four of them contained only token deposits (510, 526, 548 and 567). The fifth pit (502) contained a deposit large enough to represent a full cremation. The total weight

Table 2.1—Summary details of cremation deposits at Ballinorig West 4.

Deposit no.	Contained in:	^{14}C date (2σ) cal. BC	Weight (g)	Skull (g)	Axial (g)	Upper limb (g)	Lower limb (g)
Ditch fills rich in burnt bone							
183	Ring-ditch 522, upper fill	–	10.1	0.2	–	–	–
523	Ring-ditch 522, upper fill	–	185.3	18	–	–	–
Cremation burials within the ring-ditch fills							
549	Lower ditch fill 523	–	1.8	1.8	–	–	–
595	Upper ditch fill 183	–	128.2	8.3	–	–	–
626	Upper ditch fill 183	198–46	1287.7	114.5	–	0.3	0.3
737	Lower ditch fill 523	336–47	334.9	46	–	3.3	–
773	Upper ditch fill 183	–	54	5.7	–	–	–
775	Lower ditch fill 523	–	309.1	19	0.1	0.1	–
777	Upper ditch fill 183	–	36.1	0.3	–	–	–
191	Plough furrow 602 and upper ditch fill 183	–	106.6	16.6	–	–	–
Cremation burials within the interior of ring-ditch (522)							
184	Pit 526	–	1.1	0.3	–	–	–
185	Pit 567	–	95.1	19.1	–	–	–
186	Pit 502	–	361.7	0.5	–	0.5	3.5
512		–	29.2	-	–	–	–
187	Pit 548	355–57	51.7	2.5	–	–	–
538		–	19.2	0.9	–	–	–
503	Pit 510	–	18.8	3.6	0.1	0.2	–
Outlying cremation burials to the south and west of the ring-ditch							
193	Pit 581	–	1.4	0.1	–	—	–
584		353–56	166.5	45	–	–	–
280	Pit 495	–	143.6	7.6	–	–	–
631	Pit 630	–	10.3	-	–	–	–
767	Deposit	191–47	102.3	19.8	–	–	–
Total	–	–	**3454.7**	**329.8**	**0.1**	**4.4**	**3.8**

of cremated bone from all five pits was 576.8 g. A sample from one burial (548) produced a date of 355–57 BC (SUERC-37096). This burial also contained six small blue glass beads which seemed to have suffered fire damage, suggesting that they were present on the body during cremation (Illus. 2.18). They are all circular, measuring approximately 2 mm in diameter, and cobalt blue in colour, though their level of translucency varies. The cremations contained a mix of oak and non-oak charcoal.

A further three pit burials (495, 581, 630) and a cremation deposit (767)—all containing token amounts of cremated bone and oak and non-oak charcoal—were dispersed over a large area south and south-west of the ring-ditch (Illus. 2.15). The deposit (767) is likely to have been the base of a plough-truncated cremation pit. These produced a total of 424.1 g of cremated human bone, samples of which returned two dates of 353–56 BC (pit 581; SUERC-37092) and 191–47 BC (token deposit 767; SUERC-37091). It is clear that the pyre technology was well developed, as 97% of the bone in these deposits was completely oxidised. Characteristic dehydration evidence, such as horizontal, longitudinal and U-shaped fissuring, was present on the bone. This indicates that when the bodies were cremated there was still flesh, and particularly fat, attached to the bone.

Owing to the fragmented nature of the bone it was not generally possible to identify the age or sex of the cremated individuals, but one of the cremations from the ring-ditch (626) was probably an adult male.

Developed Iron Age charcoal-production pits and hearth

Two small charcoal-production pits (681 and 709) were excavated in Area C (Illus. 2.15). The base and perimeter of one pit (681; 1.26 m long by 1.22 m wide by 0.25 deep) showed extensive evidence of *in situ* burning, while the overlying basal deposit was rich in oak and non-oak charcoal. Alder charcoal produced a date of 397–207 BC (SUERC-37251). A small quantity of charred hulled barley grain, grass seeds and fragments of iron slag were also recovered. A number of stake-holes surrounding the pit were probably associated with it. The second, possibly contemporary, charcoal-production pit (709; 1.07 m long by 0.94 m wide by 0.26 m deep) was located 10 m to the north.

A possible metal-working hearth (010) and two adjacent stake-holes on the northern side of Area A were also attributed to this phase of activity. The hearth contained oak charcoal, occasional pieces of oxidised clay and fragments of undiagnostic slag. The charcoal was dated to 202–2 BC (SUERC-37243).

Several undated features near the hearth may have been contemporary with it and related to small-scale industrial activity; these included three hearths and a number of post-holes, pits and spreads.

Late Iron Age hearth

Excavation of a hearth (404; 1.7 m long by 0.4 m wide by 0.1 m deep) in the south-west corner of Area B (Illus. 2.15) revealed evidence of *in situ* burning on the sides and the base and yielded oak and non-oak charcoal, including hazel. A sample of hazel charcoal produced a date of AD 245–406 (SUERC-37250). It is possible that other undated features in the vicinity may be related to this activity.

Early medieval furnace and cereal-drying kilns

A slag-tapping shaft furnace (561) with an adjoining rake-out pit (617) and associated waste pit (619) were excavated in Area A (Illus. 2.19 and 2.20). The furnace comprised a circular pit (0.43 m long by 0.38 m wide by 0.42 m deep), with the remains of a collapsed clay superstructure contained within a compact burnt layer (0.12 m thick) of stone that was heavily slagged on the interior surface. The rim of the base of the clay superstructure remained *in situ* around the edge of the pit. The accompanying rake-out pit (1.44 m long by 1.39 m wide by 0.49 m deep) was heavily oxidised and

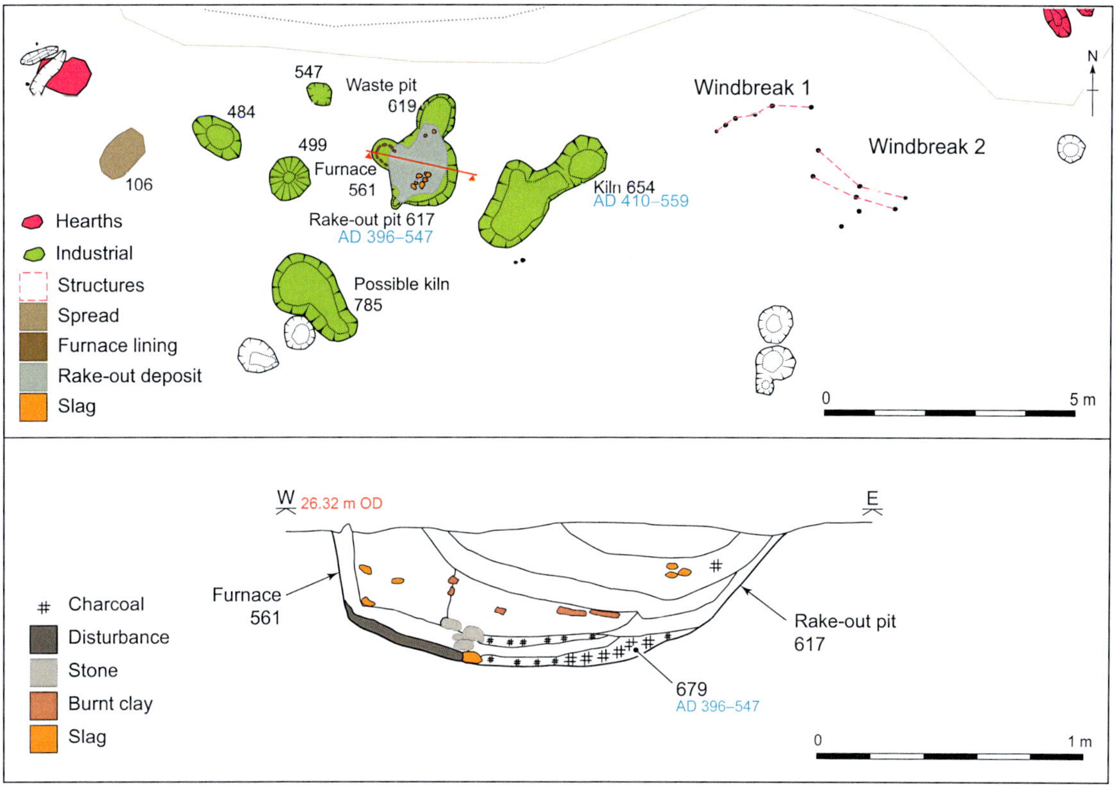

Illus. 2.19—Ballinorig West 4. Early medieval slag-tapping shaft furnace, waste pits and cereal-drying kilns, with section (below) of furnace and rake-out pit.

its fills contained oak, hazel and blackthorn charcoal, along with a large number of charred cereal grains (hulled barley, oat and emmer wheat), wild taxa (mostly grasses and sedges) and slag. A hulled barley grain from a deposit (679) in the base of this pit returned a date of AD 396–547 (SUERC-37249). The grain may have originated in a nearby cereal-drying kiln. Three nearby waste pits (499, 547 and 484) and a deposit (106) also contained slag and are likely to have been contemporary with the furnace. Two windbreaks to the east may also have been associated with this phase of metal-working. Windbreak 1 was c. 2.15 m long and consisted of an alignment of six stake-holes. Windbreak 2 was c. 2 m long and consisted of a double row of three stake-holes each.

Immediately east of the furnace was a figure-of-eight-shaped cereal-drying kiln (654; 2.9 m by 1.5 m by 0.43 m deep). It comprised three separate elements: a roughly circular drying chamber to the south-west, connected by a short, linear flue to a fire-pit at the north-east. The fire-pit displayed clear evidence of *in situ* burning, while its fills contained blackthorn and oak charcoal, charred cereal grains (hulled barley and bread/club wheat), wild taxa (wood rushes, sedges and knotweed), burnt clay, burnt stone and undiagnostic fragments of slag. Two burnt and broken rubbing stones were also recovered. A date of AD 410–559 (SUERC-37252) was returned from a hulled barley grain.

Illus. 2.20—Ballinorig West 4. Mid-excavation view of early medieval slag-tapping furnace and rake-out pit, view to north-east (Rubicon Heritage Services Ltd).

A possible second cereal-drying kiln (785) was located 2.5 m to the south-west and was probably contemporary with the first example. It was keyhole-shaped and measured 1.94 m by 1.2 m by 0.3 m deep. It did not contain any cereal remains, suggesting that it was cleaned out after its final use.

Post-medieval limekiln

A keyhole-shaped limekiln (793) was excavated in the south-west corner of Area A (Illus. 2.15). It consisted of a drystone, subrectangular walled chamber up to ten courses high (4.2 m long by 2.23 m wide by 0.85 m deep), a flue (0.84 m long by 2.23 m wide by 0.85 m deep) and a rake-out pit (6.5 m long by 2.8 m wide by 0.83 m deep), and contained varying quantities of purging buckthorn and blackthorn charcoal, lime and burnt clay. Blackthorn charcoal from the rake-out pit returned a date of AD 1667–1950 (SUERC-37244).

Undated structures and miscellaneous features

The majority of excavated features could not be attributed to a specific phase of activity. These included three structures (Illus. 2.15) that lacked datable material. Structure 1, in Area A, comprised a circular arrangement of eight stake-holes and measured 3.7 m in diameter. Structure 2, in Area C, was a rectangular arrangement of four stake-holes measuring roughly 1 m square. Structure 3, located 12.5 m south-east of Structure 1, consisted of two concentric arcs of stake-holes, 12.7 m long, enclosing an area of approximately 3 m x 4 m. For the most part, the remainder of the excavated features were pits, post holes and stake-holes of uncertain function, forming no obvious patterns.

Interpretation

The industrial activity at this site centred on the production of charcoal and iron, with some evidence for cereal drying. The charcoal was probably used for metal-working, as large quantities were needed to reach the high temperatures required for smelting and smithing. Slag-tapping shaft furnaces are a common feature of British metal-working sites from the Iron Age and medieval periods but few, if any, have been definitively recorded in Ireland.

Oak was the dominant charcoal type used at Ballinorig West, no doubt deliberately selected for its high calorific value. Given the large volumes of charcoal required, it is likely that metal-working in this period took place close to the woodland resource rather than to the iron resource, as the latter could be more easily transported. This may well have been the case at Ballinorig West, as there is no obvious source of iron ore in the immediate area.

Metal-working and cereal drying were both integral to the early medieval economy and are often found together, although both processes were commonly undertaken at some remove from the main settlement, perhaps because of the space needed to store the raw materials, as well as the smoke and other unpleasant by-products. It is possible that the produce from Ballinorig West 4 supplied the nearby ringfort (KE029-128), or perhaps the bivallate enclosure at Ballinorig West 2.

Although the Developed Iron Age ring-ditch and associated cremations pre-date the early medieval industrial activity by some 200–400 years, the industrial features do seem to respect the ring-ditch and its surrounds. The ring-ditch may therefore have still been visible at that time, and have been regarded with such significance that the early medieval population refrained from working in its immediate vicinity.

Ballingowan 1: Late Neolithic/Early Bronze Age double pit alignment; pit containing Beaker pottery, Bronze Age settlement areas, enclosure, cereal-drying kiln and drove-way; Iron Age metal-working; early medieval building and cereal-drying kiln[6]

Ballingowan 1 was a complex, multi-period site that extended across four undulating pasture fields, characterised by depressions and outcrops of limestone bedrock. These outcrops occurred throughout the area but were most prominent towards the centre of the site, from where the ground sloped away towards the north and south. The excavation was spread over c. 670 m of the bypass route and for the purposes of recording was divided into three sections—Areas 1a, 1b and 1c (Illus. 2.21).

---

[6] Ballingowan, Co. Kerry; barony: Trughanacmy; ITM 486609 613930; height 14-22 m OD; Excavation Reg. No. E4288; Ministerial Directions A056; Excavation Director: Tony Bartlett.

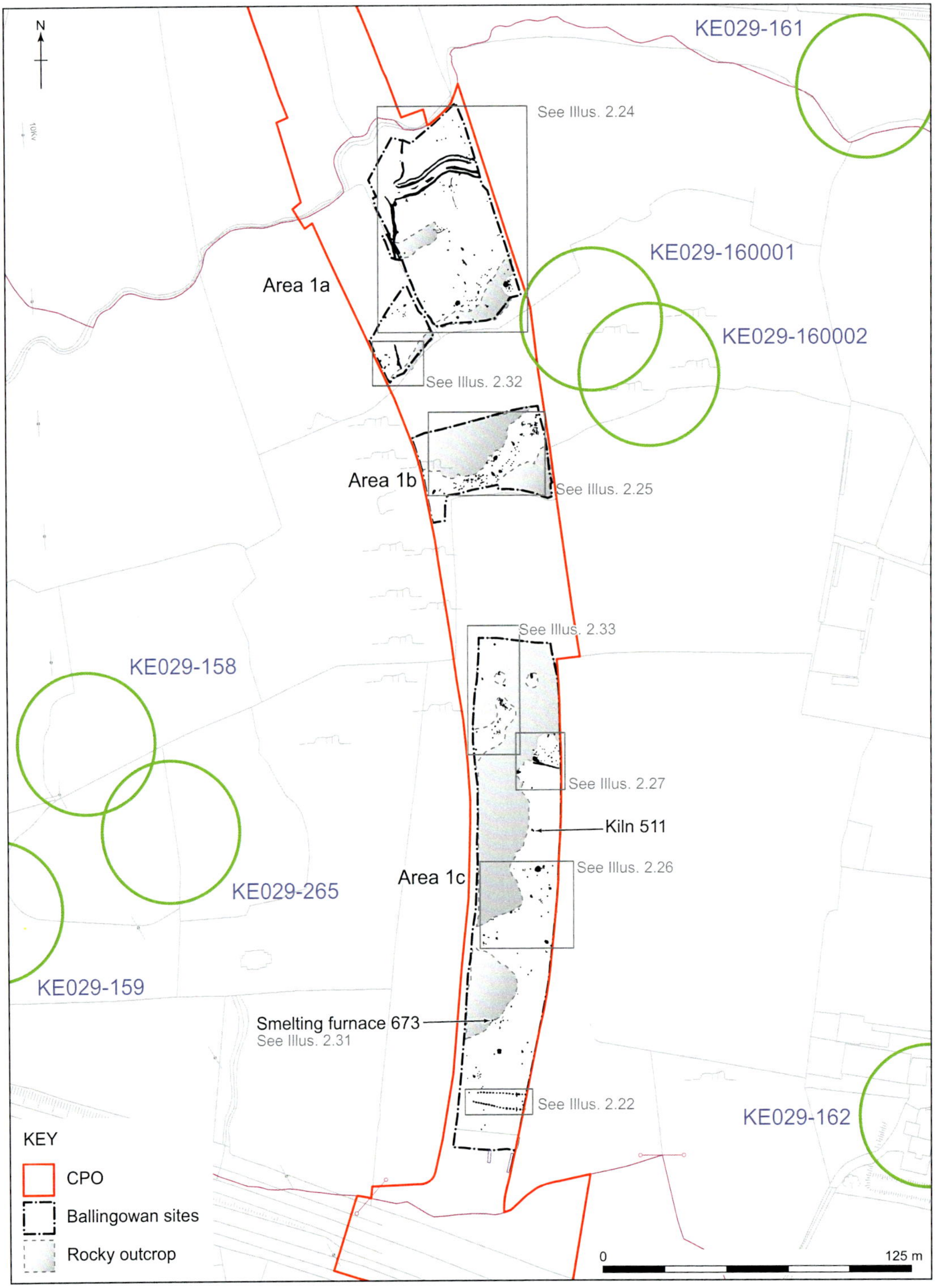

Illus. 2.21—Ballingowan 1. Overall site plan and nearby recorded monuments.

Excavation revealed at least seven phases of activity spanning the prehistoric to early medieval periods. A sherd of Early Neolithic carinated bowl was found in a pit within a possible Middle Bronze Age enclosure in Area 1c. This potsherd hints at pre-Bronze Age activity on the site, but in the absence of any related features or artefacts the precise nature of this activity is not known.

Late Neolithic/Early Bronze Age double pit alignment

A double row of pits was identified at the extreme south of the site in Area 1c (Illus. 2.22 and 2.23). It comprised two opposing rows of pits, aligned east/west (0.36–1.42 m long, 0.26–1 m wide and 0.1–0.7 m deep), a maximum of 9 m apart at the eastern limit of excavation and tapering to only 5.1 m at the western end. The northern row consisted of 16 pits, spaced on average 1 m apart (edge to edge), and was exposed for a length of 30 m. Another pit was located 6 m from the western end and may be related to this alignment. The row extended east beyond the road footprint and its full length is unknown. The southern row similarly extended east beyond the road footprint but was exposed for a length of 33 m within the excavation area. It consisted of 18 pits which became more closely spaced towards the west, where they were on average 0.7 m apart.

These pits are likely to have supported large wooden posts and there was evidence in a number of them for packing stones and the humic soil stains that result when posts decay *in situ*. Unfortu-

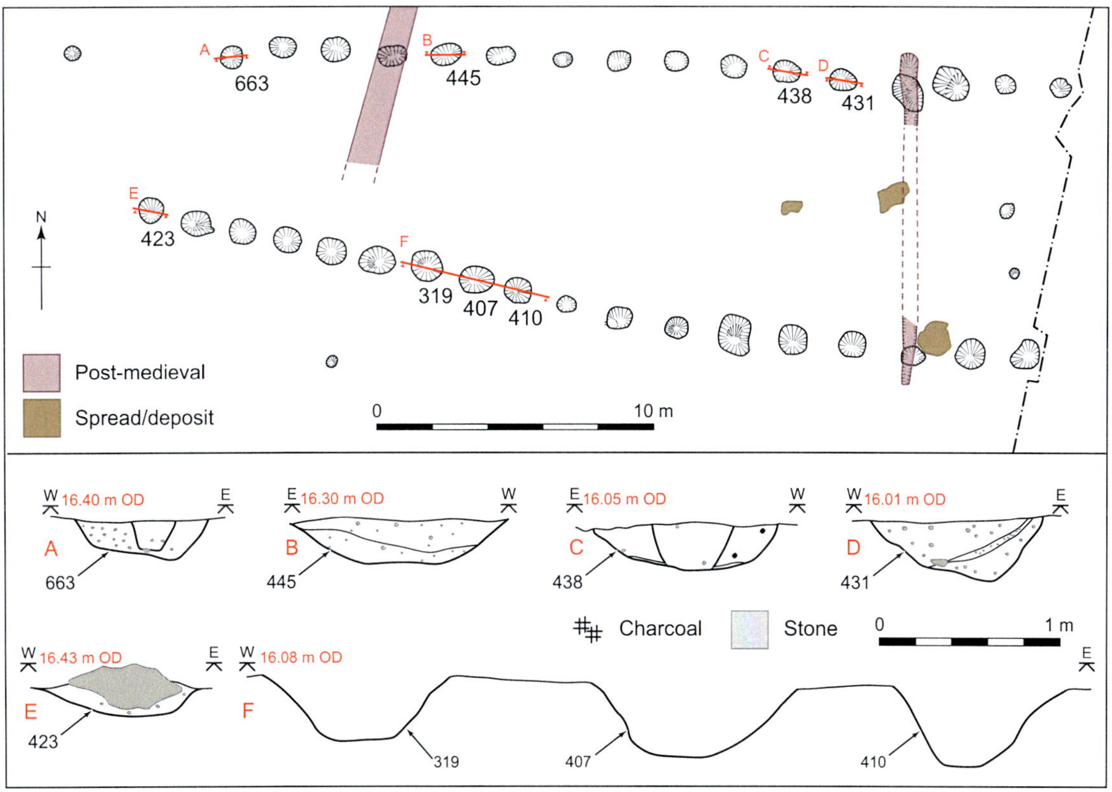

Illus. 2.22—Ballingowan 1, Area 1c. Late Neolithic/Early Bronze Age double pit alignment.

Illus. 2.23—Ballingowan 1, Area 1c. Looking west along the double pit alignment (Rubicon Heritage Services Ltd).

nately, the pits were largely sterile and no datable material was retrieved.

Parallel lines of pits/post-holes have been identified at a small number of Irish sites such as Ballynahatty, Co. Down (Hartwell 1998) and Newgrange (e.g. O'Kelly et al. 1983, 16–21), but these were elements of complex ritual monuments for which no evidence has so far been found in Ballingowan. From what we know of the alignment in Ballingowan, the closest morphological parallels are to be found in Britain, where studies of several double pit alignments have shown that they generally date from the Late Neolithic or Early Bronze Age (Waddington 1997). They have been interpreted as ceremonial in nature, possibly defining processional routes (ibid.). On this basis, the Ballingowan pit alignment is tentatively suggested to be Late Neolithic or Early Bronze Age in date.

A number of pits, post-holes and stake-holes in the immediate vicinity of the avenue are interpreted as being contemporary with it, though this is based solely on their proximity.

Early Bronze Age round-house and pit containing Beaker pottery

An oval round-house (4 m by 3.3 m), defined by eight post-holes and enclosing a central hearth, was identified in the south-east corner of Area 1a (Illus. 2.24). The post-holes contained varying

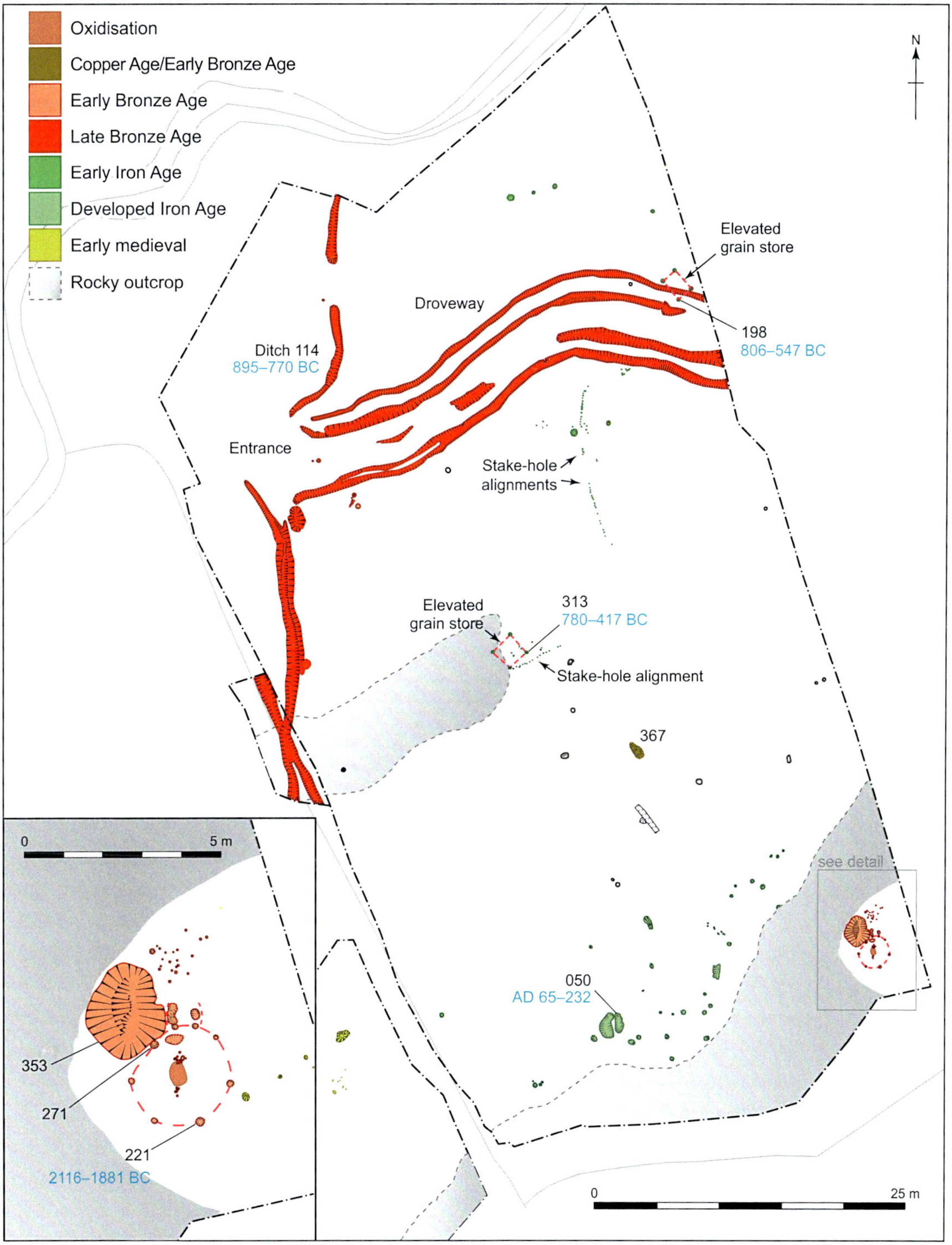

Illus. 2.24—Ballingowan 1, Area 1a. Bronze Age round-house and droveway, and Iron Age grain stores, stake-hole alignments, post-holes and pits.

quantities of charcoal (hazel) and charred cereal grain (barley), with hulled barley from one (221) returning a date of 2116–1881 BC (SUERC-37300). The base of the hearth was heavily oxidised. There were burnt animal bones in its fills, and clusters of stake-holes and post-holes to either side suggest that objects were once suspended over the fire. Two deeper post-holes on the north side are likely to have formed an entrance 0.60 m wide. Just inside this there was a spread of silty clay with charcoal inclusions, which had evidently built up on the floor of the house. Further post-holes on either side of the entrance on the outside are likely to have formed a porch-like feature. Although small by comparison with other round-houses of this period, the internal cooking hearth and the presence of burnt animal bones and cultivated cereals suggest that this was a domestic building.

Two large intercutting features (353) north-west of the house are probably the result of tree roots. One of these disturbed the edge of a post-hole (271).

An isolated, oblong pit (367; 2.4 m by 1.1 m and 0.6 m deep), approximately 30 m north-west of the house, contained three sherds of Beaker pottery—a base-angle sherd and two body sherds (E4288a:354:001–003), representing two vessels. A badly abraded but very similar Beaker sherd was also recovered from a pit (100) in Area 1c. This represents a third vessel at Ballingowan 1.

Middle Bronze Age possible enclosure, cereal-drying kiln and pits

Middle Bronze Age activity was largely represented by groups of pits or possible post-holes of uncertain function. These included four pits in the far west of Area 1b (Illus. 2.25), one of which (090) returned a date of 1411–1212 BC (SUERC-37311) from hazel charcoal. A similar date of 1436–1269 BC (SUERC-37314), from alder charcoal, was obtained for a pit (488) in Area 1c (Illus. 2.26). This was one of a number of pits and post-holes that appeared to form a band of activity orientated NE/SW across the road footprint.

There was one area of activity in Area 1c (Illus. 2.27) that may have been enclosed to some degree in this period. It seemed to have been defined by a low rock outcrop to the north and west and by a shallow ditch to the south. The ditch (476; 0.7 m wide by 0.1 m deep) was truncated by a linear feature of probable post-medieval date but was still discernible continuing under this feature for a total length of 14.5 m. It did not contain any datable material.

While the ditch itself would not have been deep enough to do anything more than demarcate an area, the concentration of activity to the north (and absence of activity to the south) does point to a deliberate effort to define and hence enclose. This area was flat and free of rock outcropping, and measured c. 20 m north/south by at least 20 m east/west. The full eastern extent of this 'enclosed' area is not known, as it extended beyond the footprint of the road on that side.

Features within the enclosed area included an L-shaped arrangement of post-holes, two hearths, a cluster of stake-holes, scattered pits and further post-holes. These produced several artefacts, including Early Neolithic pottery (thought to be residual), chipped flint, a rubbing stone, two sandstone quern-stone fragments and a number of sherds of Middle Bronze Age plain ware. They also contained varying quantities of charcoal, with charred cereal grain (hulled barley) and wild taxa (pale persicaria and violets) coming from one of the hearths. Flecks of unidentifiable burnt bone

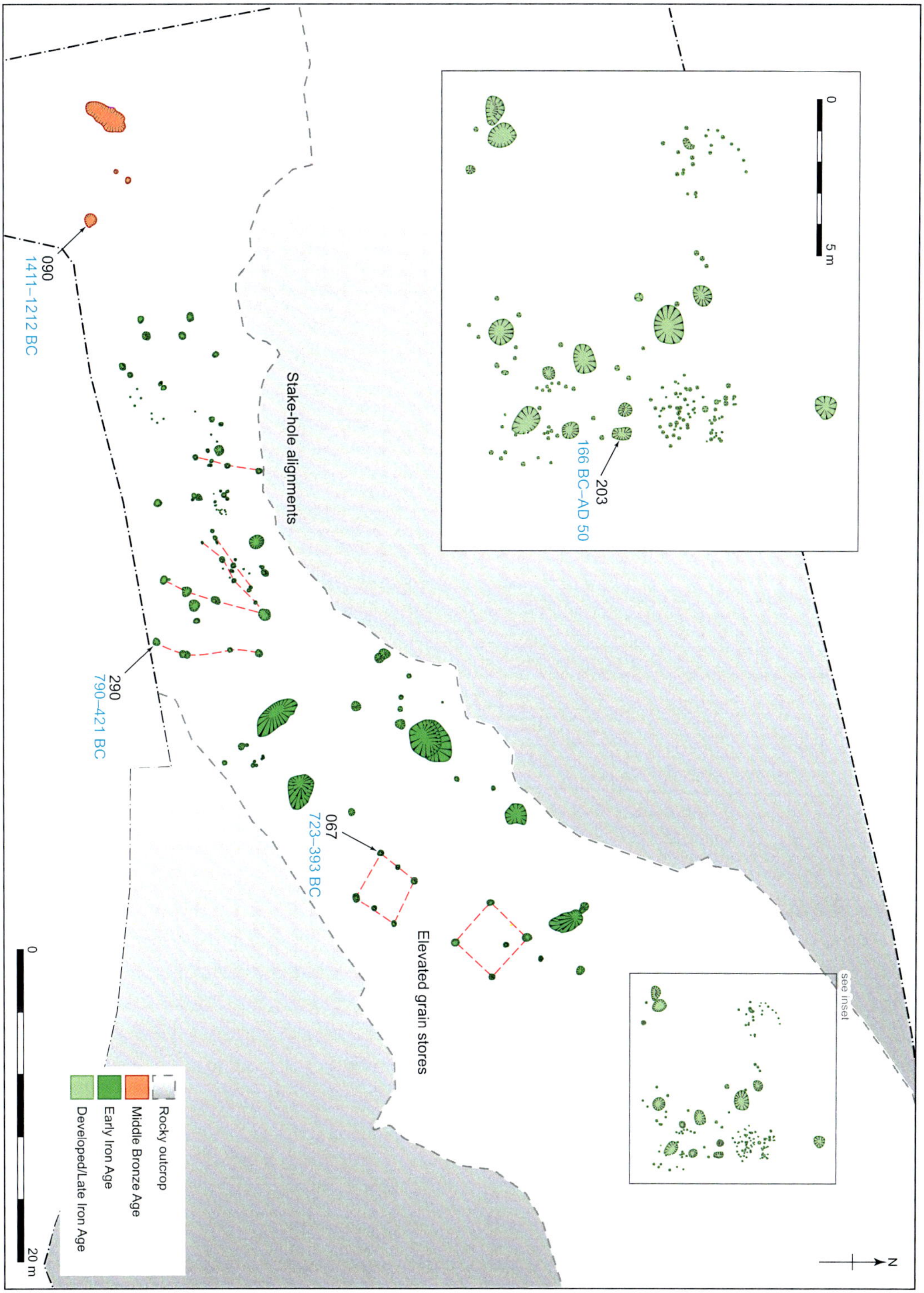

Illus. 2.25—Ballingowan 1, Area 1b. Middle Bronze Age pits and Iron Age grain stores, stake-hole alignments and associated features.

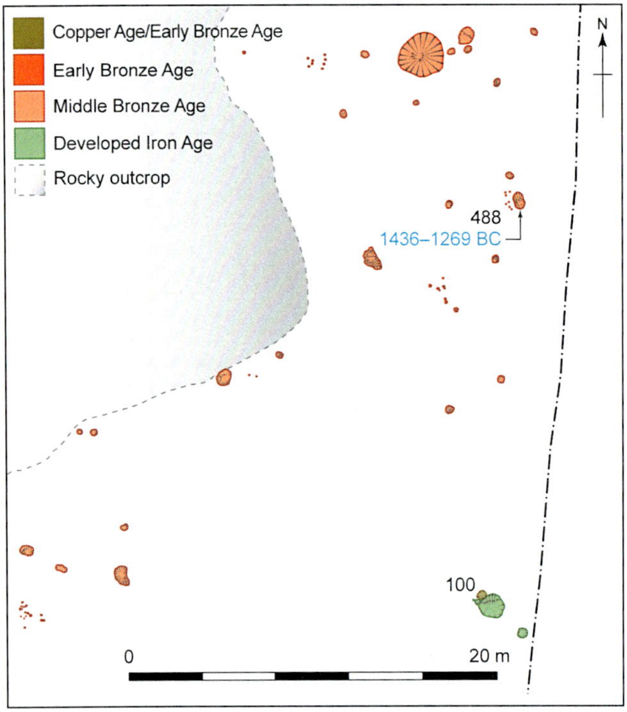

Illus. 2.26—Ballingowan 1, Area 1c. Middle Bronze Age pits and post-holes and Developed Iron Age pit.

were found in one of the pits. Hulled barley from a deposit in one of the hearths (054) was dated to 1678–1499 BC (SUERC-37312). It seems likely that the ditch to the south of the dated activity was contemporary with it and therefore Middle Bronze Age also.

A square-cut cereal-drying kiln (082; 2.3 m by 1.8 m and 0.6–1.4 m deep) was recorded 9 m to the south-west of the possible enclosure (Illus. 2.28). There was evidence of repeated burning within the main cut and its fills contained oak and hazel charcoal, as well as grains of hulled barley and oats, charred hazelnut shells and wild taxa (chickweed, mustards, pale persicaria, amphibious bistort, sedges, brambles, violets and spike rush). Hulled barley from a charcoal-rich basal layer (689) was dated to 1687–1513 BC (SUERC-37318), indicating that the kiln was broadly contemporary with the hearth in the enclosure. A ring of five stake-holes around the edge of the kiln point to a light wooden superstructure, which would have held the drying platform. The eastern edge of the kiln was truncated by a small pit, while the upper fill was truncated by a post-hole. These later features seemed unrelated to the kiln activity.

Late Bronze Age droveway

The archaeological remains in the northern part of Area 1a were dominated by a series of four curving ditches that appeared to form a Late Bronze Age droveway (Illus. 2.24 and 2.29), largely orientated WSW/ENE but turning to run WNW/ESE as it approached the eastern limit of excavation. It extended over a span of c. 57 m within the excavated area and consisted of a central area (3.2 m wide) flanked to north and south by pairs of roughly parallel ditches, each on average 1 m wide and 0.3 m deep. The ditch fills contained small stones and gravel. A sandstone rubbing stone was found in one ditch. It is likely that a bank once existed between each pair of ditches. At its western end the droveway opened out onto the floodzone of a stream (a tributary of the River Lee). On either side of this opening, other ditches extended north and south along the edges of the floodzone. They extended beyond the excavated area but probably reached to the banks of the stream. In effect, the droveway opened into a large enclosure formed by the flanking ditches in the east and the stream in the west. Hazel charcoal from one of the ditches (114) was dated to 895–770 BC (SUERC-37303). No other datable

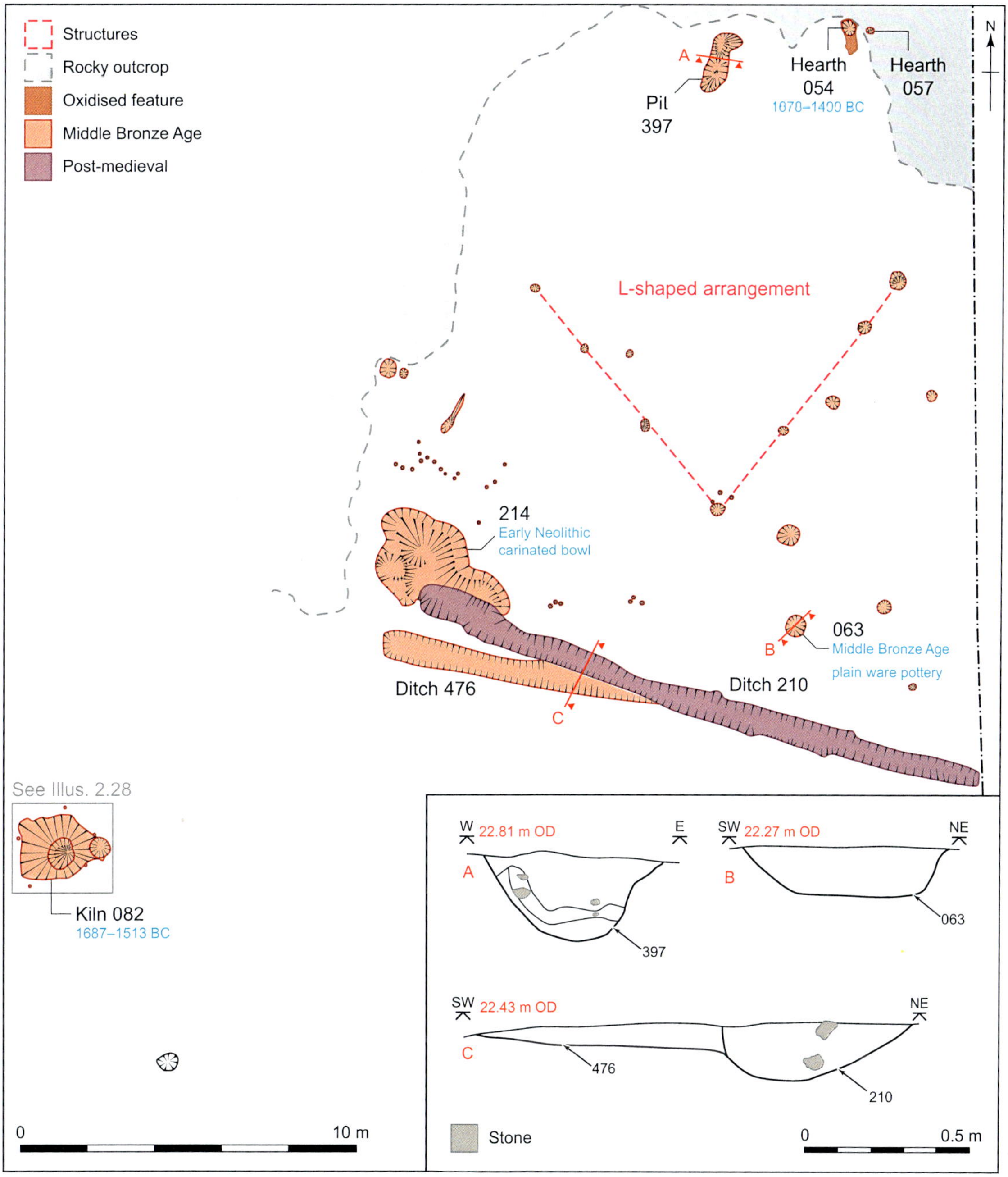

Illus. 2.27—Ballingowan 1, Area 1c. Middle Bronze Age cereal-drying kiln, possible enclosure and associated features.

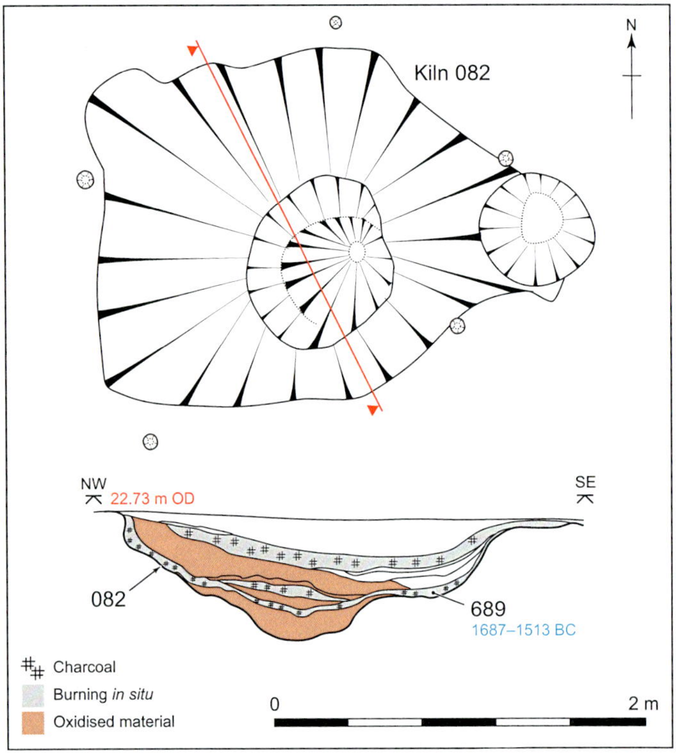

Illus. 2.28—Ballingowan 1, Area 1c. Middle Bronze Age cereal-drying kiln.

Illus. 2.29—Ballingowan 1, Area 1a. Aerial view of Middle Bronze Age droveway (outlined features overlaid) with flooding apparent within the western enclosed area (Aerialphoto.ie).

material was recovered and this single date from such a large feature must be considered with caution. An entrance break, 5 m wide, was identified between two of the ditches to the north of the droveway, indicating another point of access to/from the stream. Several pits and a possible hearth situated nearby are likely to have been contemporary with the droveway.

The droveway was probably used by herders to bring livestock to the river for watering. The single date obtained suggests that this is a very early example of this site type in an Irish context, as other known examples are all likely to be early medieval or later (Taylor 2010; Delaney 2006; Ó Faoláin 2010). This is further discussed in Chapter 5.

Early Iron Age grain stores

Two four-post structures, interpreted as elevated grain (or hay) stores, were excavated in Area 1a (Illus. 2.24). The northernmost structure consisted of a rectangular arrangement of post-holes (up to 0.4 m in diameter by 0.42 m deep) measuring 3 m long by 1.5 m wide. The post-holes contained flecks of charcoal and fragments of unidentifiable burnt bone, with hazel charcoal from one (198) returning a date of 806–547 BC (SUERC-37304). The second structure was 47 m to the south-west and was also rectangular, measuring 3.1 m long by 2.1 m wide. The post-holes were similar in size to those of the northern grain store and all contained flecks of charcoal. A small quantity of charred cereal grain (indeterminate) and straw was also retrieved from one of the post-holes, while alder charcoal from another (313) returned a date of 780–417 BC (SUERC-37302).

A large number of pits, post-holes and stake-holes in this area are thought to have been associated with the grain stores, including several stake-hole clusters and alignments. The stake-holes seemed to follow a curvilinear course between the two four-post structures and may have supported a light fence or fences.

Two more grain stores were identified in Area 1b (Illus. 2.25). Both were roughly square in plan, with one consisting of four post-holes (3.8 m by 3.7 m) and the other, located 4.3 m to the south-west, of six post-holes (3.64 m by 3.4 m) (Illus. 2.30). Post-holes from the latter structure produced a small quantity of charcoal and probable cattle bone. A sample of this bone from one of the post-holes (067) returned a date of 723–393 BC (SUERC-37678). Numerous other pits, post-holes and stake-hole alignments were identified to the west and south-west of the grain stores. A date of 790–421 BC (SUERC-37310) was obtained from charred barley grain from one of the post-holes (290) in this group.

Developed Iron Age iron-smelting furnace, pits and post-holes

A scatter of pits and post-holes extended across Area 1c from south-west to north-east for approximately 100 m. These included a roughly circular, rock-cut iron-smelting furnace (673; Illus. 2.21 and 2.31), which measured 1 m across and 0.4 m deep. It contained oak charcoal, slag and burnt clay, with a sample of the charcoal from one fill (675) returning a date of 382–186 BC (SUERC-37313). Analysis of the slag indicated that this was predominantly a smelting furnace, though the presence of a moderate quantity of smithing slag indicates that it was possibly reused as a smithing hearth once the smelting process was complete. A number of pits in the immediate vicinity are also

Illus. 2.30—Ballingowan 1, Area 1b. Early Iron Age elevated grain store, view to north-east (Rubicon Heritage Services Ltd).

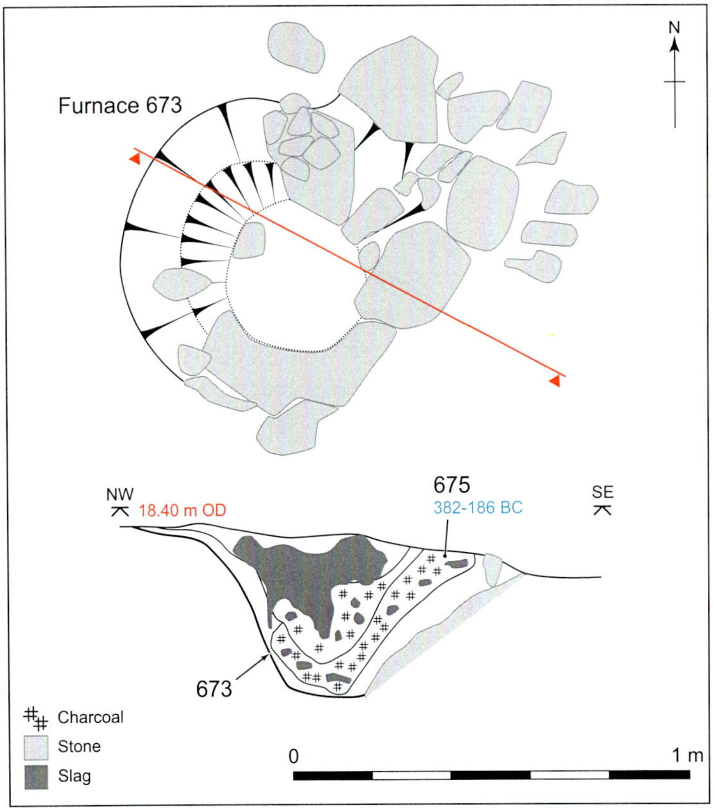

Illus. 2.31—Ballingowan 1, Area 1c. Developed Iron Age smelting furnace.

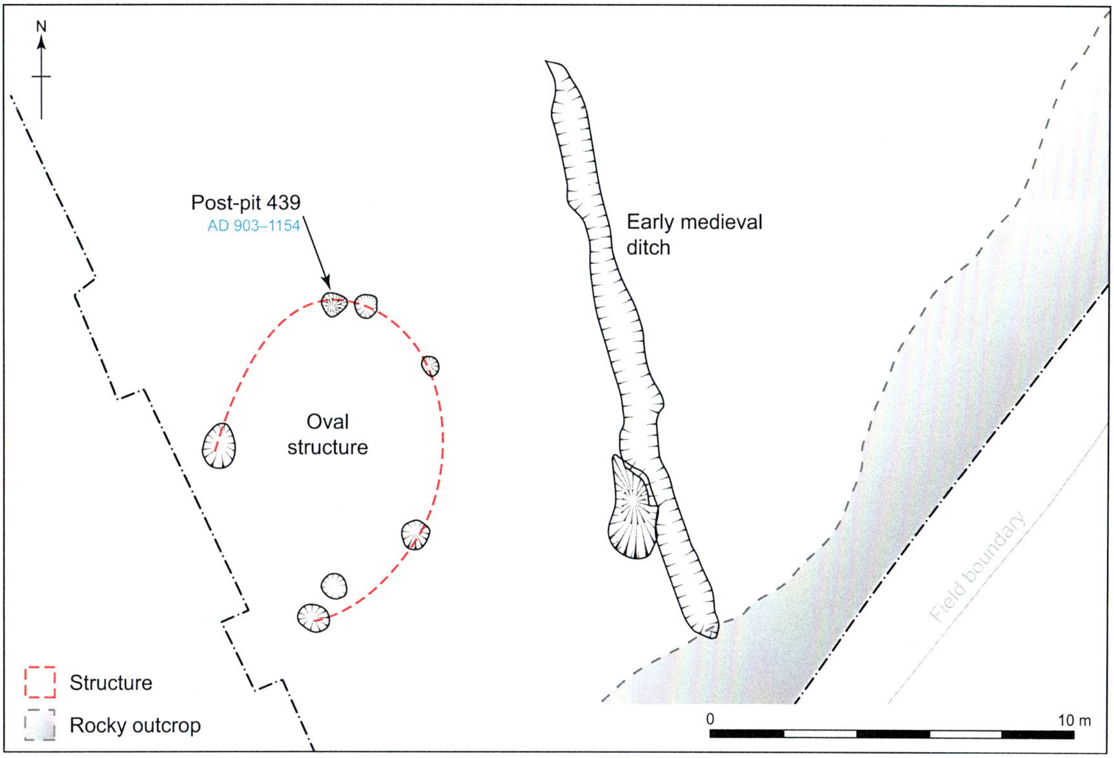

Illus. 2.32—Ballingowan 1, Area 1a. Early medieval building and associated features.

attributed to this phase of activity owing to their proximity to the furnace and the fact that some of the pits contained metal-working debris.

Late Iron Age pits, post-holes and stake-holes

Two large pits were identified in the south-west corner of Area 1a (Illus. 2.24). Blackthorn charcoal from one of the pits (050) produced a date of AD 65–232 (SUERC-37301). A large cluster of pits, post-holes and stake-holes identified to the east are also thought to be Late Iron Age owing to their proximity to the dated pit, although some are also close to the Early Bronze Age round-house and could as easily date from that period.

A dense concentration of features was identified in the north-east corner of Area 1b (Illus. 2.25). Hazel charcoal from one of them (Pit 203) was dated to 166 BC–AD 50 (SUERC-37309). At least some of the clustered features here are likely to represent the remains of insubstantial buildings, but no building plans were identified.

Possible early medieval building and cereal-drying kiln

An oval arrangement of six pits and post-holes in the south-west corner of Area 1a was identified as a possible building (Illus. 2.32). It measured 7.7 m by 5.2 m on plan but may extend slightly further west, beyond the limit of excavation. A small quantity of charred cereal grain was recovered from two pits on the northern part of the oval, including oats, hulled barley, wheat species and indeterminate cereal grain. A small quantity of naked barley grain was also recorded, which is likely to reflect its presence as a relict crop. Wild taxa of mainly arable weeds, such as goosefoot, scentless mayweed and grasses, were also recovered. Willow charcoal from one of the pits (439) was dated to AD 903–1154 (SUERC-37308). A NNW/SSE-aligned ditch to the east and a line of pits/post-holes to the north (not illustrated) may date from the early medieval period given their proximity to the building.

A dense cluster of post-holes and stake-holes as well as a number of scattered pits, two hearths and other features were identified at the northern end of Area 1c (Illus. 2.33). A charred oat grain from one of the pits (555) was dated to AD 419–574 (SUERC-37319). The other features were not directly dated but have been attributed to the early medieval period on the basis of their proximity to this pit. This cluster of features had no clear pattern and no obvious function. An early medieval spindle-whorl was recovered from topsoil in this area.

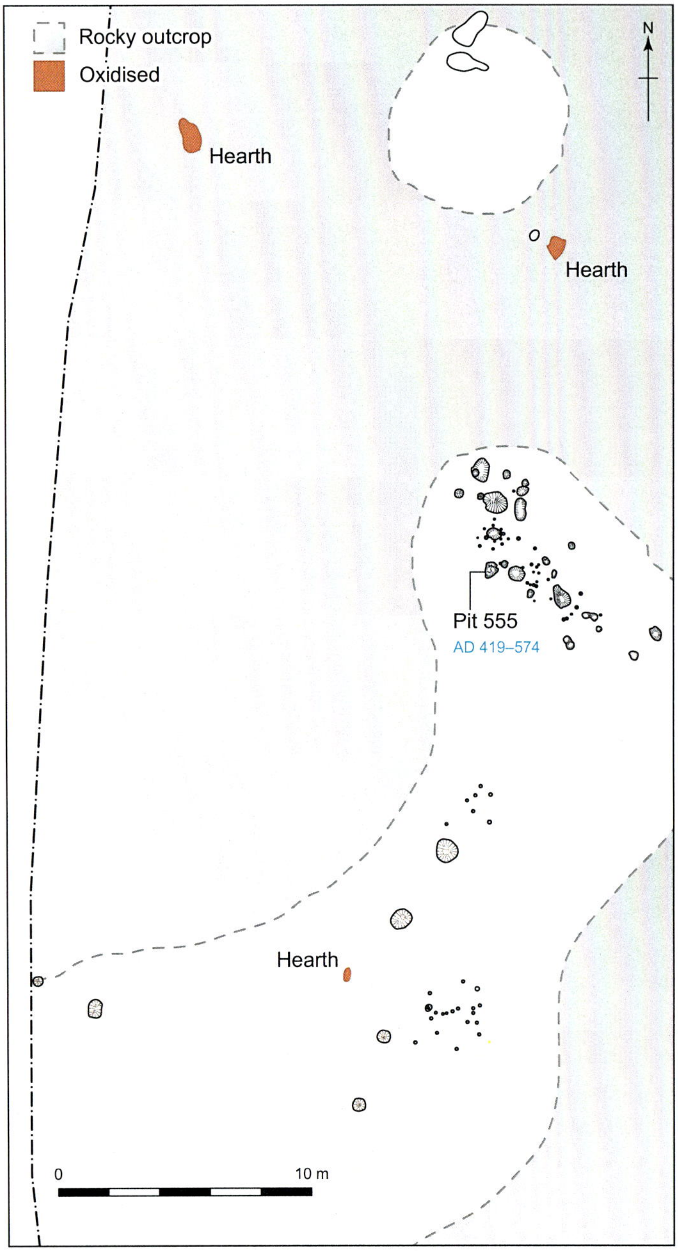

Illus. 2.33—Ballingowan 1, Area 1c. Early medieval pits, hearths, post-holes and stake-holes.

An isolated figure-of-eight-shaped kiln (511; 1.89 m by 1.02 m and 0.38 m deep) of likely early medieval date was also identified in Area 1c, 65 m south of the feature cluster described above (Illus. 2.21). Its shape was typical of a cereal-drying kiln, though it was quite small.

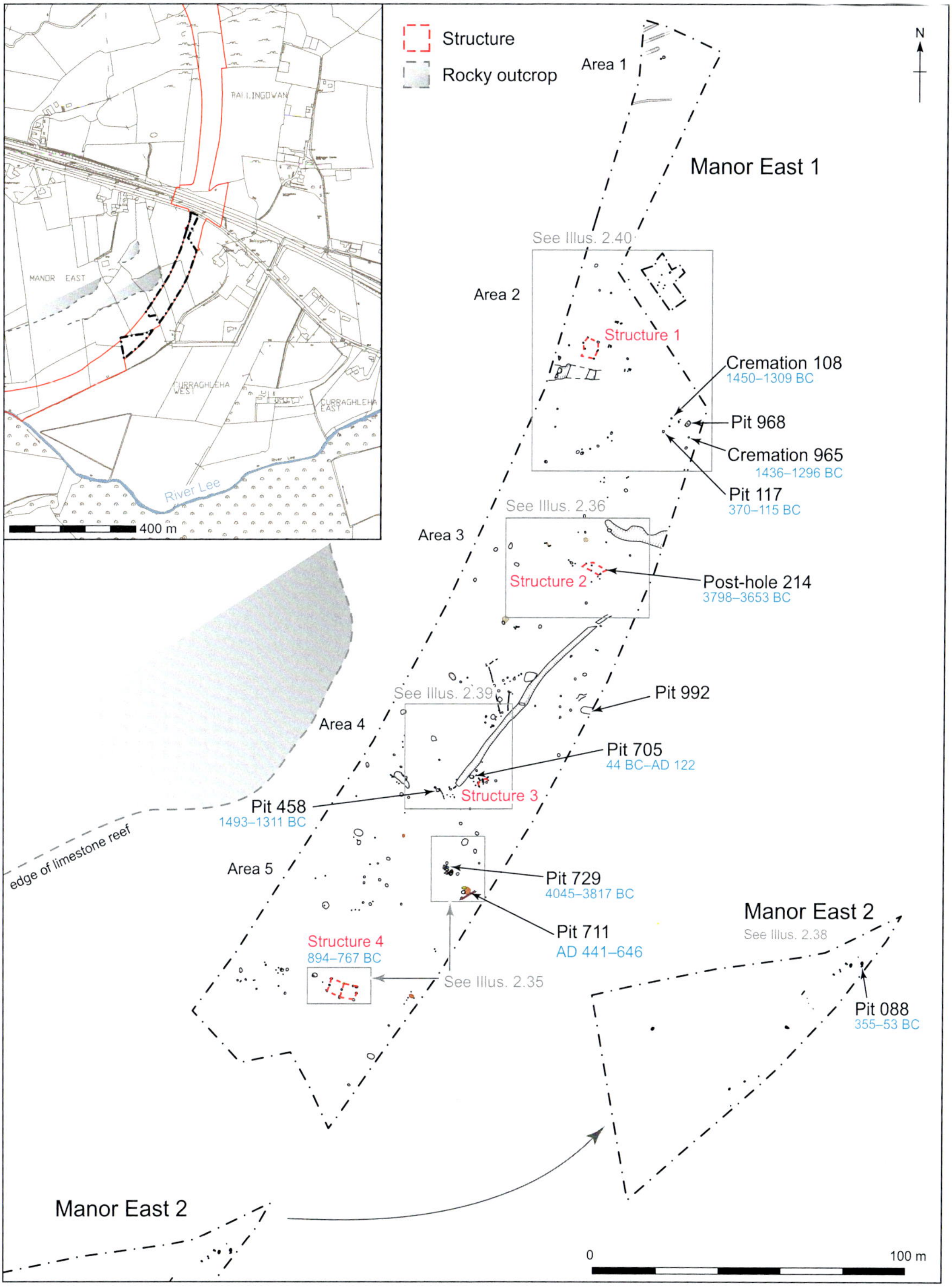

Illus. 2.34—Manor East 1 and 2. Site plan, Areas 1–5.

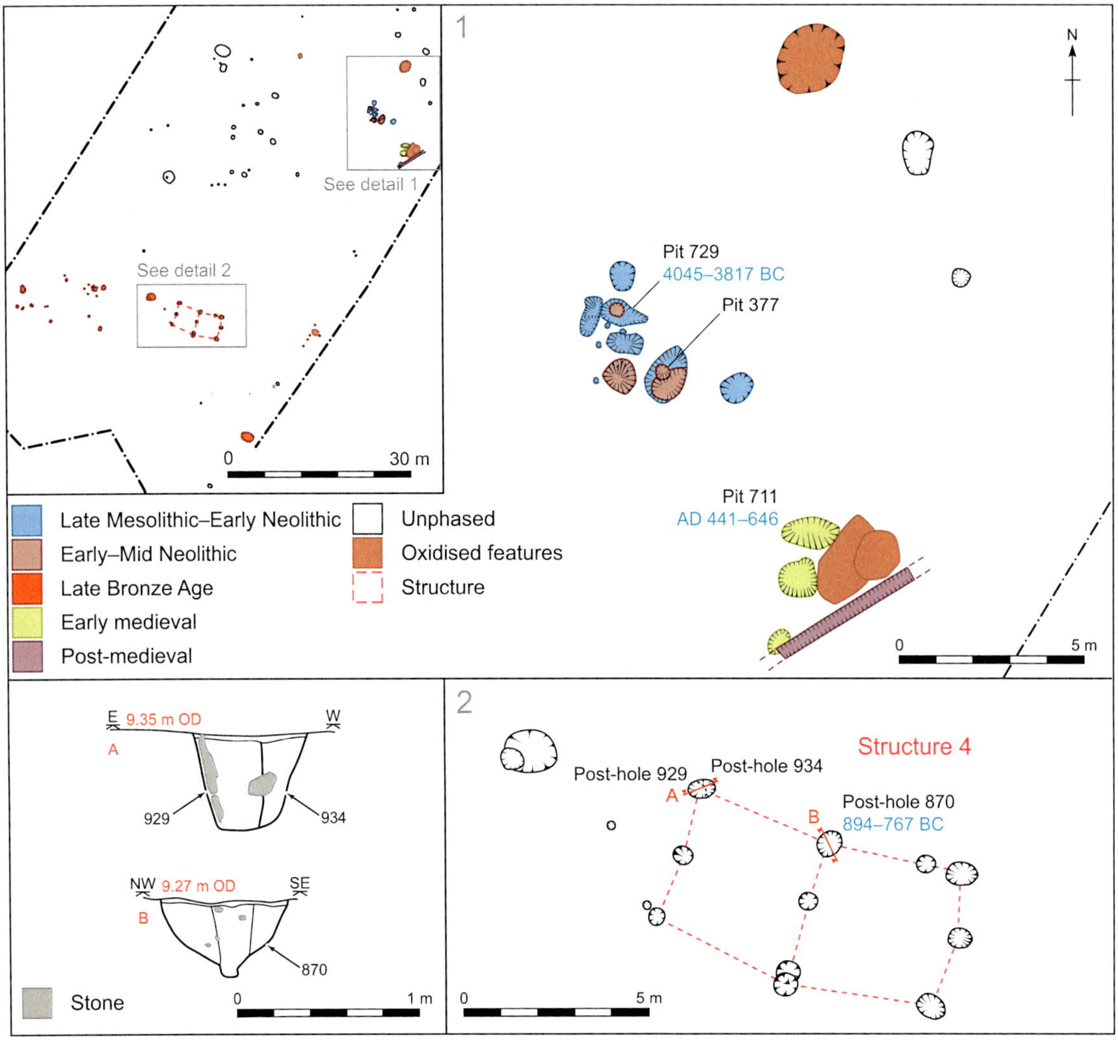

Illus. 2.35—Manor East 1, Area 5. Mesolithic/Neolithic pits and Late Bronze Age building (Structure 4).

Manor East 1 and 2: prehistoric settlement and burial; early medieval industrial activity[7]

Manor East 1 and 2 were situated in undulating pasture that sloped gently southwards from outcropping limestone, stretching as far as marshy low-lying ground close to the floodplain of the River Lee and one of its tributaries. The area of excavation was 450 m long and was divided into five areas for recording purposes. Excavations revealed the remains of Neolithic and Bronze Age settlement, Bronze Age cremation pit burials, a possible Iron Age building and early medieval industrial activity (Illus. 2.34).

[7] Manor East, Co. Kerry; barony: Trughanacmy; ITM 486502 613404 (Manor East 1) and ITM 486373 613220 (Manor East 2); height 8–12 m OD; Excavation Reg. Nos E4323 (Manor East 1) and E4322 (Manor East 2); Ministerial Directions A056; Excavation Director: Liam McKinstry.

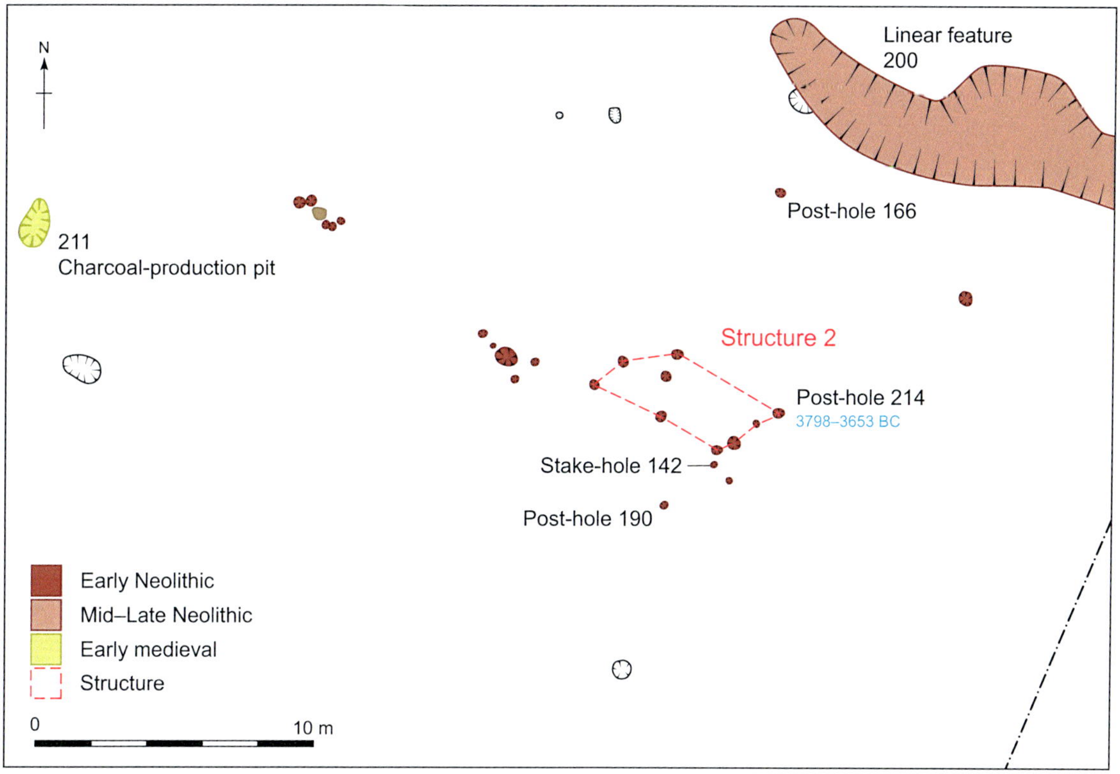

Illus. 2.36—Manor East 1, Area 3. Early Neolithic building (Structure 2) and early medieval charcoal-production pit.

Late Mesolithic/Early Neolithic pit

The earliest activity was represented by a pit (729) in Area 5, from which oak charcoal returned a date of 4045–3817 BC (SUERC-37323) (Illus. 2.35). Four nearby pits and four stake-holes have also been attributed to this phase of activity, though their function is unclear.

Early Neolithic building

A subrectangular building (Structure 2) measuring 5.2 m long (NW/SE) by 2.4 m wide was excavated in Area 3 (Illus. 2.36). It was defined by a stake-hole and seven post-holes (on average 0.32 m long by 0.26 m wide by 0.2 m deep). The fills contained hazel and oak charcoal and fragments of hazelnut shell. Hazel charcoal from one of the post-holes (214) was dated to 3798–3653 BC (SUERC-37321). The only internal post-hole was probably for a roof support. Eleven sherds of Early Neolithic carinated bowl were recovered from two nearby post-holes (190 (E4323:189:001) and 166 (E4323:167:001–002)) and a stake-hole (142; E4323:146:001–002). A rhyolite blade and quartz crystal debitage were also found in Post-hole 166, while flint and quartz debitage were found in Post-hole 190. Other nearby pits and post-holes were probably also associated with the building, though they did not contain any diagnostic material.

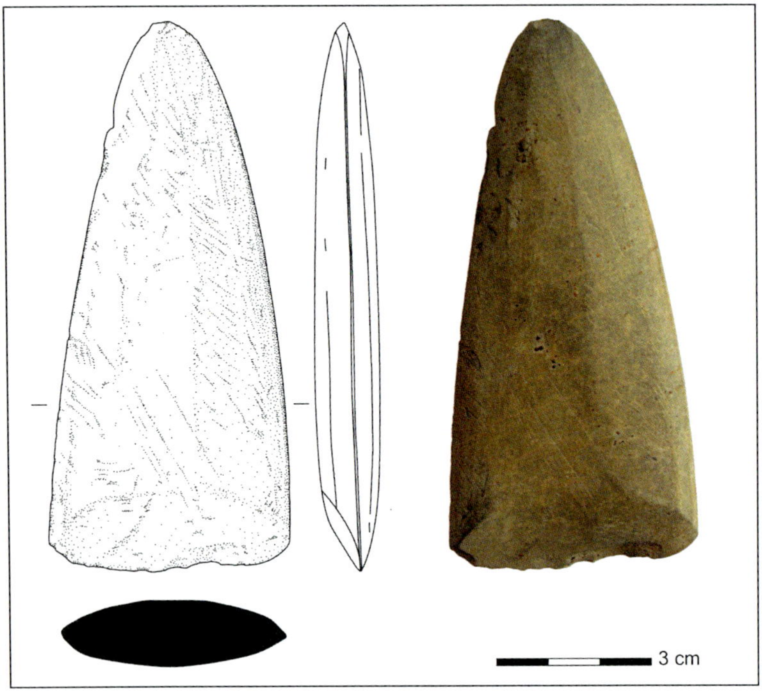

Illus. 2.37—Manor East 1, Area 4. Middle Neolithic rhyolite polished stone axe (E4323:341:001) recovered from a stake-hole (342) of a possible Iron Age building (Structure 3) (Sara Nylund).

In Area 2, 45 m north of the building, three sherds of a carinated bowl (E4323:969:001; E4323:970:001–002) were found in a pit (968) that was truncated at its centre by a circular stake-hole and which also contained unidentified charcoal (Illus. 2.34). Overall, up to seven carinated bowls are represented on the site. The fabric is very distinctive and consistent with the earliest type of Neolithic pottery, though only one of the sherds had features to indicate which part of a vessel it was from (neck sherd) (Roche & Grogan 2012a).

Middle–Late Neolithic pits and chipped-stone tools

Several features produced chipped-stone tools that are diagnostic of Middle to Late Neolithic activity. These included a hollow flint scraper (E4323:016:001) from a post-hole (017) in Area 2 and a piece of quartz crystal debitage from a linear feature in Area 3 (200). Another such piece was recovered from a pit (377) in Area 5 (Illus. 2.35), which was part of a group of features that truncated the Late Mesolithic/Early Neolithic activity there. The crystal debitage suggests that these features were at least Late Neolithic in origin.

A polished rhyolite axe of probable Middle Neolithic date (Illus. 2.37) was recovered from a stake-hole that formed part of a structure in Area 4 (below). The structure, however, was close to a pit that was radiocarbon-dated to the Iron Age, so it is possible that the axe was incorporated into the foundation of a later building.

Four probable Middle to Late Neolithic pits were also excavated at Manor East 2 (Illus. 2.38), one of which (075) contained a flint flake and a possible retouched flint artefact.

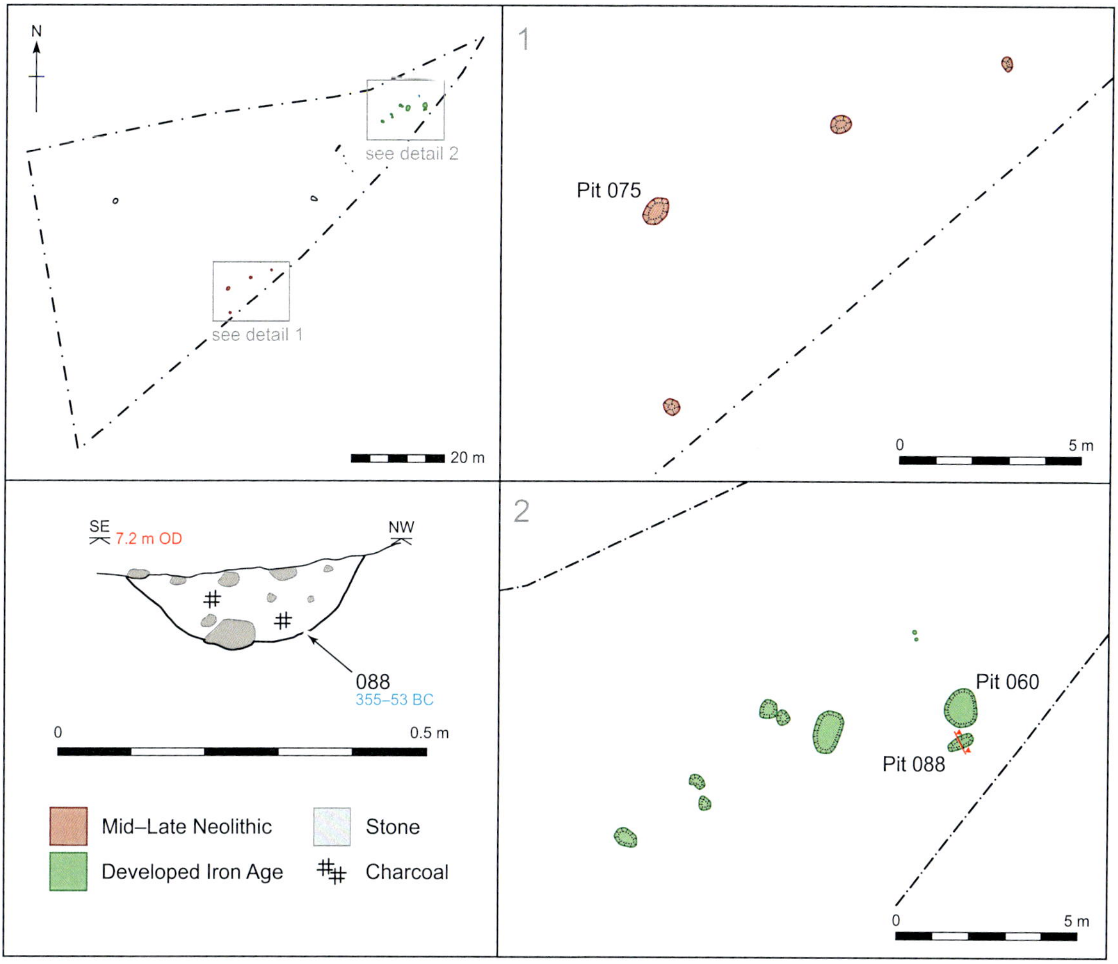

Illus. 2.38—Manor East 2. Middle–Late Neolithic pits and Developed Iron Age domestic waste pits.

Middle Bronze Age cremation pit burials, pit, stake-holes and post-holes

Middle Bronze Age activity was represented by a possible roasting pit (458) and several stake-holes and post-holes in Area 4 (Illus. 2.39), and two cremation pit burials (108 and 965) in Area 2 (Illus. 2.40). The roasting pit in Area 4 contained charcoal and heat-shattered stone and was dated to 1493–1311 BC (SUERC-37322) using alder charcoal. Nine of the adjacent stake-holes seemed to form a short alignment (3 m long) and may have been part of a light windbreak.

Cremated bone from the more northerly burial in Area 2 (108; 0.40 m in diameter by 0.51 m deep) returned a date of 1450–1309 BC (SUERC-37087), while a similar date of 1436–1296 BC (SUERC-37088) was returned for bone from the second cremation (965; 0.42 m long by 0.38 m wide).

In both cases the human remains represented the burial of an adult. It was not possible to determine the sex of these individuals or their ages at death. One of the pits (108) contained oak, ash

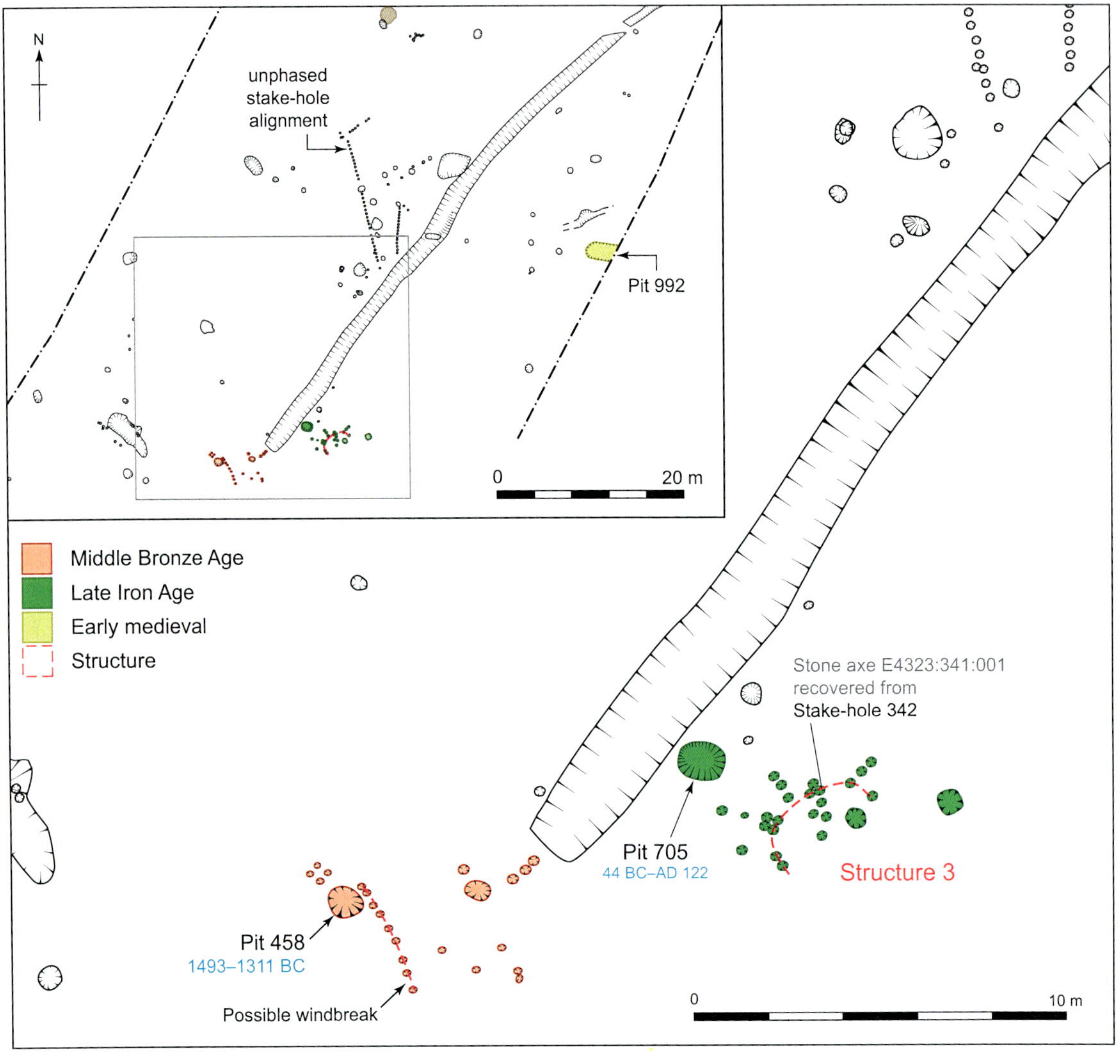

Illus. 2.39—Manor East 1, Area 4. Middle Bronze Age roasting pit and possible windbreak, possible Late Iron Age structure (Structure 3) and associated features.

and blackthorn charcoal, as well as burnt clay, charred barley grain and a chert convex end scraper. Cremated bone in the second pit (965) had been interred within a Middle Bronze Age plain vessel (Illus. 2.41). Only the distorted rim, five other fragments and several crumbs were recovered. Owing to its significance, the vessel was block-lifted by conservator Susannah Kelly for analysis and excavation under laboratory conditions.

Late Bronze Age building

The remains of a rectangular building (Structure 4), measuring 7 m long (NW/SE) by 4 m wide, was excavated in Area 5 (Illus. 2.35). It was defined by nine post-holes (on average 0.42 m long by

0.35 m wide by 0.3 m deep), two supporting or replacement post-holes and one stake-hole, the fills of which contained oak charcoal, charred cereal grain (hulled barley) and unidentifiable animal bone fragments. Oak charcoal from one of the post-holes (870) returned a date of 894–767 BC (SUERC-37328). A post-hole at the centre of the building may have served as a roof support.

A cluster of pits and post-holes to the west of the building has also been ascribed to this phase of activity. The presence of two rubbing stones in one of the pits and sandstone debitage in one of the post-holes seems to confirm a prehistoric date, although their association with the building is not conclusive.

Developed Iron Age pits, post-holes and stake-holes

A number of pits, stake-holes and post-holes dating from this period were identified at Manor East 2 (Illus. 2.34 and 2.38). One of the pits (060) contained varying quantities of unidentifiable charred cereal grain, oak and non-oak charcoal, unidentifiable burnt bone and burnt clay. Charred hazelnut shell from an adjacent pit (088) returned a date of 355–53 BC (SUERC-37299). Further north, in Area 2 of Manor East 1 (Illus. 2.40), hazel charcoal from an oval pit (117) returned a date

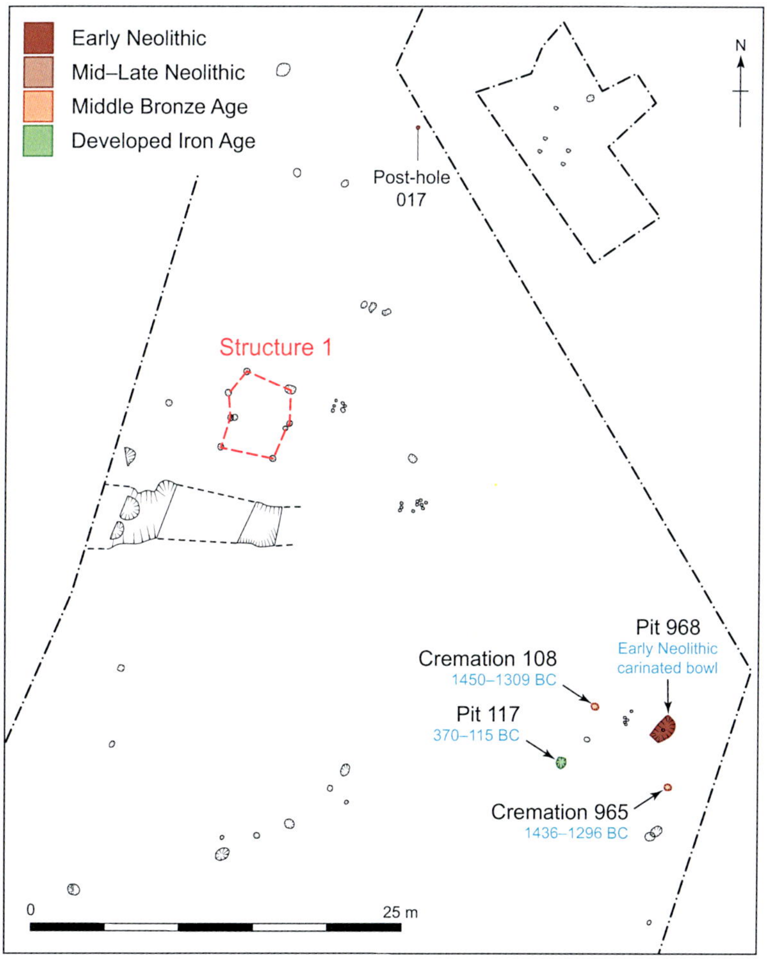

Illus. 2.40—Manor East 1, Area 2. Early Neolithic pit and post-hole, Middle Bronze Age cremation pit burials, Developed Iron Age domestic waste pit and an unphased building (Structure 1).

of 370–115 BC (SUERC-37320). Given the absence of any evidence for *in situ* burning in these pits, it is likely that they were domestic waste pits.

Late Iron Age pit and possible structure

A cluster of pits, post-holes and stake-holes in Area 4 is believed to date from the Late Iron Age owing to its proximity to a large pit (705; 1.2 m long by 0.92 m wide by 0.45 m deep) that was dated to 44 BC–AD 122 (SUERC-37329) using alder charcoal (Illus. 2.39). The pit also contained two grains of barley and some heat-affected stones. Immediately east of it was a possible building (Structure 3; c. 3 m wide) comprised of a semicircular arrangement of eight stake-holes, with further alignments of stake-holes radiating off it. Several features (four post-holes and one pit) were identified within the (projected) internal floor area, possibly representing structural timbers. The Middle Neolithic rhyolite stone axe that was recovered from one of the stake-holes (342) (above) may have been chosen for ritual burial in this Iron Age building, perhaps as a foundation deposit to bring protection and good fortune. The dating of the structure is quite tenuous, however, and it is possible that some of the features in this area, if not Structure 3 itself, were Neolithic in date.

Early medieval pits and hearth

An oval pit (711) in Area 5 (Illus. 2.35) and several nearby pits and a hearth are believed to be early medieval in date. Pit 711 contained quantities of charcoal, charred cereal grains (mainly oats and hulled barley but also five grains of bread/club wheat), wild taxa (crab-apple, violet, bramble and vetch fruits, sedge nutlets and goosefoot) and unidentifiable mammal bone, along with chert debitage. A sample of the hulled barley returned a date of AD 441–646 (SUERC-37324). A bone weaving tool/needle (35 mm long) of a type commonly found on Irish medieval settlements was found in a waste pit (992) in Area 4 (Illus. 2.39), c. 56 m north-west of Pit 711. The bone was too fragmentary to identify to species. A medieval date is also likely for a possible charcoal-production pit (211; 1.57 m long by 0.84 m wide and 0.97 m deep) excavated in Area 3.

Undated features

Many features in the excavated areas at Manor East could not be attributed to a specific phase of activity. These included the remains of Structure 1 (Area 2) (Illus. 2.34 and 2.40), which was subrectangular in plan (5.2 m long NNE/SSW by 4.4 m) and consisted of five stake-holes, three postholes and a pit. Elsewhere, a number of hearths and possible waste pits were also identified.

Interpretation

Manor East 1 presented a range of features associated with domestic, industrial and ritual activity, while features found at Manor East 2 suggested more temporary activity related to the use of the wetland for wood, foodstuffs and other materials. The limestone outcrop and the River Lee and its floodplain seem to have been the focus for this activity, which spanned the Late Mesolithic/Early Neolithic through to the early medieval and post-medieval periods.

Illus. 2.41—Manor East 1, Area 2. Middle Bronze Age vessel rim (E4323:966:001) from cremation pit burial (965) (Sara Nylund).

Clashedmond 1: Middle to Late Bronze Age pits and post-holes; enclosure; post-medieval townland boundary[8]

The site was in the north-western corner of a small pasture field, which sloped gently towards the north-west. Excavation revealed a number of Middle–Late Bronze Age pits and post-holes and part of a ditched enclosure of uncertain date.

Middle–Late Bronze Age pits and post-holes

The earliest recorded activity consisted of nine pits and three post-holes located within the area enclosed by a large curvilinear ditch (Illus. 2.42). Stratigraphic and dating evidence indicates, however, that these features were not contemporary with the ditch but rather pre-dated it. One of the pits (067) was cut by the enclosure ditch. Alder charcoal from another pit (051) returned a date of 1417–1217 BC (SUERC-37272). A slightly later date of 1257–999 BC (SUERC-37273) was obtained for hazel charcoal retrieved from another (044). These features did not form any visible patterns or alignments.

Enclosure

Approximately two thirds of a ditched enclosure (003 and 033) were excavated within the footprint of the project (Illus. 2.43). The excavated portion had an internal diameter of 35.9 m (max.) NW/SE. An entrance in the south-east was formed by an earthen causeway, 5.9 m wide, paved with rough stone.

---

[8] Clashedmond, Co. Kerry; barony: Trughanacmy; ITM 486595 611613; height 23 m OD; Excavation Reg. No. E4289; Ministerial Directions A056; Excavation Director: Liam McKinstry.

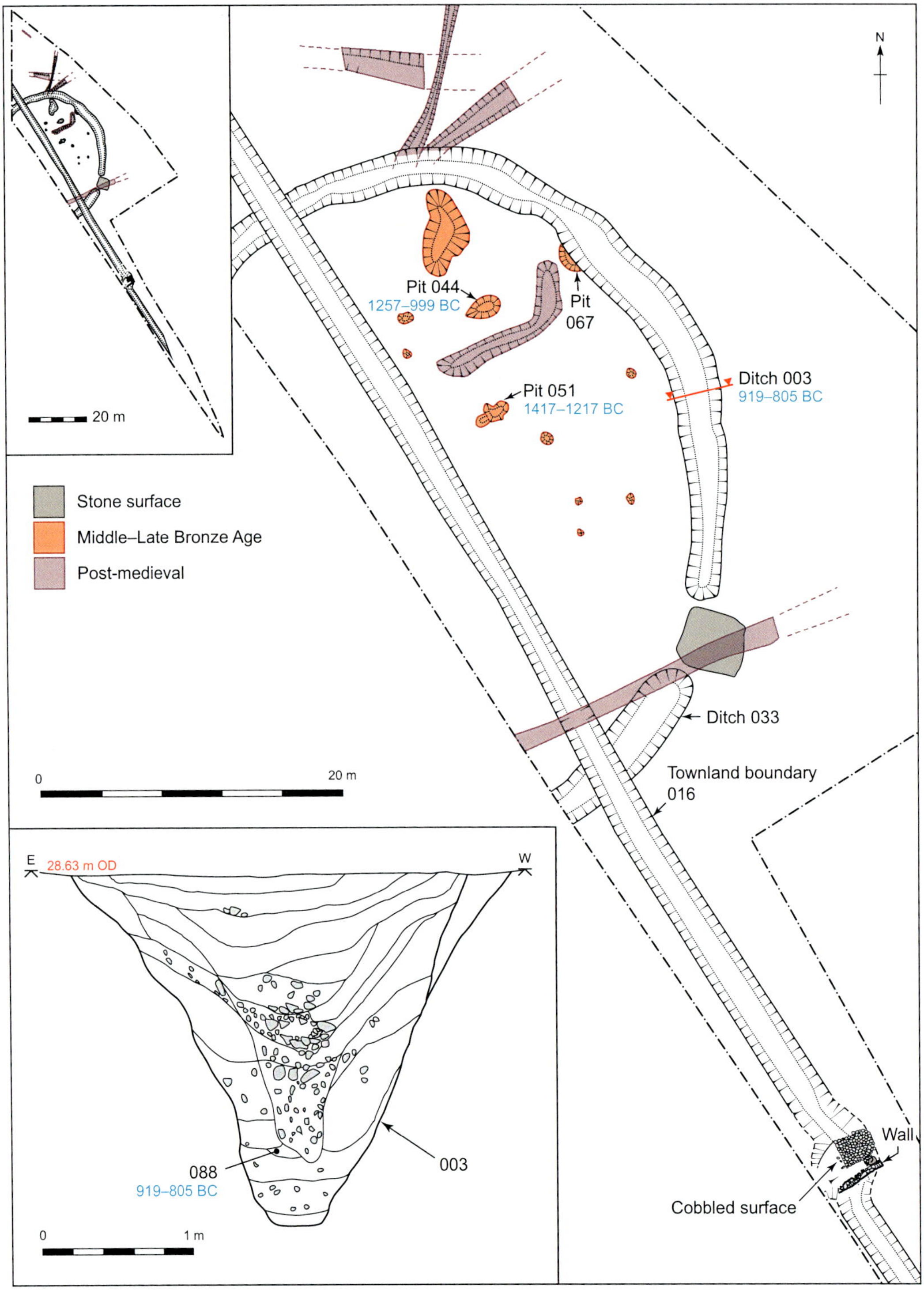

Illus. 2.42—Clashedmond 1. Middle–Late Bronze Age pits and a ditched enclosure of uncertain date.

Illus. 2.43 (above)—Clashedmond 1. Aerial view of enclosure during excavation and ringfort KE038-018 to south-east (Aerialphoto.ie).

Illus. 2.44 (left)—Clashedmond 1: 18th/19th-century glazed red earthenware dish (E4289:037:001) recovered from a drainage ditch (Sara Nylund).

The northern part of the ditch (003) had a steep, V-shaped profile and was 2–3 m wide and a maximum of 2.2 m deep. The ditch contained 23 fills, most of which were sterile. No artefacts were recovered and there was only a small amount of palaeoenvironmental material, consisting of charred hulled barley and indeterminate cereal grains, along with a small quantity of badly abraded charcoal fragments (mostly non-oak). Hulled barley from one of the lower ditch fills (088) was dated to 919–805 BC (SUERC-37271).

The southern part of the ditch (033) had a broader, shallower profile with concave sides and an uneven base. It was 1.6–2 m wide and a maximum of 0.74 m deep and contained three fills. The full extents of the ditches are unknown, as both continued beyond the limits of excavation to the west and into the neighbouring townland of Poulawaddra.

Townland boundary

The townland boundary ditch between Clashedmond and Poulawaddra (016; 1.3 m wide and 0.35 m deep) (Illus. 2.42) ran NW/SE along the western edge of the site. An associated bank was located to the west of this but has been replaced by the current, upstanding boundary, which is a mix of hedgerow and post-and-wire fence. An access point was cut into the original bank towards the southern end of the site. A small wall and cobbled surface were identified overlying the ditch at this access point. These features correspond with an entrance and lane shown on the Ordnance Survey six-inch map of 1846 and were therefore contemporary with the townland boundary.

Fourteen sherds of pottery from a red earthenware dish with a thin greenish-yellow lead glaze (Illus. 2.44) were recovered from a drainage ditch that was intercut with the townland boundary. The dish was most likely used for food preparation and storage. It dates from the 18th or 19th century and was probably locally made, though similar vessels were also imported from England and Wales during this period.

Interpretation

While a Late Bronze Age date was returned from the enclosure ditch at Clashedmond 1, there was no further corroborating evidence to support its interpretation as a prehistoric settlement enclosure. The Bronze Age pits clearly pre-date it. Moreover, the radiocarbon date was obtained from a poorly preserved barley grain that may have been exposed on the ground surface for some time before making its way into the ditch fill. It is quite possible, therefore, that the grain was residual (i.e. a stray inclusion from an earlier period) and that the date does not relate to the construction or use of the enclosure.

The absence of occupation evidence and the fact that the enclosure lies only 50 m north-west of a recorded ringfort (KE038-018) suggest an alternative interpretation, namely that it was an early medieval livestock enclosure. Although this cannot be confirmed on the basis of the present evidence, it remains the most likely interpretation for the Clashedmond enclosure.

Burnt mounds

Burnt mounds are the remains of sites where hot stones were used to heat water. They have been identified in almost every part of the country and are the most common prehistoric monument type in Ireland. They date from the Early Neolithic to the medieval period, though dated examples are largely clustered in the Bronze Age (Hawkes 2018).

The technology of burnt mounds is well known. Stones were heated in a fire/hearth and

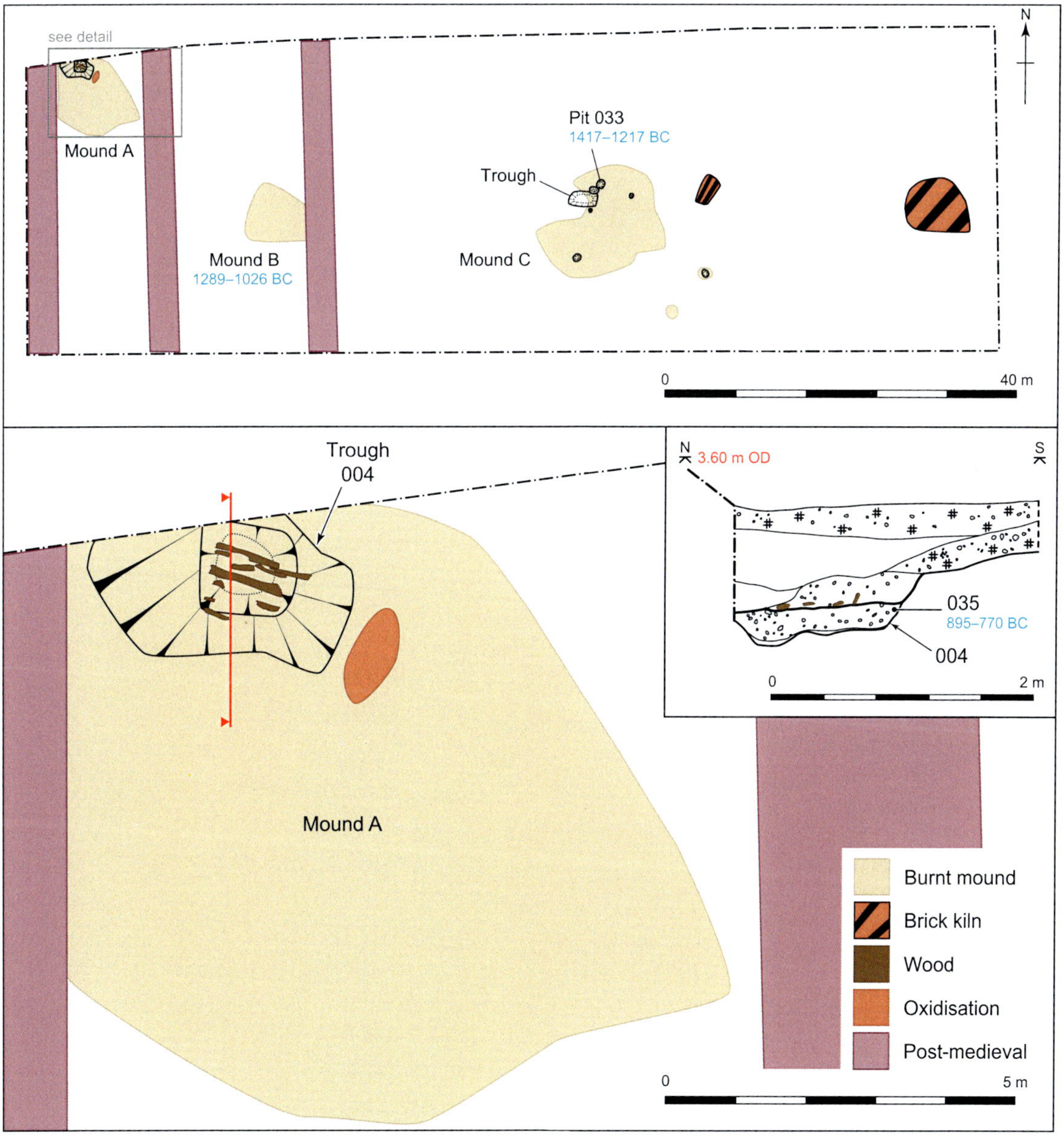

Illus. 2.45—Camp 1. Burnt mounds and troughs, with a detailed plan of Mound A and a section of the trough (004). Remnants of modern brick kilns were also recorded at this site (top right).

Illus. 2.46—Ballinorig West 1. Mid-excavation view of a burnt mound, view to north-east (Rubicon Heritage Services Ltd).

placed in a nearby water-filled trough, where the heat from the stones brought the water to boiling point. The hot stones would eventually shatter upon contact with cold water and after the trough had cooled they were removed and discarded, creating the characteristic mound/spread of heat-shattered stones. How the boiled water itself was used, however, is a matter of some debate.

Many suggestions for the functions of hot-stone technology have been put forward over the years, including cooking (O'Kelly 1954), brewing (Quinn & Moore 2007), butter-making (Sayce 1945), bathing (Ó Drisceoil 1988), dyeing and textile-processing (Jeffrey 1991; Reilly et al. 2012), butchery (Tourunen 2008), leather-working, saunas (Barfield & Hodder 1987; O'Sullivan & Downey 2004) and rendering animal fats (Monk 2007).

On the Tralee Bypass, 16 of the 37 archaeological sites excavated included remains that could be attributed to hot-stone technology. Seven of the sites consisted of at least one trough and an associated mound/spread—of these Camp 1 (Illus. 2.45) and Ballinorig West 1 (Illus. 2.46) had multiple troughs. Three sites consisted of only pits/troughs filled with heat-shattered stone and charcoal, whereas the remaining six comprised only spreads or mounds, with no associated pits/troughs identified within the boundaries of the road project.

The earliest burnt mound identified on the route (Caherleheen 1) was Late Neolithic in date, four others (Ballindooganig 1, Camp 4, Ballinorig South 1 and Ballinorig West 1) dated from the Late Neolithic/Copper Age transition period, while one site (Dromavally 2) dated from the Copper Age/Early Bronze Age. The rest of the burnt mounds from the project date from between the Early

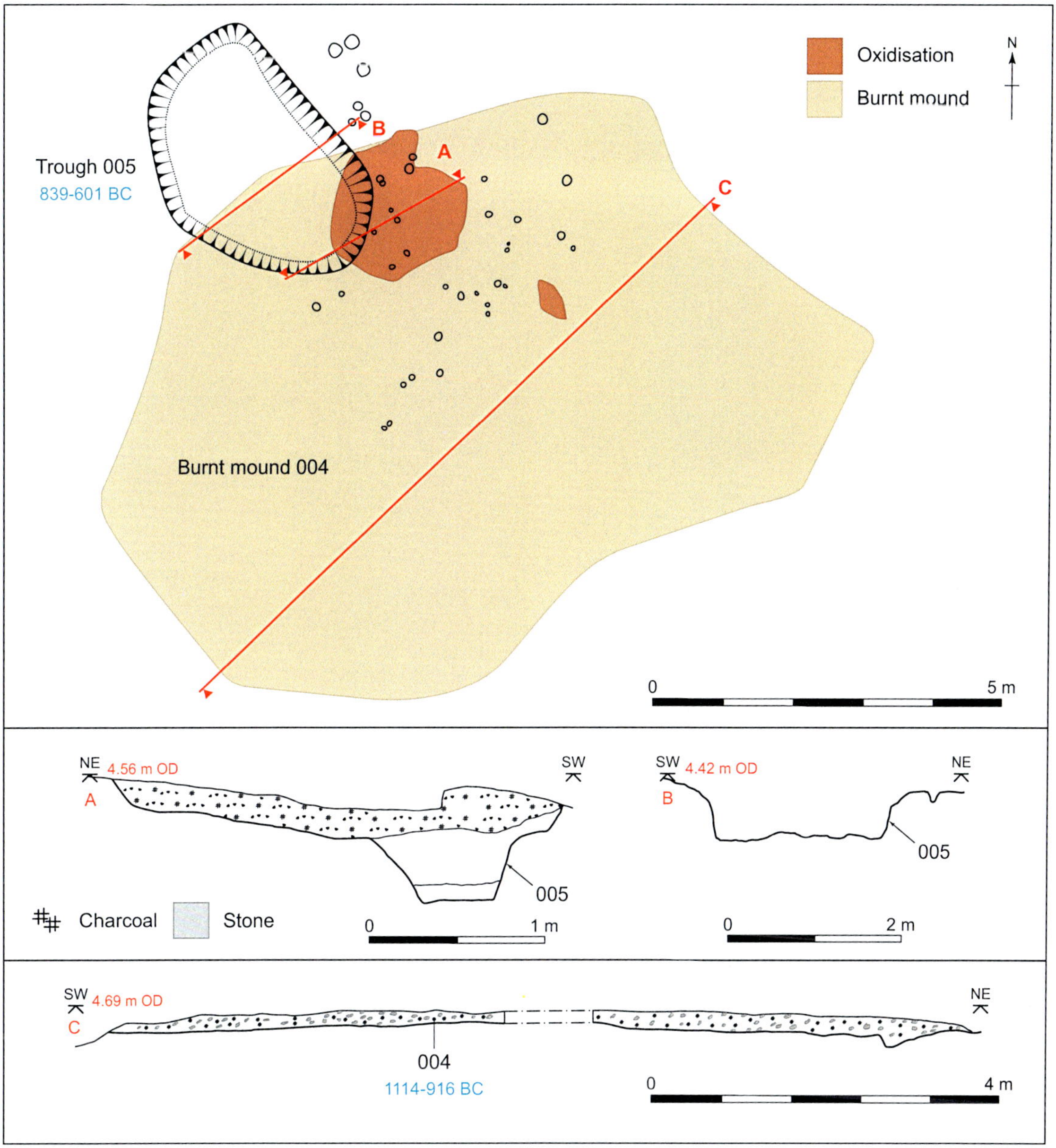

Illus. 2.47—Camp 5. Burnt mound and trough, with sections of the burnt spread (004) and the trough (005).

and Late Bronze Age, with the exception of Camp 5 (Illus. 2.47), which extended into the Late Bronze Age/Early Iron Age transition period. The burnt mounds are discussed in more detail in Chapter 5 but are also summarised here in Table 2.2.

Table 2.2—Summary of excavation results for burnt mounds excavated on the N22 Tralee Bypass (listed from north to south).

Site name	Dimensions of mound(s) (m) (L x W x D)	No. of troughs	Trough volume (Ltr)	Palaeoenvironmental evidence (charcoal, plant remains)	C14 dates
Lismore 2	11.5 x 5.4 x 0.21	1	2,109	Oak, hazel, birch and alder	Alder charcoal from pit: 900–797 BC (SUERC-37294). Hazel charcoal from basal fill of trough: 971–809 BC (SUERC-37298)
Knockawaddra Middle 1	5 x 3 x 0.5	1	1,512	Oak, hazel, holly and birch, and charred wheat grain	Alder charcoal from basal fill of trough: 1678–1499 BC (SUERC-37284)
Knockawaddra West 1	21.2 x 16.9 x 0.8	0	N/A	Oak	Blackthorn charcoal from stake-hole: 1193–930 BC (SUERC-37291)
Dromthacker 1	N/A	1	408	Oak and hazel, and charred cereal grain	Hazel charcoal from basal fill of trough: 1883–1693 BC (SUERC-37274)
Ballinorig West 1	10 x 5.1 x 0.2	1	510	Alder	Alder charcoal from basal fill of trough: 2577–2348 BC (SUERC-37233)
	9 x 4 x 0.2	3	1,060 720 2,337	Alder, hazel and holly; one trough had a timber and stone lining	Alder charcoal from single fill of trough: 1415–1215 BC (SUERC-37231). Hazel charcoal from mound: 1420–1220 BC (SUERC-37230)
	6.8 x 4.1 x 0.2	2	702 3,515	Willow, hazel, holly, oak, ash and alder	Alder charcoal from basal fill of trough: 2023–1776 BC (SUERC-37232). Alder charcoal from upper fill of trough: 1743–1535 BC (SUERC-37234)
Ballinorig West 2	N/A	1	1,118	Hazel, alder, oak, holly and willow	Alder charcoal from basal fill of trough: 1257–999 BC (SUERC-37240)
Camp 5	10.1 x 6.2 x 0.22	1	2,240	Hazel, oak and alder; trough had timber lining with corner stakes	Alder charcoal from mound: 1114–916 BC (SUERC-37270). Alder wood from a stake in trough: 839–601 BC (SUERC-38049)
Ballinorig South 1	N/A	1	2,758	Hazel, oak and alder	Alder charcoal from pit: 2460–2201 BC (SUERC-37228). Alder charcoal from trough: 2468–2210 BC (SUERC-37229)
Camp 2	15.1 x 7.8 x 0.4	0	N/A	Mainly non-oak charcoal, including alder and blackthorn	Alder charcoal from basal mound deposit: 2192–1952 BC (SUERC-37264). Blackthorn charcoal from upper mound deposit: 1249–949 BC (SUERC-37268)
Camp 1	14 x 11 x 0.30	1	285	Non-oak charcoal, including alder; trough was timber-lined	Alder charcoal from trough: 895–770 BC (SUERC-37261)
	6 x 5.5 x 0.2	0	N/A	Hazel, oak, ash and alder	Alder charcoal from only mound deposit: 1289–1026 BC (SUERC-37262)
	10.7 x 9.65 x 0.27	2	1,575 386	Non-oak charcoal, including alder; plant remains (e.g. grasses and sedges) were also present	Alder charcoal from pit: 1417–1217 BC (SUERC-37263)
Camp 4	7.6 x 4.2 x 0.18	1	841	Oak, hazel and alder, and Pomoideae (apple type)	Hazel charcoal from basal fill of pit: 2471–2235 BC (SUERC-37269)
Caherleheen 1	1.4 x 1.04 x 0.07	0	N/A	Oak and non-oak charcoal	Oak charcoal from burnt spread: 2840–2473 BC (SUERC-37260)
	2.77 x 2.62 x 0.14	0	N/A	Oak and non-oak charcoal	N/A
Dromavally 2	8 x 6 x 0.5	1	2,268	Hazel, birch, oak and alder	Hazel charcoal from basal fill of trough: 2336–2046 BC (SUERC-37281)
Ballindooganig 1	6 x 3.17 x 0.15	0	N/A	Oak	Oak charcoal from mound: 2570–2310 BC (SUERC-37223)
	12 x 7 x 0.3	0	N/A	Charcoal highly abraded and too small to identify to species, unsuitable for radiocarbon dating	N/A
Gortbrack East 2	3.2 x 2.8 x 0.09	0	N/A	Non-oak charcoal and part of a single charred oat grain	N/A
Gortbrack East 3	9 x 5.6 x 0.3	0	N/A	Non-oak charcoal, including alder	Alder charcoal from pit: 1880–1641 BC (SUERC-37283)

3

PEOPLE AND THEIR ENVIRONMENT OVER 6,000 YEARS

Scott Timpany

This chapter draws on the environmental finds (ecofacts) such as charcoal, charred cereal grains and charred seeds from the sites excavated along the new road. These ecofacts provide information on the food people were eating and the types of wood they were using for fuel and construction materials, which together help us build a picture of their local environment. In order to gain information on what changes were taking place in the wider landscape, the evidence of the ecofacts has been supplemented with information from pollen studies across County Kerry (e.g. Jessen 1949; Mitchell 1951; Lynch 1981; Barnosky 1988; Mitchell 1988; 1990; Dodson 1990; Cooney 1996; Cole & Mitchell 2003; Anderson et al. 2004). In these locations, a core (a column of soil, taken through the whole of the sediments present) was taken from either a lakebed or peatland, and subsampled at regular intervals throughout its length. At each interval, pollen grains (Illus. 3.1) were analysed to reveal how vegetation had changed over the time it took the core sediments to accumulate. In an undisturbed lakebed or peat basin this can be a period of c. 14,000 years, from the end of the last glacial period to the present day. Unfortunately, none of these pollen cores was taken from a site close to the new road but, all together, they provide a credible composite picture of the region.

How has the landscape changed?

After the last ice sheets melted (c. 15,000 years ago), the landscape would have been largely bare earth. By 11,000 years ago pollen evidence from areas such as the Dingle Peninsula and Killarney suggests that trees such as juniper and birch (probably dwarf birch) recolonised the land to form a scrub woodland, with a ground flora of grasses, together with dwarf shrubs and herbs such as crowberry, mugwort, sedges, sorrels and meadowsweet. Other tree types soon followed and by 8,000 years ago woodland including oak, hazel, elm, willow and pine had become established and shaded out much of the previous juniper–birch scrub. This woodland had a ground flora of herbs such as sedges, grasses and meadowsweet, together with ferns. By 6,000 years ago alder frequently formed canopy components of woodland in wetter areas, such as river valleys, while ash also appears around this time (Barnosky 1988; Dodson 1990; Cooney 1996).

In areas such as the Killarney National Park, pockets of yew woodland formed around 5,000 years ago. Pine is considered to have been a prominent part of this wooded landscape until around

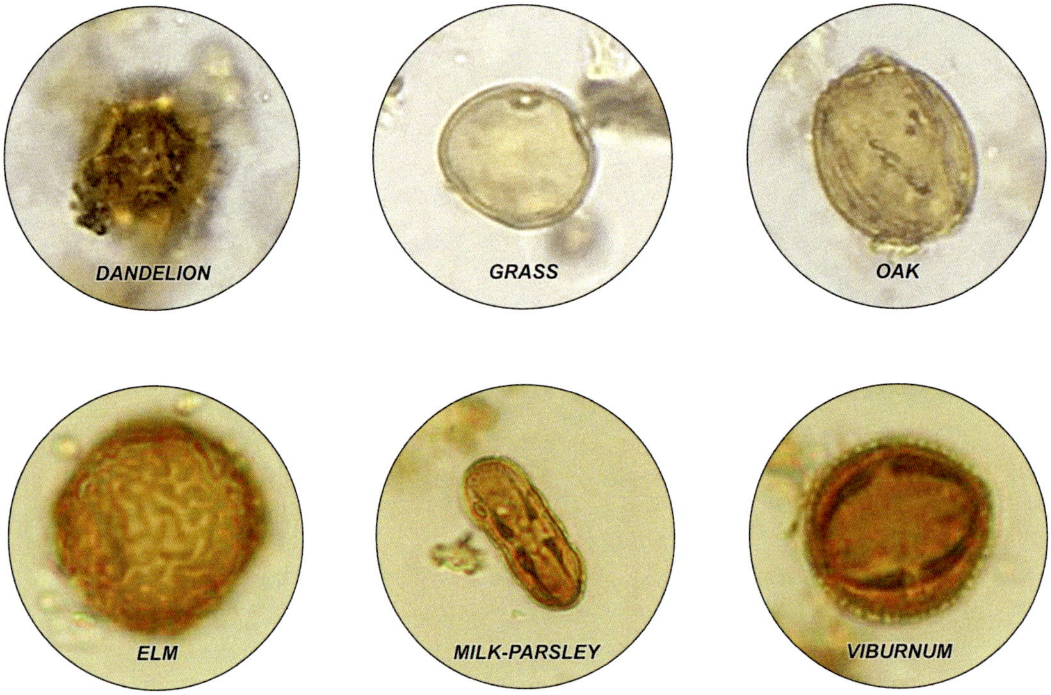

Illus. 3.1—Examples of pollen grains viewed under a microscope (Scott Timpany).

4,000 years ago, when a decline in the species occurred, an event identified in pollen records across Ireland at this time. This is likely to have been caused by a mixture of deliberate clearance by people and an increasingly wetter climate (Charman 2010), allowing for the spread of blanket bog. This deciduous woodland was the dominant vegetation cover across the region until the Bronze Age, when areas of woodland were cleared to make way for pastoral and arable farming. In areas such as the Dingle Peninsula and Cashelkeelty, on the Beara Peninsula, this clearance activity may have begun earlier, in the Late Neolithic (Lynch 1981; Barnosky 1988; Dodson 1990).

The ecofacts recovered during excavations along the new road allow us to look at how these wider changes in the landscape, indicated by pollen information, occurred within the immediate area of the road project. Charcoal and hazelnut shell fragments from Manor East 1 indicate that oak–hazel woodland was present during the Early Neolithic, with hazel being a particularly valuable resource for Neolithic people as a source of food, fuel and construction material (e.g. for making wattle panels). Oak charcoal fragments were also recovered from Ballindooganig 1 and Caherleheen 1, dated to the Later Neolithic, indicating that oak was present in the landscape throughout this period. Moving into the Late Neolithic/Copper Age period, charcoal fragments from Ballinorig West 1, Ballynabrennagh Lower 1 and Ballinorig South 1 show the use of alder for fuel, suggesting an increase of this tree type in the locality, probably forming wet woodland along river valleys.

The identification of charcoal fragments and charred/waterlogged seeds also complements information gained from pollen analysis, by revealing the presence of tree species either not recorded or occurring in low values in pollen assemblages. This can happen where species are low pollen producers or insect-pollinated, or where pollen of particular species is poorly preserved. An instance of this can be seen at Camp 4, a burnt mound dating from the Late Neolithic/Copper Age. Here, the identification of Pomoideae (apple-type) charcoal (together with hazel) indicates a local presence of apple/pear/hawthorn, which are all shrubs that are rarely recorded in pollen studies. The charcoal of these species cannot be differentiated on the basis of their cell structure.

Pollen evidence from the region suggests that it was around 2500 BC when the main phases of woodland clearance commenced, as arable and pastoral farming began to expand. Woodland clearance was not carried out solely for farming purposes, however. Pollen evidence from Shehere Bog, Killarney, suggests a phase of woodland clearance potentially associated with a demand for fuel for copper-mining at Ross Island, around 2200 BC (Cooney 1996, 30). This change to a more open landscape with increased heathland communities by the Middle Bronze Age has been recorded from pollen information across Ireland (e.g. Plunkett 2009) and is seen to some extent in the charcoal evidence from the present road project.

Early Bronze Age charcoal assemblages from a burnt mound at Ballinorig West 1 and a burnt mound and sink-hole deposit at Ballinorig West 2 indicate that a more diverse or mosaic woodland environment existed as a result of the opening up of the woodland canopy. Alder, willow, hazel, oak, ash, birch and wild cherry are all present in these assemblages. A continued reduction in woodland canopy is indicated during the Middle Bronze Age by the presence of light-demanding species such as holly at Ballinorig West 1. Blackthorn is also recorded in this period, within charcoal assemblages from a cremation pyre at Manor East 1 and a burnt mound at Camp 2, together with fruit stones of this species from a pit at Clashedmond 1. Similar assemblages are recorded from Late Bronze Age sites, with charcoal of alder, oak, holly, willow and hazel recovered from a pit at Ballinorig West 2 and alder, oak, hazel, blackthorn and ash from a trough at Camp 5. The charcoal suggests continued opening of the woodland canopy, possibly as a result of further land clearance for agriculture. An intensification of arable farming at this time is certainly indicated by the increase in the number of sites with charred cereals and the discovery of a Middle Bronze Age cereal-drying kiln at Ballingowan 1.

There is little evidence of a lull in activity during the Iron Age, with six archaeological sites providing evidence for metal-working, charcoal production and cereal cultivation, as well as the continued exploitation of hazel, alder, willow, apple-type and oak for domestic fuel. Indeed, pollen studies from the Macgillycuddy's Reeks (Anderson et al. 2004), Uragh Wood and the Killarney oakwoods (Little et al. 1996; Mitchell 1988) confirm that woodland clearance continued apace during this period. Despite this, however, the charcoal evidence indicates that areas of mixed woodland still existed locally. It is also clear that species such as oak were being deliberately selected for charcoal production for metal-working. This was the only species present in the charcoal assemblage recovered from an iron-working furnace at Ballingowan 1.

There is evidence for some recovery of woodland following clearances in the Iron Age, such as at Killarney oakwoods, where Mitchell (1988) records a general regrowth of woodland, with the notable exception of pine. This takes place during an event termed the 'pine decline', approximately 2,000 years ago, when pine pollen is observed to decline across the whole of Ireland, in some places failing to ever re-establish (Bradshaw & Browne 1987). Considering the results from our own project, there is an increase in the quantity of charred cereal grains recovered from sites such as Ballinorig West 4, Dromthacker 2 and Gortbrack East 1, indicating an intensification of arable farming during the early medieval period in the environs of the new road. Pockets of woodland were still present within this increasingly agricultural landscape, however, with pollen evidence from former stream channels infilled with peat, at Manor East 4 and 7, showing that wet woodland of alder and some birch existed along the River Lee and its tributaries in this period (Stefanini 2012a; 2012b). The worked wood assemblage, together with the pollen and charcoal evidence from Ballinorig West 4, Dromthacker 2 and Gortbrack East 1, shows that small areas of diverse woodland also existed in drier areas and included trees such as oak, hazel, cherry, holly, elder, blackthorn and apple-type.

The diversity of tree types in the wider region was to increase in the medieval period with the deliberate introduction of non-native species. Lynch (1981), for example, records the introduction of beech and walnut at Cashelkeelty, on the Beara Peninsula, in the 13th century. In our own project there is evidence for woodland management in this period from Manor East 4. Here there were remains of a 15th-century wooden platform, constructed from both worked wood and brushwood. Our analysis shows that woodland was at least partly managed through coppicing. This involved cyclical cutting of branches or stems to produce wood to a required size. The majority of the wood was alder, sourced from a local wet woodland which also contained willow. Oak, blackthorn and hazel were also used but these were more likely to have been growing on areas of drier land (O Carroll 2012).

Into the post-medieval period, the fuel used in limekilns at Knockawaddra Middle 1, Ballinorig West 4, Dromavally 1 and Lismore 1 suggests the survival of some areas of local woodland containing oak, blackthorn, common buckthorn and willow. Pollen data from sites such as Ballygisheen Bog, west of the Macgillycuddy's Reeks (Cole & Mitchell 2003), and Killarney (Mitchell 1988) corroborate the historical evidence for widespread woodland clearance during the 17th and 18th centuries to provide charcoal for the iron-working industry (McCracken 1971). This loss of woodland led to the rise of managed estates in the late 18th and early 19th centuries in order to both re-establish and conserve some remaining areas of woodland. One such example is Derrycunihy Wood, Killarney, where Mitchell (1988) records the establishment of a managed oak woodland, but also notes the planting of pine and other, exotic conifers.

Foraging and farming

Throughout prehistory and up to the present day, our diets have been influenced by what plant food we have been able to cultivate (farming) and what we have gathered from our environment (foraging). Over time, there has been a shifting balance between these two sources. Today most of our plant food comes from farming, but in the past this has fluctuated. During the Early Neolithic

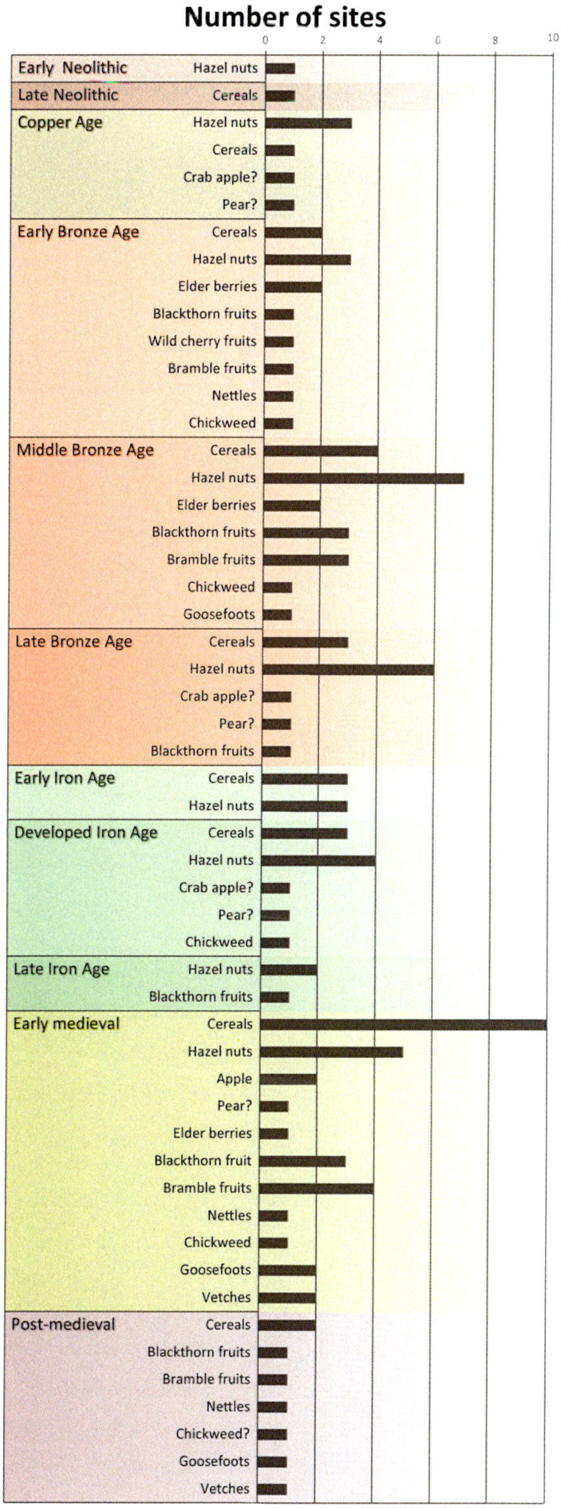

Illus. 3.2—Evidence of available foodstuffs from excavated sites on the N22 Tralee Bypass, including farmed cereal crops and wild herbs, nuts and berries.

period, some 6,000 years ago, foraging for nuts, fruits, berries, tubers and other wild plants would have been as important as farming. This is seen to some extent in the charred hazelnut shell fragments from the Early Neolithic building (Structure 2) excavated at Manor East 1. Indeed, evidence from the excavations on the new road shows that hazelnuts continued to be an important wild food until at least the early medieval period (Illus. 3.2).

Charred cereal grains provide the best evidence for the crops being cultivated in particular periods. Preservation of these remains through charring only took place, however, when accidents occurred, such as the burning of small quantities of grain in a domestic hearth or large quantities of grain in a cereal-drying kiln that was not completely raked out after its final use, or in kilns that had accidentally burnt down. This often means that only a partial representation of the cereal grains consumed by past peoples is present at any one site, thus providing us with only glimpses of a much larger picture. No cereal grains were recovered from the Neolithic building at Manor East 1, but excavation of a house of similar date at Cloghers, less than 5 km to the east, yielded a substantial charred cereal grain assemblage that included bread wheat, barley, oats (probably wild) and possible spelt wheat, alongside hazelnut shell (Dunne & Kiely 2005).

The cereal grain evidence

Along the new road, the earliest, tentative evidence of agriculture was a single grain of naked barley (a form with grains that thresh freely from the hull) from the Late Neolithic burnt mound at Caherleheen 1. A recent synthesis of charred cereal grains from Irish excavations has shown that naked barley was one of the two main cereals grown in Neolithic Ireland, the other being emmer wheat (Whitehouse et al. 2014). During the Bronze Age there was a gradual shift in cereal cultivation, with hulled barley (a form with grains held tightly within the hull) being grown alongside the naked form and then taking over as the main cultivar by the Late Bronze Age (Monk 1986). This trend can be seen to some extent in the charred grain assemblages recovered from the bypass excavations (Illus. 3.3). Small quantities of both naked and hulled barley were recovered from Early Bronze Age features associated with a round-house at Ballingowan 1, and a single grain of hulled barley was retrieved from the sink-hole at Ballinorig West 2. Into the Middle Bronze Age, cereal evidence suggests that barley was still the main cultivar but with the beginning of a shift to the hulled variety. Small quantities of naked barley (alongside grains of emmer wheat) were recorded in a pit at Ballynabrennagh Lower 1 and within cremation pyre material at Manor East 1. By contrast, a substantial quantity of hulled barley and smaller amounts of naked barley were recovered from a cereal-drying kiln at Ballingowan 1. The only cereal remains in the burnt mound at Knockawaddra Middle 1, however, were a small quantity of wheat sp., suggesting that the people here were growing wheat rather than barley. By the Late Bronze Age only hulled barley is present within the assemblages, indicating that by this time it had replaced naked barley as the favoured variety, probably because it returned higher yields.

The earliest evidence for oats comprises a single grain found in an Early Bronze Age feature at Ballingowan 1, with a further single grain with a tentative Bronze Age date found at Gortbrack East 2. These would be very early dates for oat cultivation, which is thought to have begun in the Iron Age, and thus they must be treated with some caution. Intrusive oat grains from later activity have been found in earlier assemblages, such as those recently dated from Irish Neolithic sites (McClatchie et al. 2014; Whitehouse et al. 2014). They may also represent wild oats (an arable weed) rather than the cultivated species. Small quantities of oats were also recorded from a row of Early Iron Age post-holes at Ballingowan 1, providing tentative evidence for its cultivation during this period. Hulled barley, however, remained the main cultivar during the Iron Age, with occasional grains of naked barley suggesting that this now occurred only as a remnant crop or arable weed.

The greatest evidence for cereal cultivation comes from the early medieval sites. Greater quantities of charred cereals and the cereal-drying kilns at Ballinorig West 3 and Ballinorig West 4 indicate a shift from largely subsistence-based farming to cereal-growing on a more intensive scale. A possible cereal-drying kiln was also discovered at Ballingowan 1 but no cereal grains were recovered. The kiln at Ballinorig West 4 produced a grain assemblage dominated by hulled barley, with small quantities of oats, bread/club wheat and emmer wheat. The kiln at Ballinorig West 3 produced a similar assemblage of mainly hulled barley, together with oats and smaller quantities of club/bread wheat, emmer wheat, possible spelt wheat and possible rye. As well as the kiln deposits, oats were also recorded in significant quantities from pits at Ballingowan 1 and Manor East 1 and

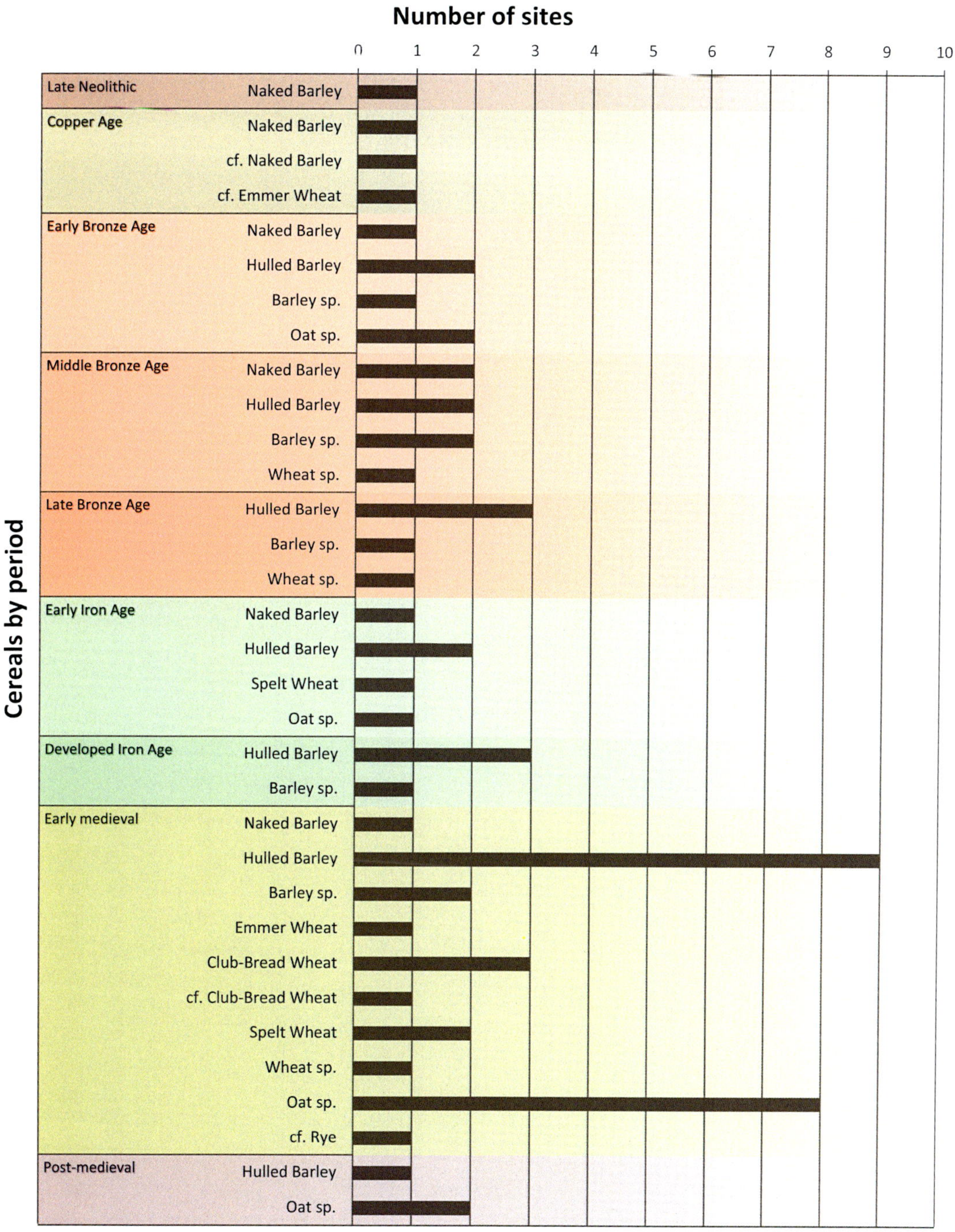

Illus. 3.3—Charred cereal evidence from the N22 Tralee Bypass excavations, showing the prevalence of different cereal types through time.

from a hearth at Dromthacker 2. Taken together, this evidence clearly identifies hulled barley and oats as the main cultivars during this period. Only small quantities of wheats, including club/bread wheat, emmer wheat and possible spelt wheat, were recovered from early medieval sites, suggesting that wheat was not one of the main cultivars in this area.

There is only limited evidence for cereal cultivation from post-medieval sites, with small quantities of hulled barley and oat grains recovered from limekilns at Dromavally 1 and Lismore 1. The small quantities of grain recovered reflect the fact that these were industrial rather than domestic settlement sites.

Wild foodstuffs

Despite the rise in cereal cultivation, wild plant foods remained an important part of the diet in all periods, and this is reflected in the charred and waterlogged plant remains and charcoal recovered from the bypass excavations. The charcoal record shows that fruits such as apple/pear were available, together with berries from trees such as wild cherry, blackthorn and possibly hawthorn. Waterlogged plant remains (e.g. seeds, fruit stones) suggest that berries from elder trees and brambles were also available, along with a range of herbs such as vetches, nettles and chickweed. At Ballingowan 1, a large number of chickweed seeds were found in an early medieval pit. This could mean that the herb was gathered for the consumption of its stems and shoots (Mears & Hillman 2007), with the seeds discarded after harvesting, although this deposit could also represent the disposal of chickweed seeds from cereal-processing waste.

With the exception of the Late Iron Age, for which no cereals were recovered, arable weed seeds were found alongside charred cereal grains from Early Bronze Age right through to post-medieval sites. The weed seeds represent plants that grew in the fields among the cereal crop—such as chickweed, goosefoots and scentless mayweed—and were collected accidentally during harvesting. The majority would have been removed by winnowing and hand-picking (Hillman 1981), but some (especially the smaller seeds) would have survived this process to become charred with the grain during drying and baking. These arable weeds are just as important as cereal grains in providing insights about agricultural practices and growing conditions. For example, the presence of herb seeds such as pale persicaria, violet, sedges and amphibious bistort in the Middle Bronze Age cereal-drying kiln at Ballingowan 1 indicates that the fields were poorly drained or prone to waterlogging. The presence of a similar assemblage in the early medieval cereal-drying kiln at Ballinorig West 4 shows that farmers still faced these problems centuries later.

The faunal evidence

Animal bone was poorly preserved on the excavated sites owing to local soil conditions, leaving little evidence of pastoral farming. Small quantities of burnt bone, identified as sheep/goat, were found in a sink-hole deposit dating from the Middle Bronze Age at Knockawaddra West 2 and in a refuse pit dating from the Early Iron Age at Ballinorig West 4, and bone fragments representative of cattle/sheep/goat were recovered from features dating from the Developed Iron Age at Manor

East 2. The greatest quantity of identifiable bone was retrieved from the early medieval ditched enclosure at Ballinorig West 2, where pastoral farming is suggested by cattle, pig and sheep/goat bones, along with horse and dog.

Hot-stone technology

The Late Neolithic period witnessed something of an industrial revolution with the development and widespread adoption of hot-stone technology. Here, the focus is on the charcoal and waterlogged wood from the burnt mound excavations on the new road and what they tell us about the character and management of local woodland, as well as the choices people made in selecting different wood types for fuel.

Sixteen sites with burnt mounds, pits, spreads or troughs with hot-stone debris were discovered along the bypass. A small assemblage of charcoal fragments from the Late Neolithic/Copper Age, consisting of oak, alder, apple-type and hazel (Illus. 3.4), suggests that woodlands on drier ground were mainly being exploited for fuelwood (Rodwell 1991; Stuijts 2005). The Pomoideae (apple-type) species only appear in the fuelwood assemblage from this period, though they have been observed in burnt mound assemblages of Bronze Age date in other locations across Ireland (e.g. Dillon & Tierney 2011).

The evidence represents a wider variety of tree types used for fuelwood in the Bronze Age. This is partly due to the greater number of charcoal fragments identified but also reflects the opening up of the woodland canopy, allowing for the formation of more diverse woodland, and the increased exploitation of wet woodland. A more open woodland canopy, probably owing to increased clearance, is indicated by the presence of light-demanding trees such as holly, which appears in the Middle Bronze Age. Blackthorn also appears in this period and may also suggest a more open canopy, being a shrub that generally favours open woodlands. A greater use of wetland resources is shown by the increased use of alder, together with trees such as willow, birch and ash, likely to have been growing along the River Lee. The overall assemblage from the excavated sites along the new road is similar to fuelwood assemblages recorded from burnt mound sites across Ireland (e.g. Stuijts 2005; O'Donnell 2007; 2009; Miller & Ramsey 2009; Timpany 2015).

Waterlogged worked wood was recovered from the trough associated with the Late Bronze Age burnt mound at Camp 5, where the wood lining of the trough and some wooden stakes were identified as alder, ash, hazel and blackthorn.

Where possible, the charcoal fragments were analysed to determine the size of the pieces of wood used to fuel the burnt mounds (e.g. trunk wood, branches, twigs). The results suggest that the wood collected for fuel was predominantly of small and medium size, most likely branches. Large pieces, such as trunk wood, were only recorded in the assemblages from Early Bronze Age Ballinorig West 1 and Copper Age/Early Bronze Age Dromavally 2 and were limited to alder, hazel, birch and oak. The near-continuous presence of oak, hazel and alder in the assemblages indicates deliberate selection of these wood types for fuel and it is possible that people were managing the woodland resource by coppicing and pollarding (removing branches) (Boyd 1988). It seems possible that, rather

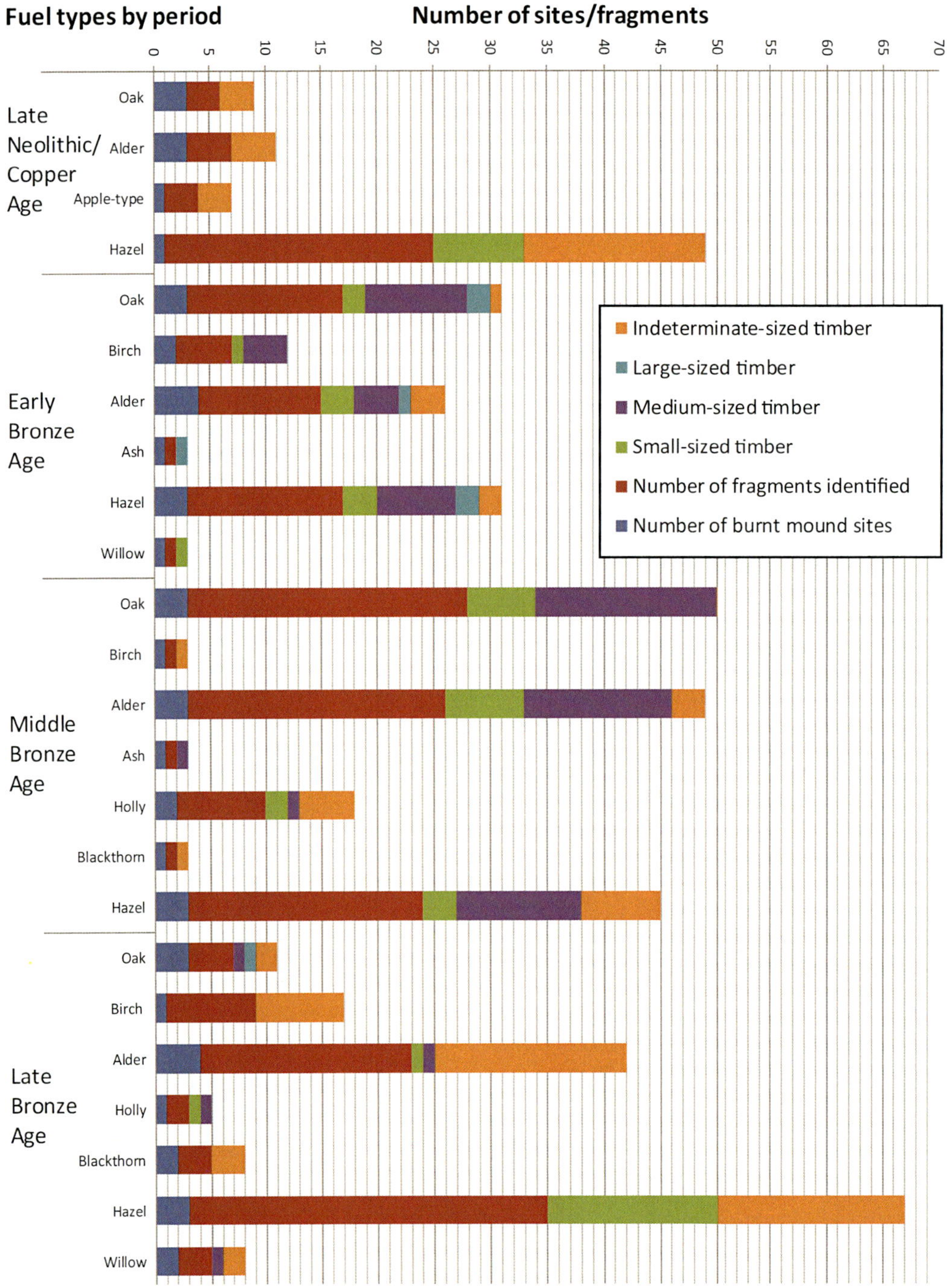

Illus. 3.4—Charcoal fuelwood identifications from burnt mound sites excavated on the N22 Tralee Bypass, by period.

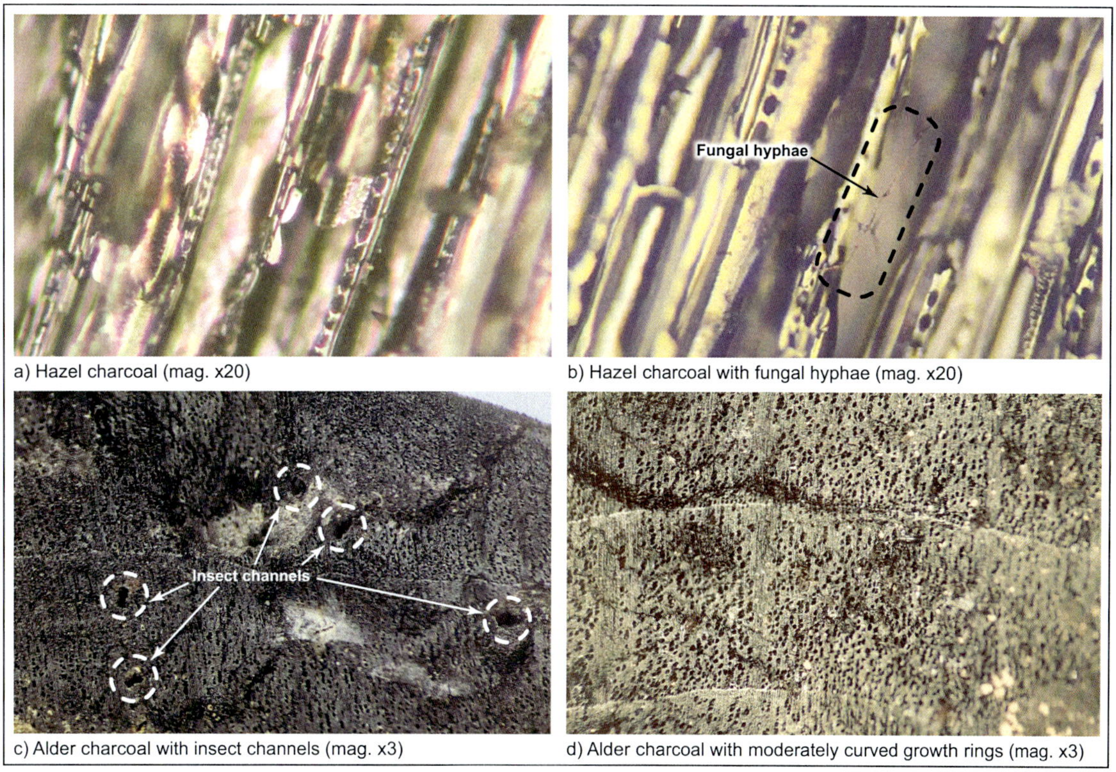

Illus. 3.5—Examples of charcoal viewed under a microscope. Fungal hyphae and insect channels indicate that the wood had begun to rot before being burned. The curvature of annual growth rings can be used to estimate the size of the piece of wood the charcoal came from; the moderately curved growth rings visible in panel (d) suggest this charcoal came from a large branch (Scott Timpany).

than cutting down entire trees, fuel was largely collected through the targeted removal of branches. These practices have been recorded from waterlogged timbers at prehistoric sites such as Lisheen, Co. Tipperary (Stuijts 2005), and Ballygawley, Co. Tyrone (Bamforth et al. 2009).

The presence of rotting wood in the charcoal assemblages suggests that firewood was also collected opportunistically. Fungal hyphae (the branching structure of fungi) were observed on charcoal fragments from some sites (e.g. Ballinorig West 1), while channels made by insects were recorded on fragments from others (e.g. Ballinorig West 2). This tells us that at least some of the wood was beginning to rot prior to being burnt (Schweingruber 1990; Marguerie & Hunout 2007), suggesting the use of dead wood collected from the woodland floor and/or wood that had been stored for some time and had begun to decay (Illus. 3.5).

Waterlogged plant remains were found on burnt mound sites at Camp 1, Camp 2 and Gortbrack East 2 and 3, all of which were located near the River Lee and its tributaries. Monocotyledon plant remains (representing sedges and grasses) were recovered, along with seeds of violets, elder, nettles and bramble fruits. These assemblages show that the local environment around these sites consisted of wet ground fringed by scrubby woodland (Clapham et al. 1962; Stace

2007). Similar siting of burnt mounds within boggy ground surrounded by partly cleared or fringe woodland has been inferred from environmental evidence from other archaeological sites in Ireland (e.g. Brown et al. 2016).

Small quantities of charred cereal grain were recovered from features associated with burnt mounds at three sites. A single oat grain (either the cultivated or wild type) was recovered from a pit fill at Gortbrack East 2. At Knockawaddra Middle 1 a small quantity of wheat sp. and indeterminate cereal grains were retrieved from the fill of a trough. A small amount of indeterminate grain was also recovered from the trough fill at Dromthacker 1. The grains showed no signs of malting (a likely indicator of brewing), which can be observed from the growth of the embryo and the presence of embryo fragments, although the poor preservation of the grains may have left little trace of this. Another possibility is that cereal straw was used as tinder for lighting fires, resulting in the odd cereal grain being preserved by charring. Despite the small quantities recorded, the presence of cereal grains (and especially wheat) means that some form of food preparation cannot be ruled out entirely.

Funerary pyres

Charcoal fragments are commonly retrieved from cremation burials. Their inclusion with the burial deposit may often have been accidental, having been gathered up with the bone after the cremation was completed. In most cases only a token amount of the cremated bone was interred; similarly, the charcoal that was included incidentally is unlikely to be fully representative of the wood used in the pyre.

Cremation burials were uncovered at three sites on the bypass: an Early Bronze Age cremation pit burial at Ballinorig West 3, two Middle Bronze Age cremation pit burials at Manor East 1, and a Developed Iron Age ring-ditch and cremation cemetery at Ballinorig West 4. Charcoal from the cremation deposits at Ballinorig West 3 and 4 was mainly oak with some non-oak fragments. A slightly more varied fuel assemblage was identified at Manor East 1, consisting of oak, ash and blackthorn. Oak has been recorded in pyre fuel assemblages from sites across Ireland (e.g. O'Donnell 2007 and 2009; Timpany 2015) and is thought to have been favoured for its high calorific value (Gale & Cutler 2000). Ash was the sole pyre fuel identified from a Bronze Age cremation at Mahanagh 3, Co. Galway (Timpany 2011), perhaps reflecting local woodland composition. Blackthorn is infrequently recorded as a cremation fuel compared to other fuels, but it has been identified in Middle Bronze Age cremation samples from sites along the Bord Gáis Éireann Pipeline to the West route (O'Donnell 2007).

Charcoal and wood identified from the burnt mounds on the bypass have shown that oak, ash and blackthorn were all growing in local woodlands in the Middle Bronze Age and presumably this is where the pyre fuel was sourced. Charcoal fragments from Manor East 1 indicate that mainly medium-sized pieces of wood, such as branches, were used for the pyre. A small number of large-sized pieces, representative of trunk wood, were also identified for ash and blackthorn, suggesting that these trees were felled to provide fuel for the pyre. A preference for ash and blackthorn, when

Illus. 3.6—People's interaction with the environment and the changing landscape from the Neolithic to the early medieval period.

other wood types were probably more abundant in the landscape (e.g. hazel and alder), may reflect some perceived cultural importance or symbolism. It has also been suggested that some Pomoideae species (apple type) were used as pyre fuel to provide a fragrant aroma during burning (O'Donnell 2007). A small quantity of charred hazelnut shell and naked barley grains found in one of the cremations at Manor East 1 may represent food tokens placed in the cremation pyre as part of the ceremony, as seen in cremations on the Bord Gáis Éireann Pipeline to the West (Johnston 2007). Alternatively, like the burnt mounds, the grain might simply represent cereal chaff used as tinder to set the pyre alight.

Conclusion

The environmental data gathered from this study have provided us with a picture of woodland change in the environs of the road project over the millennia (Illus. 3.6). Analysis of the charcoal and waterlogged wood from the excavations shows that trees such as apple type (Pomoideae) and blackthorn, which are often under-represented in pollen assemblages, were more common in ancient woodlands than previously thought. Identification of coppiced wood from waterlogged contexts, together with the ring curvature information from charcoal fragments associated with burnt mounds and cremation pyres, suggests that people in the past were actively managing and/or selectively choosing their wood resources. Farming played an important role in shaping the landscape and cereal cultivation is evidenced from the Neolithic through to the post-medieval period.

4
FIRST SETTLERS IN THE LEE VALLEY

Patricia Long
with a contribution by Eoin Grogan

The earliest definitive evidence for human habitation on this island is attributed to the Mesolithic period, though a recent study suggests the possibility of a human presence in the preceding Palaeolithic period (Dowd & Carden 2016). Following the end of the last major period of glaciation (c. 15,000 years ago), the warmer climate eventually led to dense woodland cover and an increasing variety of flora and fauna, which provided a suitable environment for human settlers arriving from the east. One of the first recorded Mesolithic habitation sites was in the north-east of the country, at Mount Sandel, Co. Derry (Woodman 1985), and for many years it was thought that hunter-gatherers did not reach the south-west until much later (e.g. Woodman & Anderson 1990). An excavation at An Baile Uachtarach Theas (Ferriter's Cove), however, on the west coast of the Dingle Peninsula, Co. Kerry, uncovered evidence of a number of temporary occupations during the Late Mesolithic, confirming that people were active here from at least 4500 BC (Woodman et al. 1999) (Illus. 4.1). A wood and stone platform excavated on Valentia Island, also dated to the Late Mesolithic period (Woodman & Anderson 1990, 386), may be another indication of coastal settlement in the region at this early stage. Late Mesolithic features possibly representing a building were identified at the Bronze Age copper-mining site at Ross Island, in Lough Leane, Killarney (O'Brien 2004, 163), indicating that people were moving inland at this time, though still remaining close to water bodies.

In the centuries before and after 4000 BC we see indications of change in the cultural landscape of the Later Mesolithic throughout Ireland. Evidence from pollen records shows increasing woodland clearance and the introduction of cereals. Cereal pollen from Cashelkeelty in south-west Kerry is among the earliest evidence we have of possible cereal cultivation in Ireland, at c. 4700 BC (Lynch 1981, 90). Domesticated animals also begin to appear in the archaeological record. Some of the earliest known cattle remains in Ireland (c. 4500 BC) were found at An Baile Uachtarach Theas (Woodman et al. 1999). All of this heralds the arrival of agriculture, which had already been spreading northward and westward throughout Europe for over two millennia.

Early visitors to the valley

Among the excavated archaeological sites along the present road project, the earliest evidence was a shallow, circular pit (729) at Manor East 1 (Illus. 4.2 and 4.3), from which oak charcoal was dated to 4045–3817 BC (SUERC-37323). Though its function is unknown, it is likely that the pit was

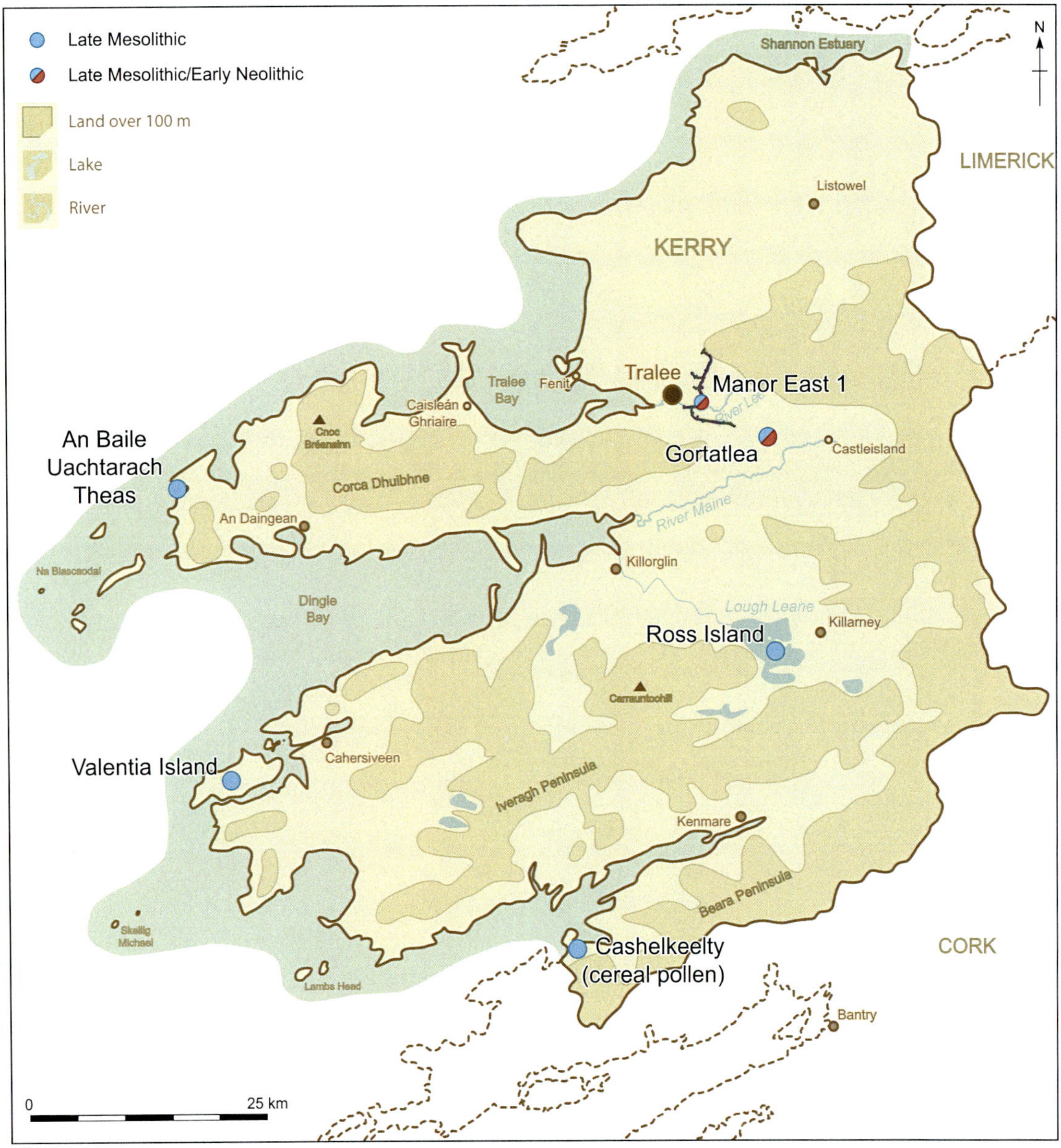

Illus. 4.1—Locations in County Kerry where traces of Late Mesolithic and/or Early Neolithic settlers have been found.

associated with a temporary habitation and may have been contemporary with a number of nearby pits and stake-holes.

Prior to this discovery there was little known evidence for human activity in County Kerry during the transitional period around 4000 BC, the exception being a number of pits excavated in Gortatlea, c. 6 km to the east (Connolly 2008). This scarcity of evidence may be due in part to relatively low numbers of excavations in the county compared to other parts of Ireland. Manor

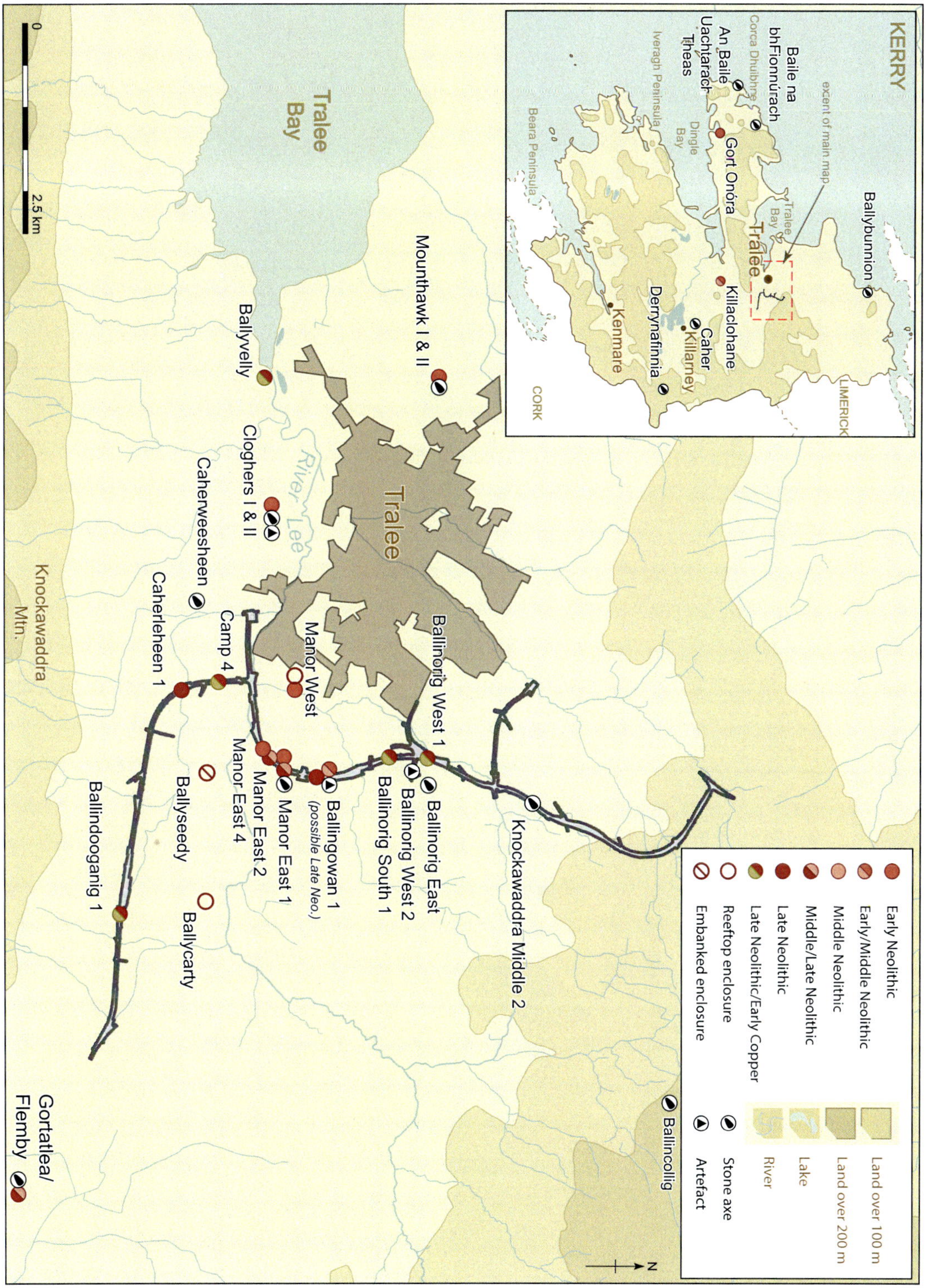

Illus. 4.2—Neolithic sites excavated on or close to the N22 Tralee Bypass and the locations of stone axes and enclosures mentioned in the text.

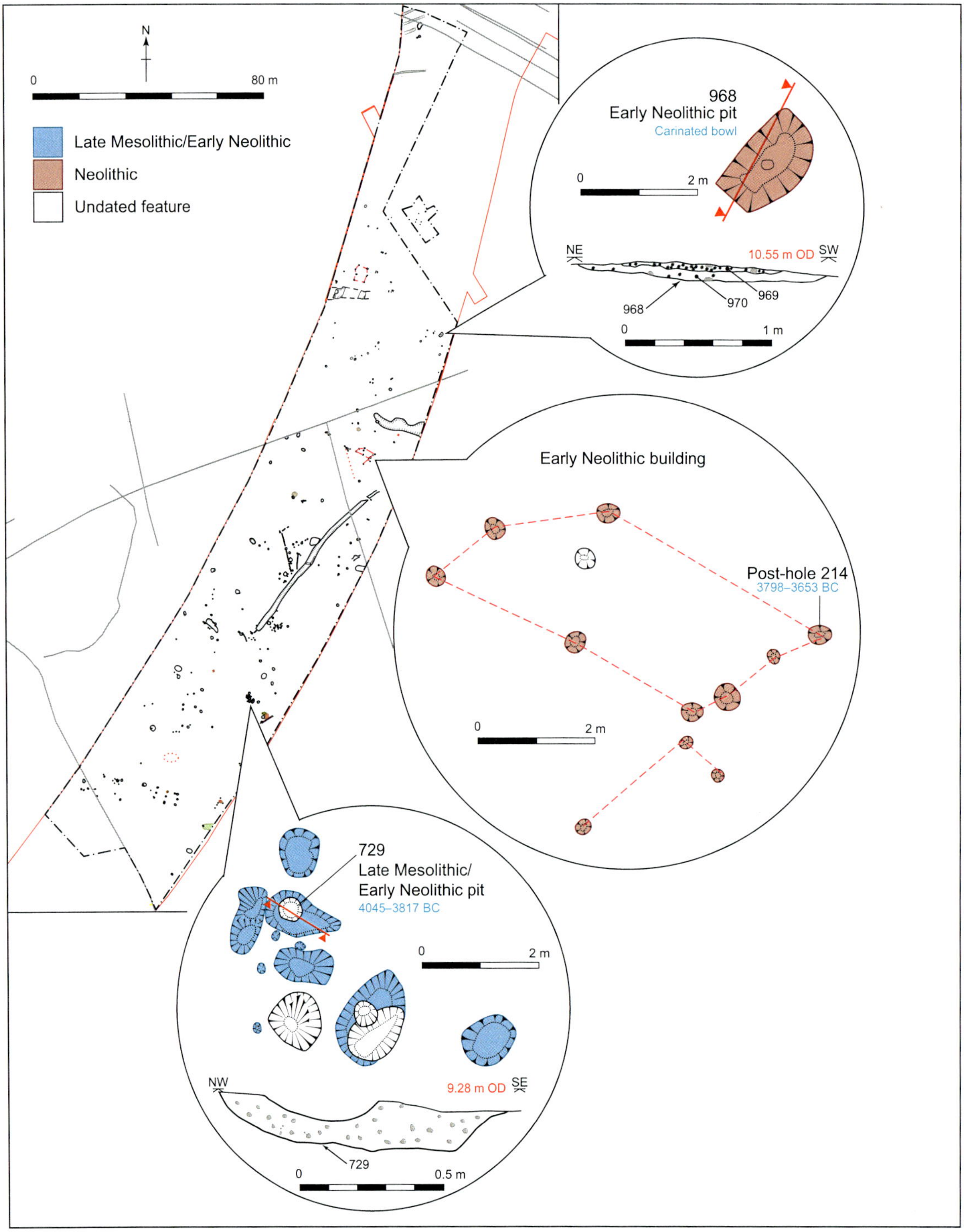

Illus. 4.3—Manor East 1. Site plan with Mesolithic/Neolithic and Neolithic features highlighted.

East 1 was a large site that included part of the wetland/dryland interface at the edge of the River Lee floodplain. Gortatlea was also located close to a major river, the Maine. It seems likely that people were navigating inland from Tralee Bay and Dingle Bay along these waterways, as with other major rivers in Ireland during the Mesolithic, when the country was still densely forested.

Changing lifeways

After 4000 BC, farming became more widespread and brought with it sweeping changes in settlement, subsistence, material culture and social organisation. The earliest Neolithic farms in Ireland may originally have been small, cultivated clearances in a predominantly wooded landscape, but even this evidence reflects the adoption of a sedentary way of life based on agriculture and livestock husbandry. This new way of producing food resulted in the development of field systems and the construction of robust wooden houses, which are more visible in the archaeological record than the temporary settlements of the Mesolithic period. Pre-bog field systems are known at a number of upland locations in County Kerry and at least some of these are likely to be Neolithic in date. A typical Early Neolithic rectangular house was excavated in Cloghers, south of Tralee (Dunne & Kiely 2005). The house was dated to 3770–3530 BC and produced a range of artefacts typical of the period, including the earliest type of pottery made in Ireland—carinated bowls. This round-based pottery, and the technology required to produce it, was introduced into Ireland around 4000 BC and is a useful indicator of Early Neolithic domestic activity (Sheridan 1995; Grogan & Roche 2010). Other small assemblages of this type of pottery have been found at Mounthawk II, Manor West and Gort Onóra (Gortonora), Co. Kerry (Dunne & Kiely 2005, 56, 59; Roche 1998 and 2001; Roche & Grogan 2007). Adjacent to the Cloghers house, another area of Neolithic activity (Cloghers II) was identified by the presence of stone tools, though it is not clear whether this was contemporary with the occupation of the house (Dunne & Kiely 2005, 53).

The pace and mechanism of the transition from a nomadic hunter-gatherer lifestyle to one of sedentary agriculture are much debated, but it is thought that by c. 3750 BC these changes had been widely adopted (e.g. Cooney et al. 2011, 668). In tandem with sedentary settlements, people now had a heightened sense of place and began to create the first permanent public monuments, including court tombs, passage tombs and portal tombs. There were no recognised Early Neolithic funerary monuments (court/passage/portal tombs) in County Kerry prior to the discovery and excavation of a passage tomb at Ballycarty (Connolly 1999), less than 2 km east of the present project, in the mid-1990s (KE038-074). The tomb sits atop a limestone reef enclosed by up to three stone and earth ramparts and appears to be part of a ceremonial complex that includes cairns, a possible henge, causeway and enclosures. Unfortunately the tomb was extensively disturbed and there was no hard dating evidence for any of the three main phases of activity, though the main structural features of each phase can be paralleled among the Irish and European passage tomb series (ibid., 69).

The presence of an embanked enclosure 1 km to the west, at Ballyseedy (KE038-093), may indicate a wider ceremonial landscape. The discovery of the Ballycarty tomb within a reeftop enclosure led to an extensive survey of the Lee Valley. This identified a total of 283 monuments suggested to be of prehistoric date (Connolly 2008, 133). The discovery of two cairns just below the summit of Knockawaddra Mountain (342 m OD), a reeftop enclosure at Manor West and the presence of other large cairns in the area have led Connolly to suggest that Ballycarty may be just one element of a sizeable passage tomb cemetery. Six embanked enclosures were among the features identified during the survey, which might mirror the association between embanked enclosures and passage tombs in the Boyne Valley (ibid., 93).

Two portal tombs have also been recognised in Killaclohane near Milltown, Co. Kerry. Killaclohane I (KE047-052) was excavated and conserved, as it was in danger of collapse. The excavation recovered cremated human remains, numerous pottery fragments, flint artefacts and a broken saddle quern. The pottery indicates that Killaclohane I was in use from around 3900 BC to 3300 BC, with a secondary use in the Middle Bronze Age (Connolly 2015). Excavations at Killaclohane II (KE047-059), a collapsed tomb located 1 km to the east, uncovered a single cremation deposit accompanied by fragments of poorly preserved pottery (Connolly 2017; 2018).

Settling down by the Lee

Our own excavations on the Tralee Bypass project produced evidence at 11 sites for Neolithic or Late Neolithic/Copper Age activity (Table 4.1). Three of these sites—Manor East 1, 2 and 4—were within about 400 m of each other.

Six sites produced evidence of activity in the Early or Middle Neolithic—Manor East 1, 2 and 4, Knockawaddra Middle 2, Ballinorig West 2 and Ballingowan 1. The earliest building was Structure 2 at Manor East 1, which was dated to 3798–3653 BC (SUERC-37321). Its setting is in keeping with previously excavated buildings of this period, which generally display a preference for slightly elevated, south-facing slopes with ready access to water (Cooney & Grogan 1999, 42–7; Cooney

Table 4.1—Sites with evidence for Neolithic activity, listed from north to south.

Site name	Neolithic features
Knockawaddra Middle 2	Middle Neolithic stone axe fragment from topsoil.
Ballinorig West 1	Late Neolithic/Copper Age burnt mound phase.
Ballinorig West 2	Sherd of Middle Neolithic globular bowl from a sink-hole; three further sherds representing a second bowl, along with a Middle/Late Neolithic hollow scraper, from an early medieval ditch.
Ballinorig South 1	Late Neolithic/Copper Age trough and pits containing burnt mound material.
Ballingowan 1	Early Neolithic carinated bowl sherd from a pit, possibly residual.
Manor East 1	Early Neolithic building and pits, potsherds representing an estimated seven carinated bowls; Middle to Late Neolithic scattered pits, post-hole and linear feature.
Manor East 2	Middle to Late Neolithic pits located on a natural hillock in the River Lee floodplain.
Manor East 4	Early Neolithic pits and post-holes, one containing carinated bowl sherds, on a hillock in the River Lee floodplain.
Camp 4	Late Neolithic/Copper Age burnt mound and pits containing burnt mound material.
Caherleheen 1	Late Neolithic burnt spread.
Ballindooganig 1	Late Neolithic/Copper Age burnt mound.

2000, 74). Its position in a river valley is also quite typical of the period (Smyth 2013). Small quantities of flint, chert and quartz debitage were associated with the building, as well as a rhyolite blade. Eleven sherds of pottery from an estimated seven Early Neolithic carinated bowls were recovered from features associated with the building, while a further three sherds were found in a pit 45 m to the north.

The pottery and the radiocarbon date from this building both indicate that it was broadly contemporary with the only other Early Neolithic building to have been excavated in County Kerry, the rectangular house at Cloghers, less than 5 km to the west. This house is typical of the Early Neolithic, with its characteristic shape and walls formed of split oak planks and posts, together with post-and-wattle set into slot-trenches. Approximately 90 such houses are known from Ireland and they have a very narrow date range of c. 3715–3625 BC (Smyth 2014). While the Manor East 1 building falls largely within this date range, its irregular shape and manner of construction—comprising free-standing uprights rather than a slot-trench—make it difficult to say with certainty whether it was a house. Structurally, it seems much flimsier than the house at Cloghers and would have taken less effort to construct. At 5.2 m by 2.4 m (internal area 6.9 m^2), it is also considerably smaller than typical Early Neolithic houses, which range from 6 m to 12 m in length by 4 m to 8 m in width (ibid., 303). While the pottery, stone tools, hazelnut shell and unidentified cereal grains recovered are consistent with domestic occupation either inside or immediately adjacent to the building, the very small quantities in which they were found indicate that any occupation would have been short-lived. It is possible that the building was never a house but some kind of outbuilding or temporary shelter, built at a remove from the permanent habitation site.

At Manor East 4, 350 m to the south-west, a number of randomly placed post-holes and pits were found on a natural hillock, next to a former stream channel. One of the pits contained sherds of a carinated bowl. These remains suggest that, as well as occupying the dryland/wetland interface on the north side of the River Lee floodplain, Early Neolithic people were also exploiting the floodplain itself, perhaps using this small raised area as a temporary camp. Carbonised residue on the interior of the pottery suggests a domestic use (e.g. cooking), though the character of the residue was not ascertained by analysis.

A carinated bowl sherd was also recovered from a pit located within a Middle Bronze Age enclosure at Ballingowan 1. If the pit was contemporary with the enclosure, this pottery was only a residual inclusion. Nevertheless, it is suggestive of Early Neolithic activity at the edge of the limestone outcrop that dominates this site and overlooks the River Lee floodplain and Manor East sites to the south.

Significance of the Early Neolithic pottery

Eoin Grogan

While the quantities of pottery from Ballingowan 1, Manor East 1 and Manor East 4 were small, representing about nine vessels in total, these are important discoveries. The vessels are all Early Neolithic carinated bowls (Illus. 4.4). These have simple, often everted rims, gently curved necks,

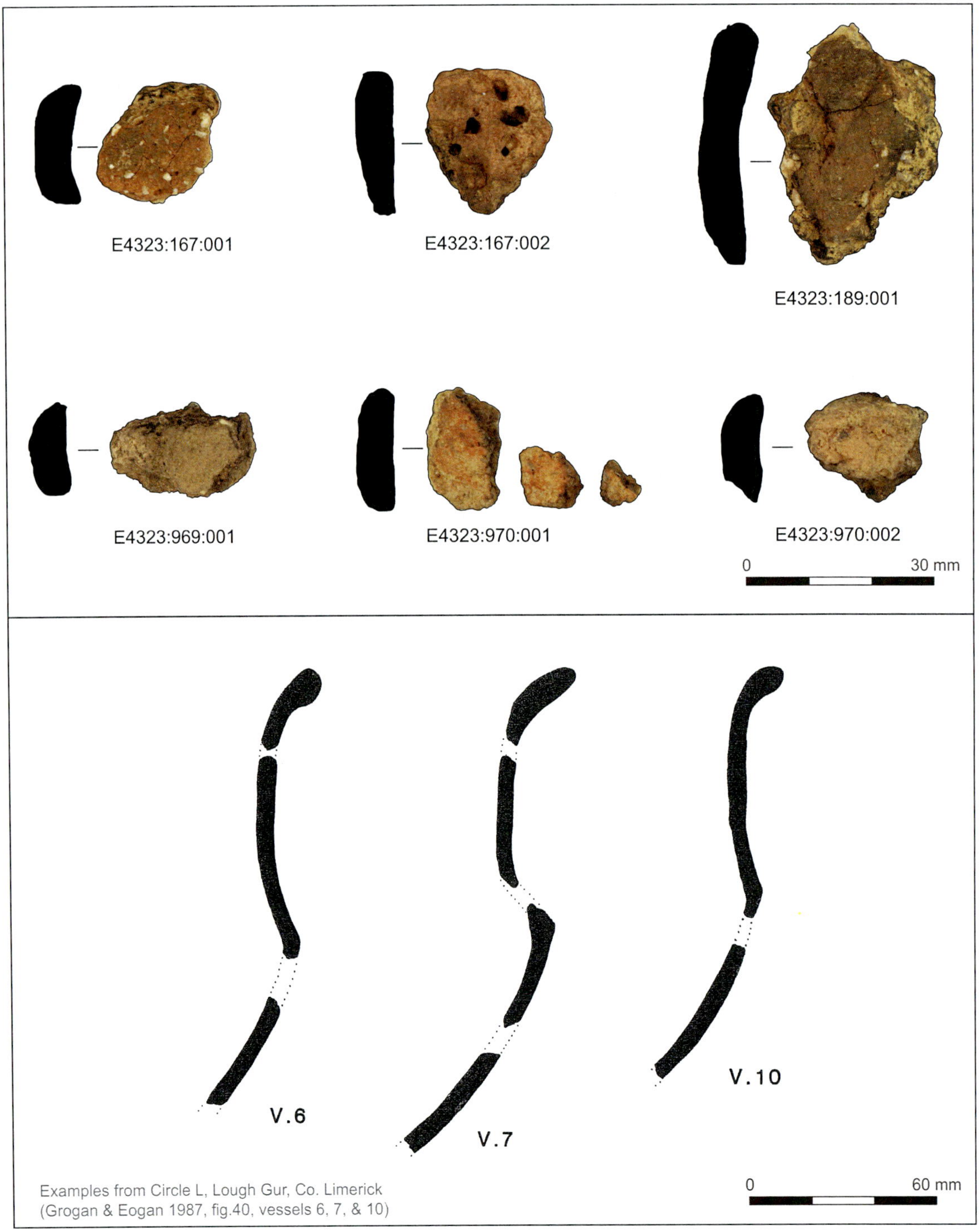

Illus. 4.4—Manor East 1. Early Neolithic carinated bowl sherds, and examples of profiles of this bowl type. The sherds are from post-holes associated with a building (Structure 2) and a pit nearby (Hannah Sims).

simple or slightly stepped shoulders and deep, rounded bowls. As is typical throughout the country, they are well fired with thin walls (4–8 mm) and finely crushed quartzite inclusions. The small number of sherds from each vessel and the extensive wear and traces of carbonised residue on the internal surfaces of Vessels 1, 5 and 7 from Manor East 1 indicate that they are domestic debris. This material is dated to the period c. 3900–3650 BC (Grogan & Roche 2010; Cooney et al. 2011).

These three sites along the road project form part of a cluster of Early Neolithic sites in the Tralee area and indicate very early settlement. This includes a significant assemblage (10 vessels) from the rectangular house at Cloghers (Dunne & Kiely 2005, 53, 48; Roche 1999) and a small quantity from Manor West (Dunne & Kiely 2005, 53 and 59; Roche 2001). Similar pottery also came from the south side of the Dingle Peninsula at Gort Onóra (Gortonora) (Roche & Grogan 2007). Three sherds of possible carinated bowl (highly degraded) came from a pit at Mounthawk II, where it was found in association with a lozenge-shaped arrowhead (Dunne & Kiely 2005, 56). The nearest contemporary activity is in mid- to north Cork and east Limerick (Grogan & Roche 2010); this suggests that the Kerry sites are a result of coastal landfall, a feature—together with riverine spread—of the Irish Early Neolithic.

Scattered traces of ongoing settlement

While there was some degree of continuity from the Early to the Middle Neolithic, by about 3625 BC the robust rectangular houses were no longer being constructed and had been replaced by more *ad hoc* methods of construction (Smyth 2013). Much Middle Neolithic settlement is represented by spreads of occupation material, pits and occasional hearths or areas of burning. Evidence for buildings is typically slight and often consists only of clusters of stake-holes (Smyth 2011a, 14). There is also evidence from the pollen record that agricultural activity may have waned, with countrywide indications of less intensive use of the landscape and possible reafforestation (e.g. Whitehouse et al. 2014, 199–200). Court and passage tombs continued in use, with the complex at Brú na Bóinne, Co. Meath, reaching its peak towards the end of the Middle Neolithic (Cooney 2000, 16). There also seems to have been increasing regionality, perhaps as a result of communities becoming more established and rooted in the land. This is especially apparent in the development of different styles of carinated and globular bowls. The hollow scraper, a distinctive type of stone tool, also seems to have developed during this period (Woodman et al. 2006, 163–6).

During the Later Neolithic, grooved ware pottery (flat-bottomed pots with grooved line decoration) was introduced, most likely from the Orkney Islands off the north coast of Scotland, apparently signalling a cultural shift (Smyth 2013, 318). This pottery is associated with new forms of ceremonial sites, consisting of large timber posts set in circular or four-post arrangements, both of which can occur on the same site (Smyth 2011a, 20). Roughly contemporary with these are the large circular enclosures known as embanked enclosures; Ballyseedy (KE038-093) is one possible example, located c. 800 m east of the bypass (Connolly 2008). Late Neolithic domestic houses are elusive in the archaeological record (Smyth 2011a) and, again, this is probably a result of construction methods that leave little archaeological trace.

Illus. 4.5—Flint hollow scrapers from a post-hole at Manor East 1 and the inner enclosure ditch at Ballinorig West 2 (Sara Nylund).

A variety of stone tools and associated waste products, diagnostic of the Middle to Late Neolithic, were recovered from widely scattered features at Manor East 1. These include a rhyolite blade made from a reworked polished stone axe, two flint flakes, two chert flakes, a quartz crystal flake, a flint hollow scraper fragment (Illus. 4.5), a chert convex end scraper, and 17 pieces of flint, chert, sandstone and quartz crystal debitage. The end scraper was found in a cremation pit burial that was dated to the Middle Bronze Age and so it is clear that at least this stone tool had been incorporated into a later feature, though it is not known whether this was deliberate or accidental. While no clear focus of Middle/Late Neolithic settlement was identified, these objects indicate that stone tools were being made and reworked here, suggesting ongoing habitation on the margins of the floodplain.

Also at Manor East 1, a polished rhyolite stone axe (Illus. 2.37) was found in one of the stake-holes of a tentatively dated Late Iron Age structure. The axe itself is probably Middle Neolithic and was finely made, possibly reworked from a larger axe. It measures 85 mm by 42 mm by 24 mm. Cooney & Mandal (1998, 10) suggested that axes 80–200 mm in length were predominantly used for small-scale woodworking, with those towards the upper end of this range being used for tree-felling. Smaller examples, like the Manor East 1 axe, were probably used for carpentry (ibid., 53). The careful positioning of the axe in the stake-hole may reflect a practice identified at numerous prehistoric sites throughout Britain and Ireland, whereby Neolithic axes were deliberately placed in later features (Cooney 2000, 189), perhaps for good luck or to invite the protection of the ancestors who were represented by the ancient object.

A fragment of a rhyolite stone axe that had been made in the Middle Neolithic, and then reworked and reused as a pestle in the Bronze Age, was found in topsoil at Knockawaddra Middle 2 (Illus. 2.4). Over 20,000 stone axes have been recovered in Ireland to date. Only a small proportion of these were found in County Kerry—including examples from An Baile Uachtarach Theas, Mounthawk I, Cloghers, Caherweesheen, Derrynafinnia, Caher, Gortatlea/Flemby, Ballybunnion, Ballincollig, Ballinorig East and Baile na bhFionnúrach (Woodman et al. 1999; Dunne 1998; Kiely 2000 and 2002; Dowd 2004; Coyne 2003; O'Callaghan 2011; Coyne 2002; Dunne 2003a; Connolly 2008; ibid.; and Isabel Bennett, pers. comm.).

At Manor East 2, a semicircular grouping of four pits/post-holes has been tentatively dated to the Middle–Late Neolithic on the basis of two flint artefacts found in one of the features. This site (like the earlier Manor East 4) was on a natural hillock in the River Lee floodplain. These hillocks provided elevated, dry ground in otherwise marshy surroundings and would have been attractive as bases from which to exploit the flora and fauna of the floodplain. They are unlikely, however, to have been permanently occupied owing to difficulties of access in the winter months, when the surrounding area was flooded. There are other Middle and Later Neolithic sites in Ireland that demonstrate seasonal and specialised use in riverine environments, such as Carrigdirty, Co. Limerick, in the Shannon Estuary (O'Sullivan 1997), and Bay Farm II, Co. Antrim (Mallory 1992). This seasonal exploitation of natural resources would have been carried out in parallel with agricultural activity, supplementing the diet of Neolithic people with fish, game, wildfowl and plants.

Pits of Neolithic date, such as the Early and Middle Neolithic examples identified in Manor East 4 and 2, are a common occurrence on archaeological sites and are found both in isolation and in association with houses and megalithic tombs (Smyth 2011b). There is a recognised practice of placing domestic waste such as pottery, stone and other tools, as well as food remains, in the ground (ibid.). This may simply have been a method of rubbish disposal but, given that it would have been easier to throw material into the adjacent swamp, there may have been a specific significance in the way used/broken objects were deposited. Digging and filling pits may have been a ritualised act, though the contents of the Manor East pits give no clear indication of this. Although Neolithic pits are generally indicative of habitation, it can be difficult to understand their exact function or their relationship to settlement, particularly when found on sites with little other evidence for occupation.

At Ballinorig West 2 (1.6 km north of Manor East 1 and 2), a sherd of Middle Neolithic pottery, representing a globular bowl (E4306:264:001; Illus. 4.6), was recovered from an infilled sink-hole complex. Sink-holes are a common geological feature in the Tralee area. They occur when the ground surface collapses into voids in the underlying limestone and can vary considerably in size, from less than a metre to several metres across. Some of the sink-holes on the bypass route appeared to have filled naturally over time, whereas others contained archaeological material such as charcoal and artefacts. This could represent both deliberate deposition into open sink-holes and accidental inclusion when they collapsed. The Neolithic bowl sherd from Ballinorig West 2 is the earliest pottery type found within any sink-hole on the route. The same sink-hole also contained Early and Middle Bronze Age material.

Four further sherds (E4306:314:001–004, two of which refitted), representing a second globular bowl, were recovered from the inner enclosing ditch of an early medieval enclosure at the same site. The ditch also contained a flint hollow scraper and two pieces of flint debitage. These artefacts were clearly in a secondary context and we can only assume that Ballinorig West 2 had formerly been a site of Middle–Late Neolithic occupation, the evidence for which was removed by the construction of the medieval enclosure.

Early hot-stone technology

A burnt mound at Caherleheen 1 was the only site on the bypass that was dated to the Late Neolithic (2840–2473 BC; SUERC-37260), but burnt mound sites at Ballindooganig 1, Ballinorig West 1,

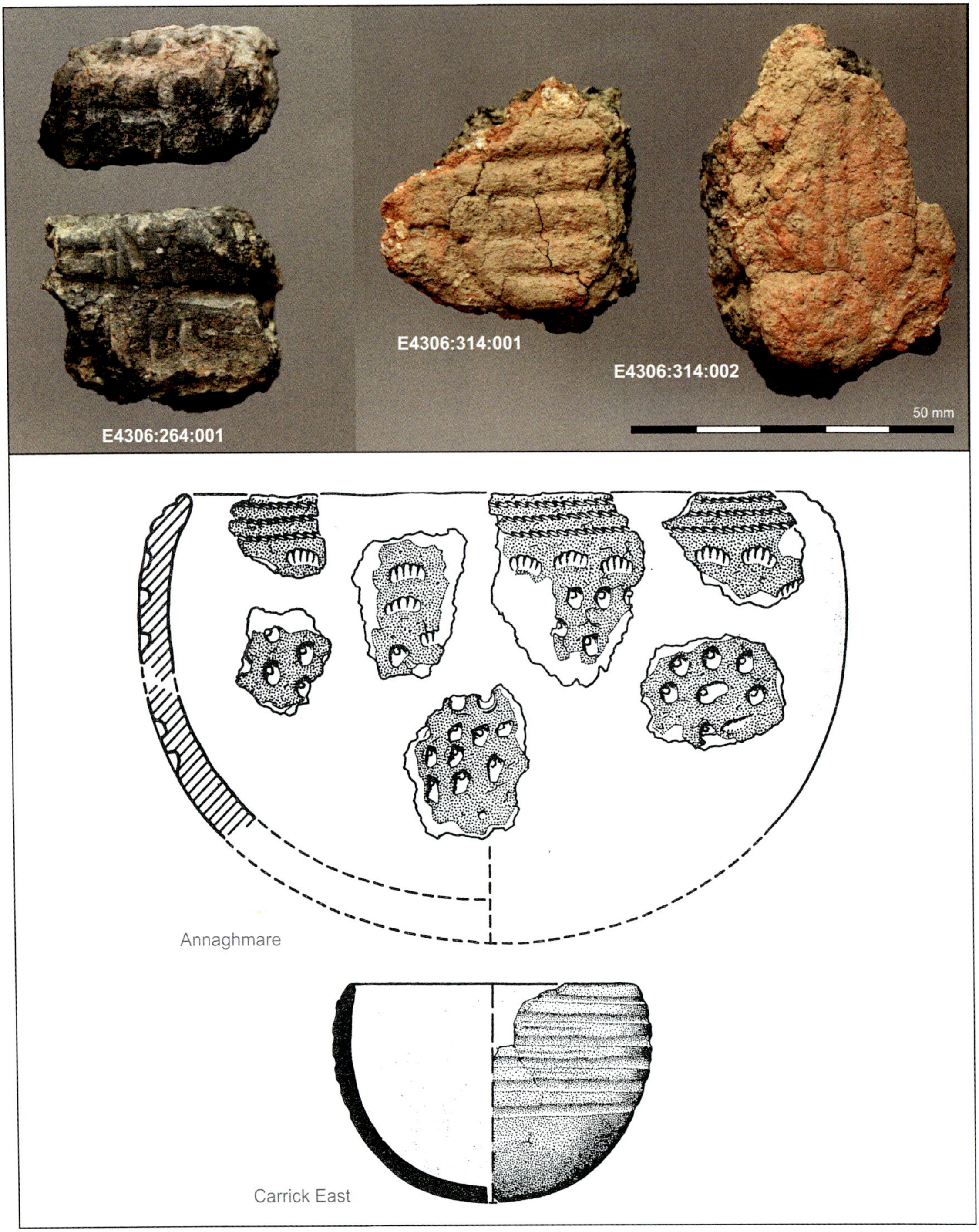

Illus. 4.6—Ballinorig West 2. Middle Neolithic globular bowl sherds and illustrations of similar globular bowls, with examples (below) from Annaghmare, Co. Armagh, and Carrick East, Co. Galway (after Herity 1982, figs 49.3 and 50.1) (Hannah Sims).

Ballinorig South 1 and Camp 4 all produced dates spanning the Late Neolithic/Copper Age transition. These sites indicate that hot-stone technology (the use of heated stones to boil water or heat roasting pits) was used in this part of south-west Ireland from around the middle of the third millennium BC.

While these sites lacked any direct evidence for settlement (i.e. houses or other structures), it is probable that the people who used them were living in the immediate vicinity. Elsewhere in the Lee Valley, possible Late Neolithic/Early Bronze Age settlement in the townland of Ballyvelly, to the west of Tralee, is suggested by the discovery of a cluster of pits, post-holes and stake-holes containing stone tools diagnostic of the period (Dunne & Kiely 2005).

A Late Neolithic/Copper Age date (2471–2213 BC; SUERC-37259) was also obtained from a round-house excavated at Ballynabrennagh Lower 1. The date is problematic, however, because the dated charcoal came from the same pit as several sherds of Middle Bronze Age pottery. It is likely that the charcoal was residual and that the date does not relate to the construction or occupation of the house, and so it is not considered further in this volume.

An enigmatic monument at Ballingowan

A double pit alignment (two parallel rows of pits, more or less evenly spaced) on the southern side of a low limestone outcrop at Ballingowan 1 was a particularly interesting find, as nothing exactly like it has been found in Ireland before (Illus. 4.7). In the absence of any datable material, it has been

Illus. 4.7—Ballingowan 1, Area 1c. Double pit alignment with outcropping limestone in the background (right), view to north-west (Rubicon Heritage Services Ltd).

tentatively ascribed to the Late Neolithic or Early Bronze Age on the basis of comparable sites excavated in Britain. The recognition of these pit alignments is a relatively recent phenomenon in Britain; the majority of them have been identified from aerial photography. They can largely be divided into single and double alignments, with the latter being far less common (Waddington 1997). Single pit alignments are thought to have played some role in the agricultural landscapes of the Iron Age, whereas double alignments, like Ballingowan, are thought to be earlier (Late Neolithic or Early Bronze Age) and more specifically ceremonial (ibid.).

In Britain, many pit alignments appear to run for several hundred metres or more, in straight or curving lines, and clearly represent massive undertakings by large numbers of people or construction over long periods of time. There are a few examples in upland areas, such as at Ebberston Common in the North York Moors (Ainsworth 2009), where banks have been preserved alongside the pit alignments.

A double pit alignment with some similarities to the Ballingowan example was excavated in 1998–9 at Thornborough in North Yorkshire, England (Harding 2003), where 88 pits were uncovered over a distance of 350 m. The alignment was dated to the Early Bronze Age (on the basis of dates and diagnostic artefacts) and the pits originally held large upright posts, as also seemed to be the case at our site in Ballingowan. Both monuments, therefore, would have consisted of two parallel lines of posts, forming an avenue c. 9 m wide and narrowing towards one end. Thornborough is the largest of four known examples in the Ure–Swale catchment area of North Yorkshire. They are believed to have had a ritual purpose relating to processions through sacred landscapes. The Thornborough alignment was found alongside a complex of three Neolithic henge monuments. There are a number of probable Bronze Age barrows scattered nearby and at each end of the pit alignment. The Thornborough landscape clearly had a ritual life that endured from the Neolithic period to the Bronze Age. Evans & Knight (2001, 85) argue convincingly that similar pit alignments in Cambridgeshire defined 'vast ceremonial spaces' related to large-scale gatherings of people during the Bronze Age. These Cambridgeshire pit alignments were located on the edge of a floodplain, as is the case with the Ballingowan example.

It is difficult to find comparable Irish sites for a double pit alignment of this type. Parallel lines of pits/post-holes have been identified in association with Late Neolithic timber enclosures at Ballynahatty, Co. Down (Hartwell 1998) and Newgrange (O'Kelly et al. 1983, 16–21; Sweetman 1985; Smyth 2009), but these were elements of complex ritual monuments. There is currently no known evidence for similar monuments in the vicinity of Ballingowan, though the possibility cannot be ruled out. Geophysical survey of the field immediately to the east was inconclusive, other than a slight suggestion that the alignment terminates a few metres beyond the boundary of the road project (Bonsall 2011).

We do know that the limestone reefs in the area were the focus of burial and ceremonial activity from the Early Neolithic, the most significant examples being the passage tomb and ceremonial complex at Ballycarty, c. 2 km to the south-east, and another reeftop enclosure site at Manor West (KE039-304) (Connolly 2008, 93). It is unsurprising that these monuments and their environs would have retained a significance for later communities, whose own monuments should perhaps be viewed

Illus. 4.8—Ballingowan 1, Area 1c. Artist's impression of the type of ritual activity that may have taken place along the timber-post avenue represented by the double pit alignment (Jonathan Millar).

as additions to rather than replacements for existing sacred sites. The pit alignment at Ballingowan was near the edge of outcropping limestone on relatively flat ground. We currently have no clear idea where the avenue may have led, or with what monuments it might have been associated. Besides the Neolithic complexes at Ballycarty and Manor West, there are also numerous cairns, barrows and enclosures in the general area. Many may be Late Neolithic or Early Bronze Age funerary and/or ceremonial monuments. Some of these may well have been linked by a sacred processional route demarked, at least in part, by an avenue of posts.

Alternatively, the avenue may have been aligned on a celestial body at a significant time of the year (Illus. 4.8). The sun breaks the horizon in line with the avenue on 21 March, and the sun, moon and Mercury all break the horizon at this point around 16 September. Computer modelling using the on-line, open-source site Stellarium indicates that, at the beginning of the second millennium BC, the moon would have risen at this point on the horizon on 31 October.[1] This was an important time in the pastoral calendar, as it marked the end of the grazing season, when flocks and herds were brought together and animals that could not be maintained over the winter months were slaughtered and consumed in feasting (Moloney 2012, 57).

[1] Stellarium (http://www.stellarium.org, accessed April 2014).

Conclusion

The Neolithic activity identified during these excavations was generally small-scale and probably transient. In some cases, *ex situ* artefacts were the only indication of activity. Nevertheless, these discoveries provide us with a glimpse of daily life in an area where our knowledge of the Neolithic has previously been focused on prominent ceremonial monuments. The Ballingowan avenue, while

Illus. 4.9—A natural limestone reef at Ballycarty, c. 2 km east of the N22 Tralee Bypass, is the location of a prehistoric ceremonial complex. The summit is enclosed by earth-and-stone ramparts (RMP KE038-136), surrounding a passage tomb (RMP KE038-074) and a circular enclosure (RMP KE038-022). Associated features include an embanked causeway leading to the enclosure, and a number of small cairns, enclosures and quarry ditches. View from west (Michael Connolly, Kerry County Council).

Illus. 4.10—Limestone reef on the north-west side of Manor East 1, view to south-east. The summits of these natural outcrops were favoured for ritual monuments in the Neolithic period; occupation evidence is more likely to be found on the flanks (Rubicon Heritage Services Ltd).

not definitely dated to the Neolithic, provides a hint of the unknown extent and complexity of the ritual landscape and of possible interconnections between monuments. Connolly (1999 and 2008) highlighted a pattern of elevated limestone reefs being used for ceremonial monuments during the Neolithic. He noted that 80% of the reefs surveyed were crowned by archaeological features and the larger reefs followed the Ballycarty model, with cairns, quarry ditches, enclosures and ramparts (Illus. 4.9). The bypass route did not traverse the summit of any pronounced reefs but did skirt the edges of limestone outcrops at Ballingowan and Manor East (Illus. 4.10), which is where the Early Neolithic evidence from the bypass was concentrated. This association of Neolithic features with limestone reefs is also evident from other excavations in the area, such as the Early Neolithic house at Cloghers (Kiely 2003) and the pits and stake-holes at Manor West and Ballyvelly (Dunne & Kiely 2005). It seems that, while the summits of the raised limestone areas were being used for ceremonial purposes, it was the lower slopes of these reefs and outcrops that were more suitable for habitation. These areas were well drained, less exposed and on the margins of more fertile low-lying ground.

Manor East 1 and Cloghers remain the only known Early Neolithic buildings from the Lee Valley. As we have seen with the presence of carinated bowl sherds at Manor East 4 and Ballingowan 1, however, Early Neolithic occupation is not solely represented by clearly defined structures. This was also the case at other excavated sites in the area, such as Mounthawk II and Manor West. This pattern continues into the Middle and Late Neolithic, where no houses or other buildings are yet known from this part of the country but habitation has instead been identified from the evidence of clustered pits, post-holes and stake-holes, as at Manor East (2 and 4) and Ballyvelly, with further activity represented by artefacts from scattered features at Manor East 1 and a stray axe fragment at Knockawaddra Middle 2. Several burnt mound sites were dated to the Late Neolithic or Neolithic/Copper Age transition period and are also likely to have been associated with nearby habitation sites.

5

UNCOVERING A BRONZE AGE COMMUNITY

Stephen Hourihan and Patricia Long
with contributions by Katharina Becker, Eoin Grogan and Carmelita Troy

The spread of metallurgy in the Copper Age and Bronze Age is associated with other notable changes in material culture, burial traditions and settlement. The knowledge of how to extract copper from ore and how to manufacture copper implements is thought to have been introduced from the European mainland and coincides with the first appearance of Beaker pottery. This pottery is characterised by fine, decorated vessels with S-shaped profiles and flat bases. It was used in Ireland from about 2450 BC until c. 1900 BC, though its deposition within burials appears to have ceased around 2170 BC (Brindley 2007, 321; Mount 2011). Beaker pottery was a Europe-wide phenomenon often associated with distinctive artefacts such as tanged copper knives, awls, wristguards and barbed-and-tanged arrowheads (Gibson 2002, 87). In Ireland at this time a significant sheet-goldworking tradition emerged, which produced lunulae, discs and earrings. Along with the continued development of wedge tombs as communal grave monuments, there are individual burials also dating from this period. Domestic buildings were not substantial and there is no single recognised architectural form (Carlin & Brück 2012).

Archaeological evidence for the Bronze Age in Ireland (c. 2200–700 BC) is much more plentiful than for the preceding periods and this is thought to reflect a significant increase in population. The reason for this is not clear, but it might be partly due to a warmer climate in the Early Bronze Age, which may have facilitated year-round grazing and increased yields (Feehan 2003, 44). Technological advances, including those associated with the use of metal, may also have facilitated increased food production. This higher rate of representation in the archaeological record is also reflected on the Tralee Bypass, where Copper Age, Bronze Age and/or Beaker evidence was found on 21 sites (Table 1.1; Illus. 5.1), compared to just seven with Neolithic and four with Late Neolithic/Copper Age material.

While the archaeological evidence for the period varies considerably, some key elements can be seen as characteristic of different stages of the Bronze Age. For example, as well as occasional objects made from copper, bronze and gold, the Early Bronze Age (2200–1600 BC) is typified by both inhumation and cremation burials. These were accompanied by, or contained within, decorated pottery vessels and often associated with barrows or cairns of earth or stone. Among other changes, towards the end of the Early Bronze Age we see the introduction of round-houses (Carlin & Brück 2012). Burnt mounds, which we first see in the Neolithic period, continued in use throughout this period.

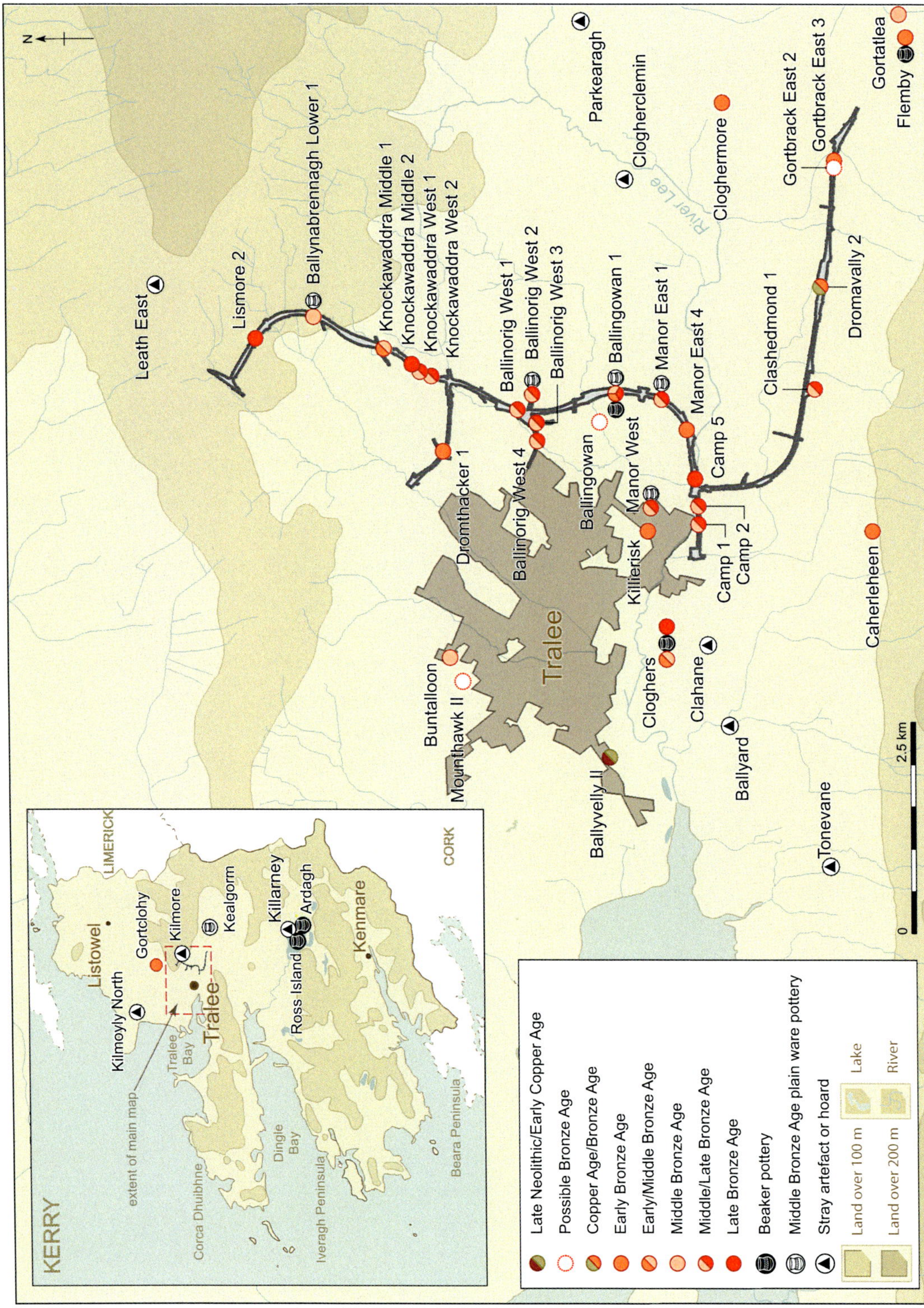

Illus. 5.1—Locations on or near the N22 Tralee Bypass where traces of Copper and Bronze Age settlers have been found.

The Middle Bronze Age (1600–1100 BC) saw much diversity in burial practices but there was a general reduction in the use of highly decorated pottery (Cooney & Grogan 1999, 135) and a move towards cremation as the exclusive burial rite. Burnt mounds were extensively used during this period and round-houses were the most common form of domestic dwelling (Doody 2000, 139). The emergence of defended hilltop enclosures in the Late Bronze Age (1100–700 BC), alongside developments in weaponry, suggests that society became increasingly more stratified and warlike (Waddell 2010, 205).

Excavations on the Tralee Bypass revealed traces of human activity in the Lee Valley throughout the Copper Age and Bronze Age. This evidence was distributed along the full length of the route and points to widespread activity in the area during these periods.

Bronze Age settlement in the Tralee area

Bronze Age habitation sites take various forms, ranging from open to enclosed settlements and from isolated houses to house clusters and even small villages (Carlin 2006). Prior to the bypass excavations, eight sites with signs of habitation had been identified in the Lee Valley (Illus. 5.1). The most substantial of these was Cloghers II, where four post-built, probable round-houses were excavated (Dunne & Kiely 2005). Three were clustered together, while the fourth was some 150 m to the east. One had a central hearth, two had porch-like entrance features and one had external gullies. Very small quantities of cremated bone, which might be human, were found scattered about the site, and nearby pits contained material that might represent ritual deposits. In general, however, the stone tools, pottery, grain and charcoal recovered throughout the site point to domestic activity. Beaker pottery was found in three of the round-houses, yet samples from two of them were radiocarbon-dated to the Middle and Middle/Late Bronze Age. The excavators contend that the houses were constructed during the Copper Age/Early Bronze Age (i.e. during the period when Beaker pottery was in use) and that the dated material derives from later activity (ibid.). A concentration of three pits and numerous stake-holes to the north of the houses was also associated with Beaker pottery.

A similar round-house, with porched entrance, internal hearth and beaten clay floor, was identified by test excavations in Ballingowan (Dunne & Buckley 2010). Another was found in Killierisk, defined by a circular slot-trench and an arc of post-holes and enclosing a possible central hearth; this house was dated to 1760–1600 BC (Lynch 2010).

Elsewhere in the Tralee area, habitation is also suggested by the discovery of Late Neolithic/Early Bronze Age stone tools in a cluster of pits, post-holes and stake-holes at Ballyvelly II, as well as pits of possible Bronze Age date at Mounthawk II, a saddle quern and rubbing stone from Middle Bronze Age pits in Buntaloon, and Middle and Late Bronze Age domestic pottery and stone tools from pits, post-holes and stake-holes in Manor West (Dunne & Kiely 2005). In addition, Beaker pottery was recovered from a pit in Flemby to the east of Tralee (Coyne 2002) and Early Bronze Age radiocarbon dates were returned from a burnt spread at Caherleheen and a furnace pit at Cloghermore, while a slot-trench with stake-holes at Gortatlea was dated to the Middle Bronze Age (Connolly 2008, 162).

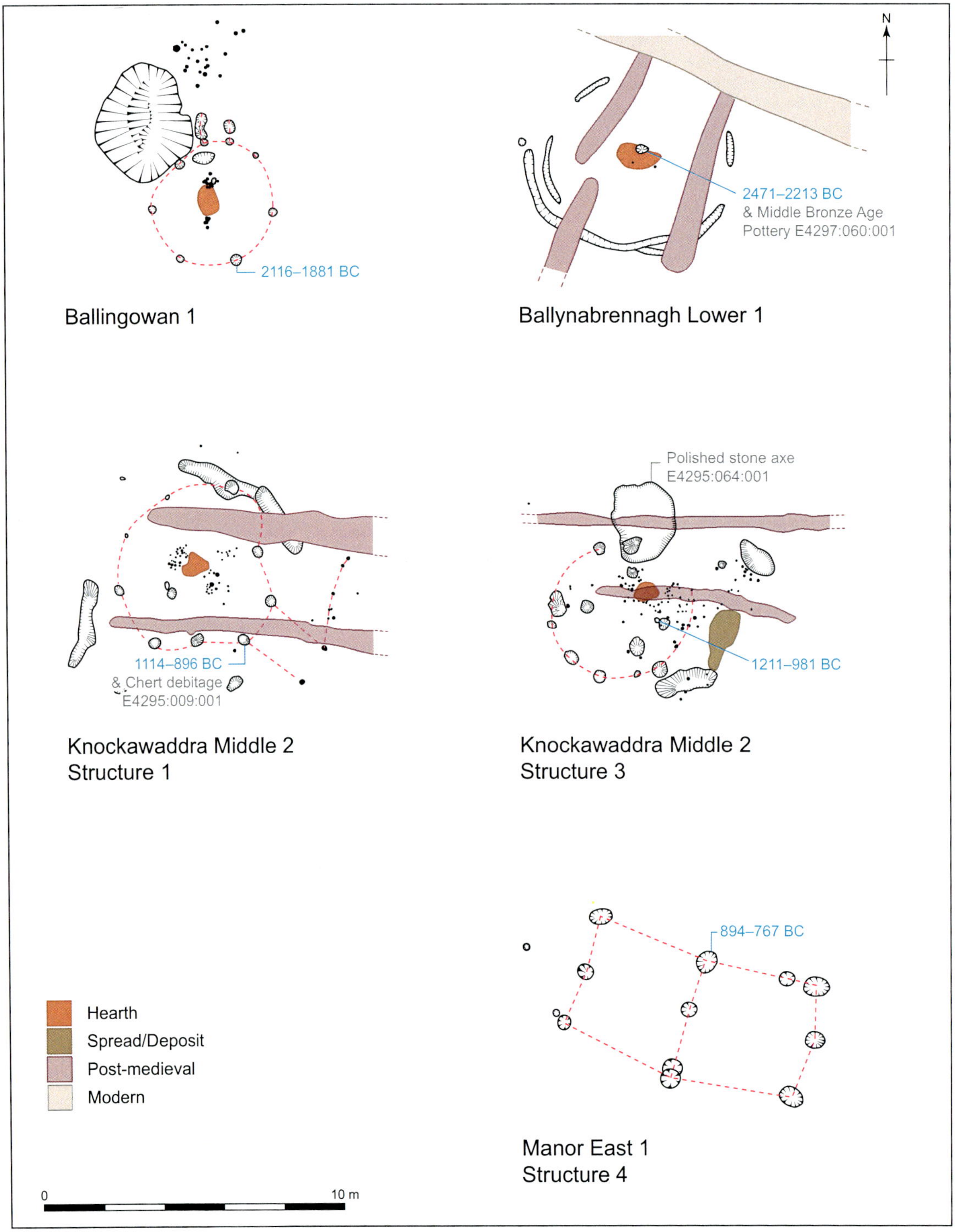

Illus. 5.2—Bronze Age round-houses and a rectangular building excavated on the N22 Tralee Bypass.

Bronze Age buildings on the bypass route

Four round-houses were identified on three sites along the bypass—Ballingowan 1, Ballynabrennagh Lower 1 and Knockawaddra Middle 2 (Table 5.1; Illus. 5.2). In addition, a rectangular building dating from the end of the Late Bronze Age was found at Manor East 1. As discussed in Chapter 4, the construction of robust rectangular houses ceased during the Middle Neolithic period (Smyth 2013) and a preference for circular structures emerged (Grogan 1996, 59). This preference continued through the Bronze Age, although rectilinear structures continued to be built into the Iron Age (Doody 2000, 137).

Approximately 85% of the Bronze Age houses known in Ireland are round (circular or oval) in plan (Carlin 2006, 10). These tend to vary structurally, with some consisting of a single or double ring of posts, or a single or double footing trench, sometimes accompanied by an inner setting of roof supports (ibid., 8). The house at Ballynabrennagh Lower 1 is an example of single footing-trench construction, though in this case the trench was discontinuous (Illus. 5.3). It is not clear whether this is a reflection of the original construction or whether the trench only partly survived. The slot-trench presumably held timber planks or wattle panels to form the house walls. The lack of evidence for an entrance or internal roof supports, while perplexing, is not unusual.

Three of the round-houses on the bypass route were defined by a single ring of posts. The intervals between the posts ranged from 0.28 m to 1.8 m and also varied within each individual house. This may be a reflection of the original construction method—rather than, say, the result of later truncation by tillage—as the spacing of uprights has been found to vary considerably in many excavated Bronze Age houses (Doody 2000, 144).

The internal diameter of the round-houses varied between 4 m and 6 m, with Ballingowan 1 (Illus. 5.4) and Structure 3 at Knockawaddra Middle 2 being the smallest. These were smaller than the

Table 5.1—Bronze Age buildings excavated on the N22 Tralee Bypass.

Site and building	Description	Radiocarbon date
Ballingowan 1	Oval round-house (4 m by 3.3 m; int. area 9.8 m^2) defined by eight post-holes and enclosing a central hearth. Entrance porch on north side.	2116–1881 BC (SUERC-37300)
Ballynabrennagh Lower 1	Circular house (int. diam. 6 m; int. area 23 m^2) defined by discontinuous footing trench. Central hearth but no identifiable entrance. Repair/improvement suggested by later footing trench on south side.	2471–2213 BC (SUERC-37259) (Dated material probably residual. Middle Bronze Age pottery recovered from same pit.)
Knockawaddra Middle 2 (Structure 3)	Circular house (int. diam. c. 4.6 m; int. area c. 8 m^2), defined by seven post-holes/pits and at least four stake-holes. No identifiable entrance but north-east side seemed open. Internal hearth and four large post-holes that may have held roof supports.	1211–981 BC (SUERC-37290)
Knockawaddra Middle 2 (Structure 1)	Subcircular house (5.2 m by 5 m; int. area 17.5 m^2), defined by nine post-holes and enclosing a central hearth. Entrance porch on south-east side.	1114–896 BC (SUERC-37288)
Manor East 1 (Structure 4)	Rectangular building (7 m by 4 m; int. area 22.5 m^2) defined by nine posts with two supporting/replacement posts and a stake-hole; central post that may have held a roof support. No identifiable entrance or hearth.	894–767 BC (SUERC-37328)

Illus. 5.3—Ballynabrennagh Lower 1. Bronze Age round-house and internal hearth, view to south-east (Rubicon Heritage Services Ltd).

majority of known Bronze Age round-houses, which range from 5 m to 7 m in diameter, though houses as small as 2 m in diameter were excavated at Laghaunstown, Co. Dublin (Carlin 2006, 10). Elsewhere in the Lee Valley, the Killierisk round-house was only 2.6 m in diameter (Lynch 2010), while the round-houses at Cloghers II fell within the more typical range at 5–6 m (Dunne & Kiely 2005).

Rectangular buildings are in the minority in the Bronze Age, with only 12 of the 114 buildings examined by Carlin (2006, 10) being rectangular or subrectangular in plan. It is more common for rectangular buildings to include a footing trench, such as at Chancellorsland, Co. Tipperary, and Coney Island, Lough Neagh (Doody 2000, 141), rather than free-standing posts as we have in the rectilinear structure at Manor East 1. This building was one of only two excavated on the bypass that had evidence for internal roof supports, the other being Structure 3 (a round-house) at Knockawaddra Middle 2. The absence of roof supports in the other three buildings suggests different methods of roof construction, but as we are left with just the footprints of the buildings we can only speculate as to what the roofs may have looked like (Illus. 5.5).

Of the houses on the bypass, only Ballingowan 1 and Structure 1 at Knockawaddra Middle 2 had identifiable entrances. Both had external porches, facing north and south-east respectively. At

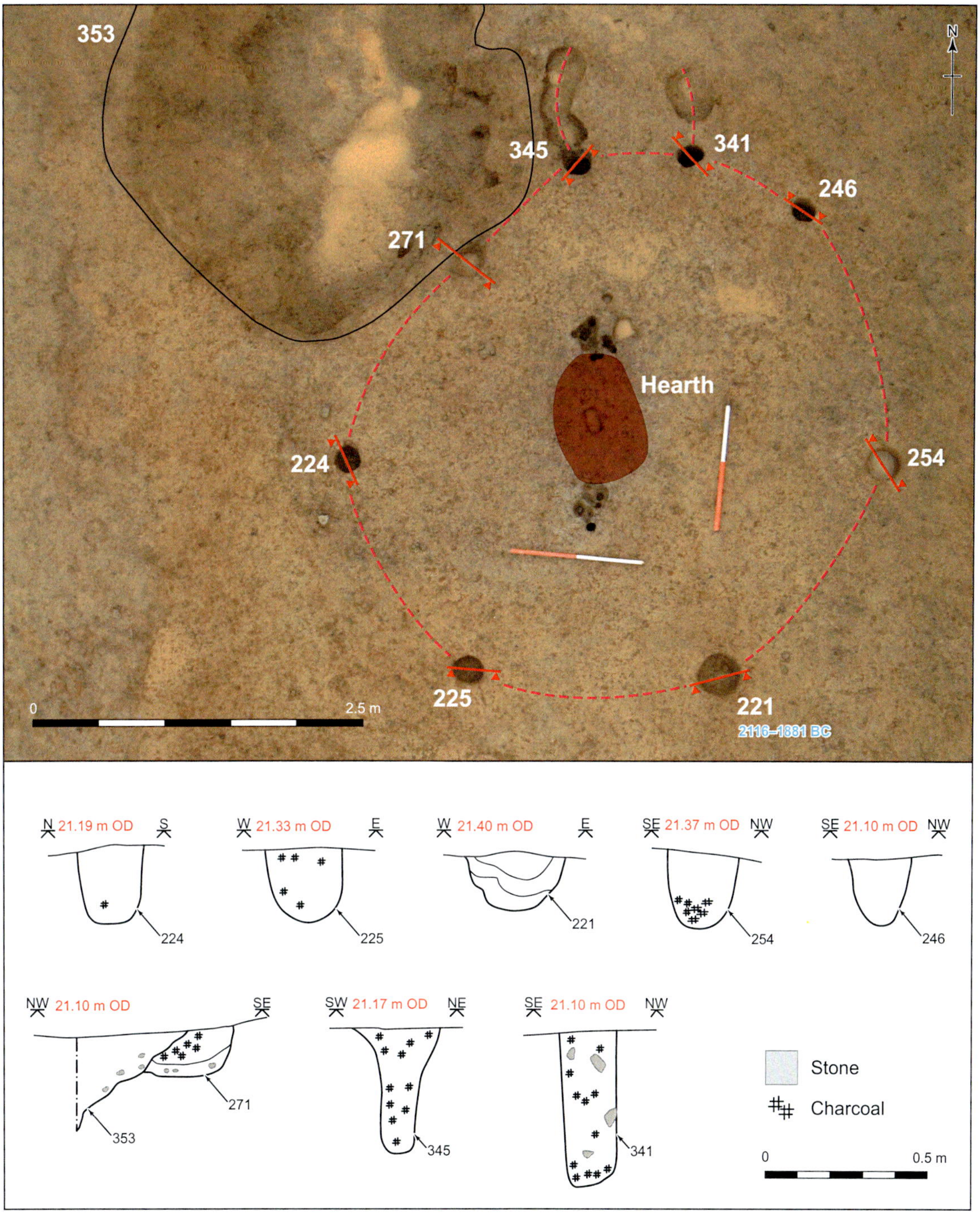

Illus. 5.4—Ballingowan 1, Area 1a. View of Early Bronze Age round-house from above and section drawings of post-holes (Rubicon Heritage Services Ltd).

Illus. 5.5—Knockawaddra Middle 2. Artist's impression of Structure 3, showing possible roof supports and entrance screens (windbreaks) supported on posts (Hannah Sims).

Knockawaddra Middle 2, Structure 1, a line of stake-holes formed a windbreak that would have created a sheltered area on the north side of the porch. No definite entrance was identified for Structure 3 at this site, though it may have been on the north-east side of the house, where there was no discernible wall line. A linear cluster of stake-holes, possibly forming a windbreak or small fence, was also identified on this side. The rectangular building at Manor East did not have an obvious entrance, though a seemingly extra post-hole near the north-east corner may have been part of a doorway.

Inside the buildings

A hearth was identified in all four of the round-houses, but not in the rectangular building at Manor East (Structure 4). At Knockawaddra Middle 2 (Illus. 5.6) and Ballingowan 1, the hearths were accompanied by dense clusters of stake-holes. These probably held spits or tripods from which cooking pots or meat joints were suspended over the fire. In a previous study by Carlin (2006, 11), of 104 buildings for which detailed information was available 23% had an internal hearth. The absence of hearths is seen to an even greater degree in the Bronze Age village at Corrstown, Co. Derry, where only 14 out of the 74 round-houses excavated had possible hearths (Ginn & Rathbone 2012, 208). A hearth is generally seen as evidence of domestic occupation in a building (Doody

Illus. 5.6—Knockawaddra Middle 2. Hearth and surrounding stake-holes in Structure 1, view to east (Rubicon Heritage Services Ltd).

Illus. 5.7—Manor East 1, Area 5. Late Bronze Age rectangular building (Structure 4), view to north-west. The central post suggests that the building was internally divided into two spaces (Rubicon Heritage Services Ltd).

2000, 145), but the apparent absence of a hearth does not automatically mean that a structure was not a domestic building. A hearth on a raised bed of stones would leave no trace on a site that was subsequently ploughed out, and small, portable cooking fires could have been maintained in ceramic vessels, rekindled when needed from their embers.

The majority of excavated Bronze Age rectangular buildings seem to lack internal features, with very few producing evidence of subdivisions. Doody (ibid.) suggests that this lack of internal division may be a reflection of the size of the structures, with most being too small for more than a single room. At 7 m long, however, the rectilinear building (Structure 4) at Manor East 1 was large enough to be divided in two, in line with its internal post (Illus. 5.7). The lack of a hearth or other internal features suggests that it is more likely to have been a byre or store rather than a dwelling house, though it is also possible that it provided sleeping quarters, with food being prepared and eaten outdoors, perhaps at the hearth 10 m to the east.

Apart from hearths, stake-holes and roof supports, internal features were limited to a pit with some stake-holes in the round-house at Ballingowan 1 and a single pit in the house at Ballynabrennagh Lower 1. The exact function of these features is unknown.

Similarly, the various pits, post-holes and stake-holes identified in the immediate environs of all the round-houses had no obvious purpose, though it is likely that they too represent aspects of domestic life in and around the buildings.

Enclosed and open settlements

The enclosure of domestic spaces with ditches, banks and/or fences had become common practice by the Middle and Late Bronze Age (Carlin 2006). Enclosures associated with ceremonial and funerary activity, on the other hand, are found throughout the Bronze Age and, obviously enough, are usually distinguishable by the presence of burials and ritual deposits.

A possible Middle Bronze Age enclosure was identified and partly exposed at Ballingowan 1 (Illus. 2.27 and 5.8). It was quite unusual in that it was defined on the north and west by low outcropping bedrock and by a very shallow ditch to the south. It would have offered little or nothing in terms of defence or the control of livestock, suggesting that its only purpose was to define a domestic space. Internally, there was an L-shaped arrangement of post-holes and stake-holes (c. 8.5 m by 8.5 m), as well as a cluster of stake-holes, scattered pits, post-holes and hearths. These are all typical features of domestic spaces, though no building plans were identified. A date of 1678–1499 BC was returned from a hulled barley grain recovered from one of the hearths.

A Late Bronze Age date was obtained from an enclosure ditch at Clashedmond 1, but the dating and interpretation of this site are problematic, as discussed in Chapter 2. As there is insufficient evidence regarding the date of the Clashedmond 1 enclosure, it is classified as undated for the purposes of this volume and is not discussed further here.

A small number of sites along the bypass route pointed to domestic activity but without an enclosure or even a recognisable dwelling house. These include an Early Bronze Age hearth at Manor East 4 and Middle Bronze Age pits, post-holes and stake-holes occurring both in isolation

Illus. 5.8—Ballingowan 1, Area 1c. Possible Middle Bronze Age enclosure, view to north. This large, irregular space (diameter >20 m) was bounded by outcropping rock on the west and north and by a shallow ditch on the south side (Rubicon Heritage Services Ltd).

and in small clusters at Ballingowan 1, Clashedmond 1 and Manor East 1. Further Bronze Age dates were returned from sink-hole deposits at Ballinorig West 2 and at Knockawaddra West 2.

The idea that a settlement site must include at least one dwelling house is often ingrained in archaeological thought, but we need to recognise that different aspects of domestic life may leave varied signatures in the archaeological record. Thus the scattered features on these sites may well represent temporary occupation or activity on the periphery of large settlements that remain undiscovered.

Remnants of domestic life

Although the quantity of artefacts and palaeoenvironmental material recovered from the Bronze Age settlements on the bypass route was small, it does give us an indication of the day-to-day activities that were taking place.

Stone rather than metal would still have been the primary raw material used for domestic tools—for cutting, woodworking and grinding. A piece of chert debitage was found in a post-hole

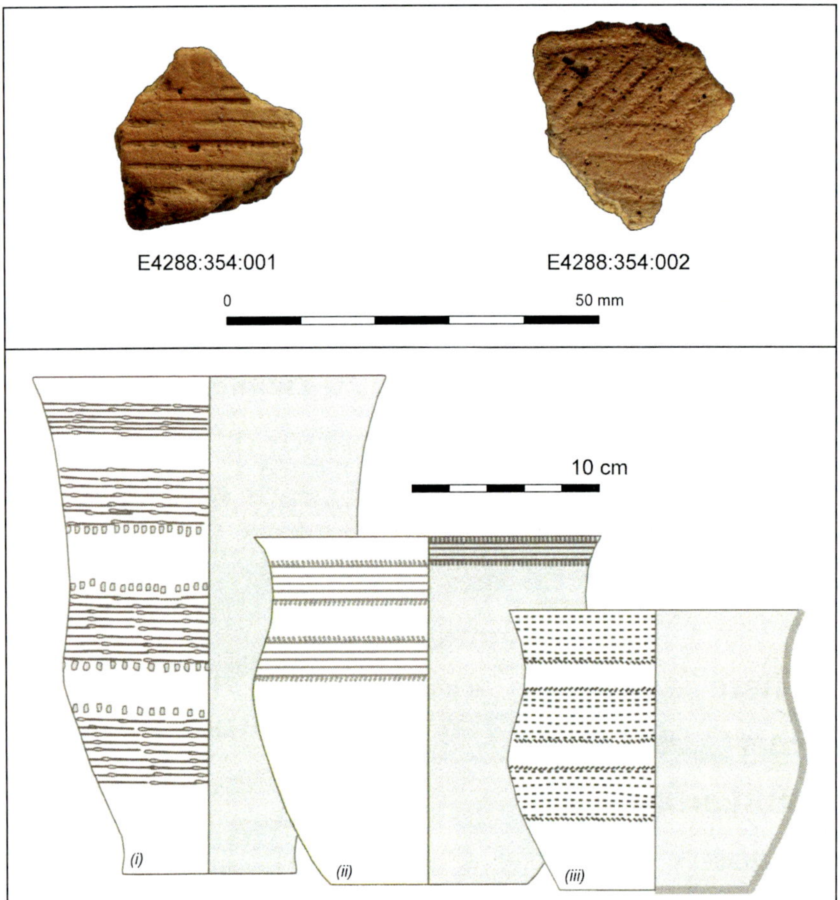

Beaker pottery from (i) Windmill, Co. Tipperary; (ii) Farranamanagh, Co. Tipperary; (iii) Kilgobbin, Co. Dublin.

Illus. 5.9—Ballingowan 1, Area 1a. Beaker pottery showing decoration consisting of horizontal rows of fine comb impressions (Vessel 1) and banded lines of fine impressed cord and comb (Vessel 2) and (below) examples of these vessel types found elsewhere (after Grogan & Roche 2010, illus. 7) (Rubicon Heritage Services Ltd).

of Structure 1 at Knockawaddra Middle 2, and a possible stone axe and a rubbing stone or pestle were found in features within 10 m of Structure 3 at the same site. Chipped flint, a rubbing stone and two sandstone fragments were recovered from features within the possible enclosed space at Ballingowan 1.

Further evidence of domestic activity is present in the palaeoenvironmental and faunal assemblages. Features associated with all four round-houses, the rectangular building and the Ballingowan 1 enclosure produced charred cereal grain and animal bone. A small number of cereal grains were identifiable as barley and hulled barley, but none of the burnt bone was identifiable to species. These assemblages are too small and poorly preserved to draw any overarching conclusions about agriculture and subsistence but they do at least indicate that food was being prepared and/or consumed in the vicinity of, or within, the houses.

Pottery was used extensively for storage and cooking during the Bronze Age. Beaker pottery, which dates from the Copper Age/Early Bronze Age, is generally found in domestic contexts in

Ireland and is seen as an indicator of settlement, even on sites where there is no clear evidence for houses or buildings. Ballingowan 1 is one such site.

Beaker pottery

Eoin Grogan

Three Beakers, represented by just four sherds, were recovered from two pits on Ballingowan 1 (Illus. 5.9). They represent three very fine, expertly made vessels that probably had soft, S-shaped profiles. On two sherds the horizontal ornament is dominated by banded lines of fine, impressed cord and comb lines (Roche & Grogan 2012c). This Beaker form is one of the most common and widespread in the Irish repertoire (Grogan & Roche 2010, illus. 7A, C and T), while the decoration on the third pot—rows of shallow horizontal grooves bordering short oblique grooves, forming a ladder motif—also occurs in early assemblages that are closely dated to the beginning of the period (2450–2300 BC).

Beaker pottery is a rarity in the south-west but small quantities have been recorded in the area around Killarney at the early copper-mines of Ross Island (O'Brien 2004) and just 3 km to the east at Ardagh (Dunne 2003b). Another small cluster occurs at Tralee, with a large assemblage of up to 13 vessels from Cloghers II (Kiely 2002, 149), the Ballingowan 1 site 2.5 km ENE of this and another site that yielded Beaker pottery from a pit at Flemby, 5.5 km to the ESE (Coyne 2002).

While the discovery is itself an important addition to the evidence from the south-west, the particular significance is the style of the Ballingowan Beaker pottery, which firmly establishes the Tralee cluster as occupied in the early Copper Age.

Other Beaker evidence in the area

Artefacts typically associated with Beaker pottery-using groups include a stone wristguard from Leath East and a barbed-and-tanged arrowhead from Clahane (Connolly 2010, 12). In Gortclohy, 13 km south-west of Listowel, flint and chert waste flakes typical of the period were found in a pit that was dated to 2132–1920 BC, using alder charcoal (Long 2012, 47). Though the evidence is scattered, it is clear that the Beaker phenomenon was influential in the region, perhaps owing to the arrival of migrants from Britain and mainland Europe and/or the spread of ideas and technologies via long-established trade routes. The early miners at Ross Island may have been at the forefront of this, bringing with them the requisite skills to mine and work copper ore and, over time, passing on their knowledge and the trappings of their lifestyle to the neighbouring communities.

Middle Bronze Age domestic pottery on the bypass

Eoin Grogan

During the Middle Bronze Age, and certainly by 1400 BC, plain domestic pottery emerged from a background of domestic cordoned urns (Grogan & Roche 2009a, 131–2). These vessels are straight-sided to slightly barrel-shaped, with flat, unfooted bases. The rims are generally rounded, pointed or slightly flattened, with very occasional internal bevels. The pots are well and evenly fired.

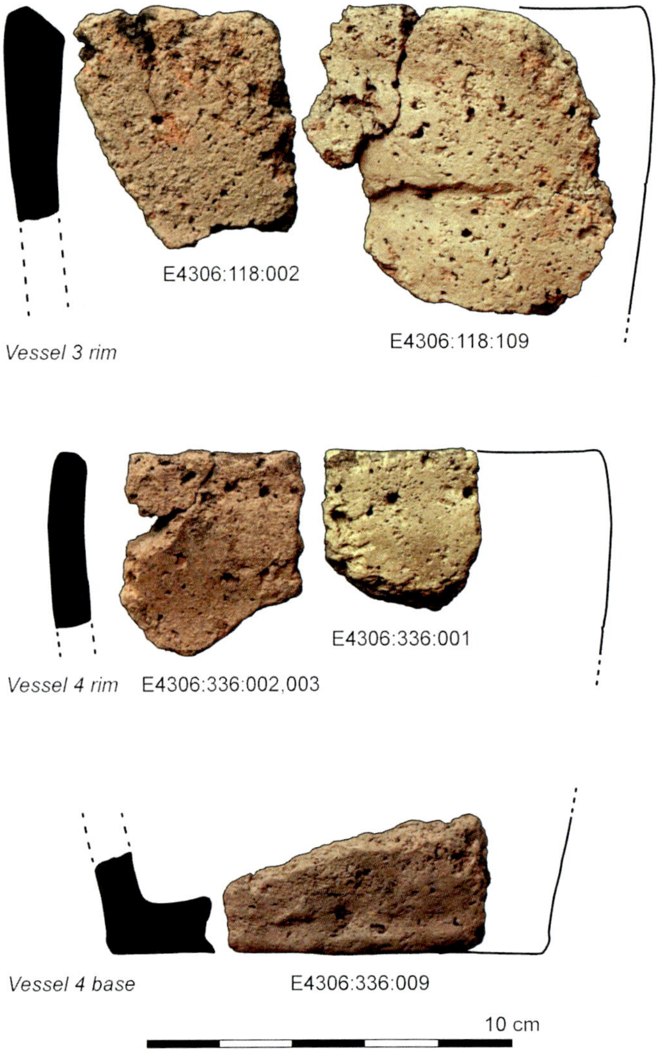

Illus. 5.10—Ballinorig West 2. Middle Bronze Age plain ware Vessel 3 and Vessel 4 (sample of recovered sherds) (Sara Nylund).

This pottery has an increasingly widespread distribution, augmented by the re-identification of material from earlier excavations.

This pottery was represented on the bypass, with sherds of two vessels found in the backfill of a sink-hole at Ballinorig West 2 (Illus. 5.10), sherds of another two found at Ballingowan 1 (Roche & Grogan 2012b; 2012c), and a fifth vessel represented by a single sherd recovered from Ballynabrennagh Lower 1 (Roche & Grogan 2012d). West of the bypass, at Manor West, a much larger domestic assemblage produced evidence for at least eight plain pots (Dunne 2002; Roche 2001). Further south, at Kealgorm near Castleisland, sherds from at least three vessels were identified (Grogan & Roche 2011); this material also came from the backfill of a sink-hole. As discussed above, a backfilled sink-hole at Knockawaddra West 2 produced a Middle Bronze Age radiocarbon date. Evidently these natural features had a particular fascination for prehistoric people and, at least during the Middle Bronze Age, special deposits—rather than simple domestic waste—were being placed in them.

This cluster of sites in the Tralee area—including well-dated examples without ceramic associations—is an important addition to the record and indicates a thriving Middle Bronze Age community.

Bronze spearhead fragments

Katharina Becker

There are a small number of Bronze Age metal finds known from the Lee Valley area, including three Early Bronze Age bronze axes (Kilmore, Ballyard and Parkearagh) and a small copper knife from Tonevane (Connolly 2010, 12). The only metal artefacts discovered along the bypass route were two tiny fragments of a probable spearhead from Knockawaddra Middle 2.

The two joining copper-alloy fragments were recovered from a stake-hole at Knockawaddra Middle 2 (Illus. 5.11). The fragments are heavily corroded, with the surviving blade half-width reduced to a maximum of 5 mm near the base of the larger fragment. The heavily worn surface allows the reconstruction of a blade of lozenge-shaped cross-section with a raised midrib of consistent width for most of its length of about 45 mm and flattening near the tip. In spite of the high degree of damage, it is likely that the fragments represent a formerly rather slender blade.

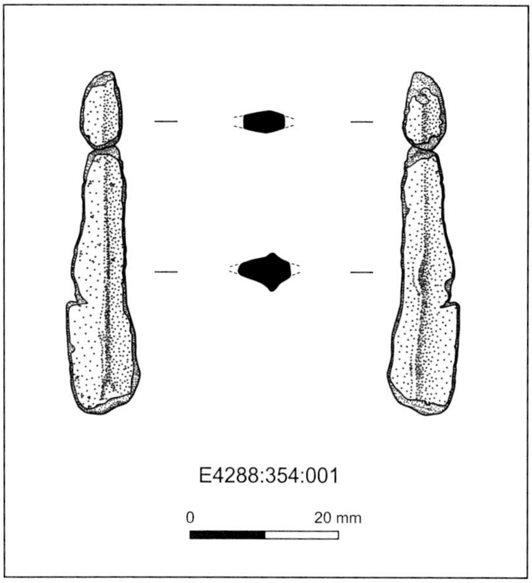

Illus. 5.11—Knockawaddra Middle 2. Bronze Age spearhead fragments (Hannah Sims).

A variety of bladed artefacts is represented in the corpus of known Bronze Age artefacts in Ireland. While the dimensions and possible proportions of this artefact would agree with those of a knife, dirk or rapier tip, those tend not to have midribs (cf. Ramsey 1989). Narrow and raised midribs of relatively consistent width on flattish blades, as in the example from Knockawaddra Middle 2, can be found particularly on Middle Bronze Age looped spearheads, whereas Dowris period (c. 900–600 BC) forms tend to be round and integrated into flat blade wings (e.g. Eogan 1964, fig. 1). On balance, it is most likely that here a finely worked spearhead tip is represented. While good parallels for finely raised midribs can be found on Middle Bronze Age spearheads in particular, the Knockawaddra Middle fragments are too small to be representative of the midrib of the object and thus it is possible that they represent a Middle or Late Bronze Age spearhead.

Finding a prehistoric metal artefact on an excavation is a rare occurrence. The fragments discussed here were recovered from one of several stake-holes truncating the base of a pit (066), which was situated near two Late Bronze Age houses (Structures 1 and 3) and a D-shaped building (Structure 2) dated to the early medieval period. The pit showed evidence for episodes of high-temperature burning and was probably a hearth. As it was not directly dated, it cannot be definitely attributed to either phase. The blade fragments are probably Middle to Late Bronze Age and most likely associated with the Bronze Age phase of the site. Their very fragmentary and abraded condition suggests, however, that they may have been residual objects only incidentally incorporated in the hearth and so they cannot be used to date the use of the hearth more precisely.

Cattle and cereals: agriculture in the Bronze Age

The small quantities of cereal grains found on the Bronze Age settlement sites indicate that crops were being grown and consumed by those who lived there, but there were also other signs of arable and pastoral activity on the large multi-period site of Ballingowan 1. A cereal-drying kiln containing hulled barley and a very small quantity of oats (possibly the wild rather than the cultivated variety) was excavated immediately south-west of the possible Middle Bronze Age enclosure. This is clear evidence of cereal processing. A grain of hulled barley from a basal layer

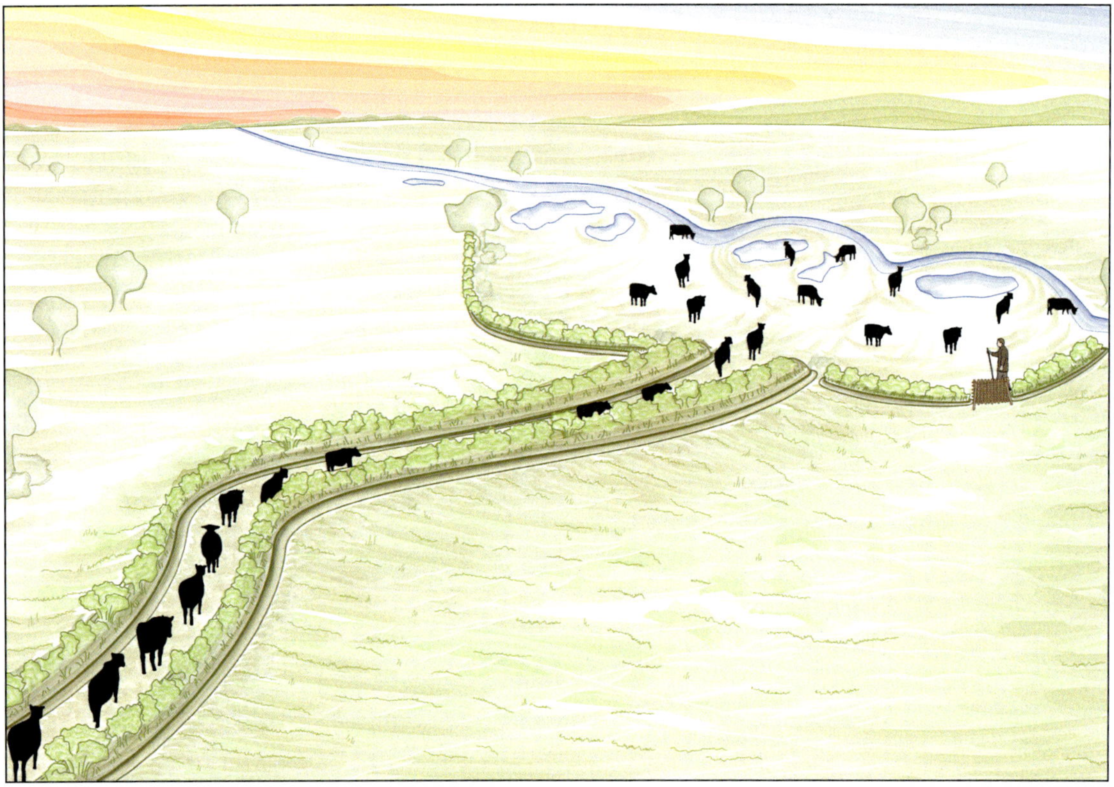

Illus. 5.12—Ballingowan 1, Area 1a. Artist's impression of the droveway. The excavated ditches are interpreted here as the flanking ditches to an embanked hedgerow lining either side of the droveway (Hannah Sims).

in the kiln returned a date of 1687–1513 BC (SUERC-37318). This kiln can therefore be added to the small body of Irish cereal-drying kilns dated to the Bronze Age, including those at Knockgraffon, Carrigatogher and Parkstown, all in Co. Tipperary, Moone, Co. Kildare, and Caherdrinny, Co. Cork (Monk & Power 2014). Monk and Power (ibid., 40) have questioned the reliability of these radiocarbon dates because the majority of excavated kilns date from the Iron Age or early medieval period, but the secure context from which the dated barley grain was retrieved at Ballingowan suggests that there is little reason to doubt the dating of this kiln. Moreover, the fact that hulled barley was the most commonly occurring cereal on the excavated

Bronze Age sites confirms that it was being grown in the area, while the recovery of quern-stone fragments from the adjacent enclosure is further evidence that cereals were being processed at this specific location during the Middle Bronze Age.

Tantalising evidence of pastoral farming on a large scale was also revealed at Ballingowan 1. Here a droveway formed by two parallel boundaries, each comprising a set of double ditches, was exposed for a length of 57 m where the bypass intersected it. If the single Late Bronze Age date obtained from one of the ditches is a reliable indicator of when it was constructed, this is a very early example of a droveway in Ireland. Other excavated droveways are believed to be early medieval in date and are associated with enclosures and field systems, such as those at Balriggin 1, Co. Dublin (Delaney 2006), and Killeisk, Co. Tipperary (Ó Faoláin 2010). Another at Ballynahinch, Co. Tipperary (Taylor 2010), returned radiocarbon dates in both the early and late medieval periods. In England, Francis Pryor (1999, 89–108) has argued that these double-ditched trackways were droveways for livestock and formed the principal elements of large field systems. Each side of the Ballingowan droveway is likely to have consisted of a low bank with dense hedging, flanked by ditches (Illus. 5.12). As well as increasing the height of the physical barrier, the hedging would have restricted views out of the droveway, thereby encouraging the animals to proceed along the defined route. The end of the droveway opened out to form an enclosure along the edge of a seasonally flooded area adjacent to a stream, suggesting that the objective was not just to guide livestock to the watering area but also to contain them there. This may have been an important factor in avoiding conflict with neighbouring landowners over water or other resources during a period when the archaeological evidence suggests a significant population increase throughout the country. The effort that went into constructing this droveway suggests that a sizeable number of cattle were kept here, requiring a correspondingly large grazing area in its environs.

Burnt mounds in the Bronze Age

Prior to the bypass excavations there were 24 known examples of burnt mound sites within 1 km of the route (five of these have more than one mound) (Illus. 5.13). A further 16 have been identified during the bypass investigations. The possible uses of these sites have been discussed above (Chapter 2). It is likely that many burnt mound sites were multi-functional and that not all were used for the same purposes. Determining that purpose is difficult because burnt mounds typically yield little in terms of artefacts or palaeoenvironmental remains, and this was also the case with the excavated burnt mound sites on the bypass.

Classic burnt mounds survive as low grassy mounds of crescent or U-shaped plan with a sunken, earth-cut trough at the centre, although those that were not used for long and those levelled by later ploughing often do not have any visible surface expression. Troughs are generally rectangular, circular or oval in plan and are sometimes lined with clay, wood and/or stone. They have been defined as having a steep-sided cut with a minimum length of 0.75 m and a flat base (Eogan 2011, 264). On the bypass, 17 troughs were excavated at 10 sites. They were not evenly distributed. Camp 1 and Ballinorig West 1 had three and six troughs respectively, while the other eight sites had only

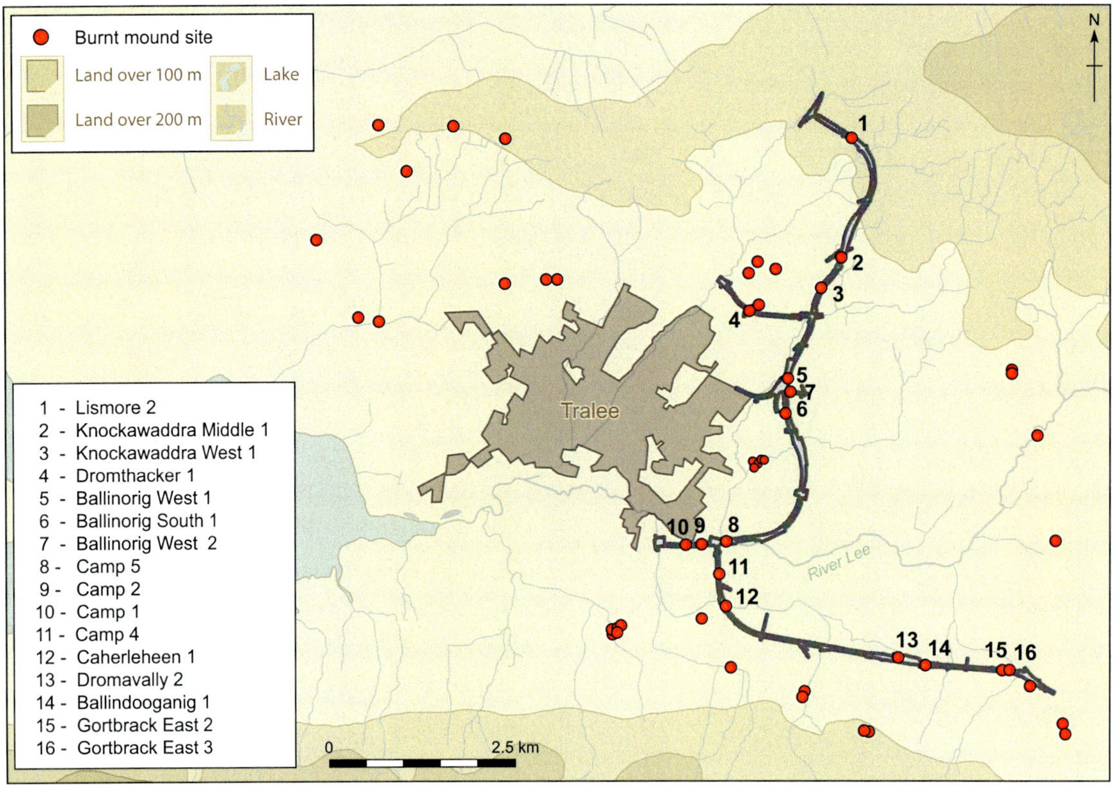

Illus. 5.13—Known burnt mound sites in the Lee Valley area, including those discovered on the N22 Tralee Bypass.

one trough each. The troughs were rectangular, oval or irregular in shape and measured between 1.29 m and 2.45 m in length and between 0.27m and 0.9 m in depth.

The subrectangular trough at Camp 5 was lined with wood (Illus. 5.14). This survived as 17 base planks and two side planks, all held in place by a wooden stake in each corner. The trough cut was larger than the wooden lining. The sides of the cut may have been partly infilled with silty material after the lining was inserted. Four wood species were represented: alder, hazel, ash and blackthorn. Traces of wood lining also survived in the trough at Camp 1 but it was very poorly preserved. Wood lining in a similarly poor condition was uncovered at Ballinorig West 1, though here a large stone slab also formed part of the lining on the south-east side (Illus. 5.15). There was no evidence of trough lining at any other site.

At Camp 5 and Lismore 2, the hearth used to heat the stones—indicated by a patch of burnt soil—was located directly adjacent to the narrow end of a rectangular trough (Illus. 5.16). In both cases the hearths sloped into the end of the trough, and this presumably allowed the heated stones to be easily rolled in while ensuring minimum heat loss. Similar trough-edge hearths have been identified at burnt mounds around the country, for example at Ballyduff East, Co. Waterford (Hegarty et al. 2011, 21). A large number of stake-holes around the hearths indicate that they may

Illus. 5.14—Camp 5. Mid-excavation view of trough, showing alder planks lining the base and an adjacent hearth with stake-holes, view to south-east (Rubicon Heritage Services Ltd).

have had a secondary function, such as spit-roasting of meat, heating suspended pots or drying hides. Some of the stake-holes may also have supported a windbreak to shelter the hearth.

Pits associated with the burnt mounds were found at Ballinorig West 1, Camp 1, Camp 4 and Knockawaddra Middle 1. None were of a size or shape typical of a conventional trough, nor was there evidence of any linings. Stake-holes and post-holes (i.e. other than the hearthside examples just described) were found in association with burnt mounds at a number of sites, including Knockawaddra West 1, Dromavally 2, Camp 4 and Gortbrack East 2, but there was no evidence as to their use.

The mounds themselves consisted of dark, charcoal-rich deposits with heat-shattered limestone and sandstone. They were generally irregular in shape and varied in size from 5 m to 21.2 m across and from 0.15 m to 0.8 m in thickness. Their shape and profile had undoubtedly been affected by later agriculture and none retained any surface expression prior to excavation.

In addition to Caherleheen 1, mentioned in the previous chapter, five of the bypass sites—Ballindooganig 1, Camp 2, Gortbrack East 2, Gortbrack East 3 and Knockawaddra West 1—comprised burnt mounds/spreads without an associated trough. At Ballindooganig 1, Camp 2 and Knockawaddra West 1 it is possible that associated troughs are lying undiscovered beyond the road footprint, as the mounds extended beyond the road boundary and were therefore only partly

Illus. 5.15—Ballinorig West 1. Mid-excavation view of trough, showing stone slab and timber lining, view to east (Rubicon Heritage Services Ltd).

excavated. It is possible that at least some of the pits excavated at Gortbrack East 2 and 3 served as troughs, though they were certainly not typical examples in terms of size or shape.

No mounds/spreads were uncovered at Dromthacker 1, Ballinorig West 2 or Ballinorig South 1, nor was there any sign in the surrounding topsoil of mounds having been ploughed out. The use of hot-stone technology at these sites was represented only by pits filled with heat-shattered stone and charcoal. The lack of a mound/spread indicates that these features may only have been used once or for a very short period of time. Some of these pits, particularly those at Dromthacker 1 and Ballinorig West 2, may have functioned as troughs, while others were probably roasting pits or earth ovens (e.g. the pits at Ballinorig South 1). These latter pits did not involve boiling water; instead, items such as pots or joints of meat were heated directly on the hot stones.

Dating the Lee Valley burnt mounds

Excavations throughout the country have revealed that burnt mounds were in use from the Early Neolithic to at least the Iron Age (Hawkes 2018). Radiocarbon dating has consistently demonstrated, however, that by far the greatest number were in use during the Bronze Age, in particular the Middle Bronze Age, with a noticeable fall-off towards the Late Bronze Age. For example, the majority of

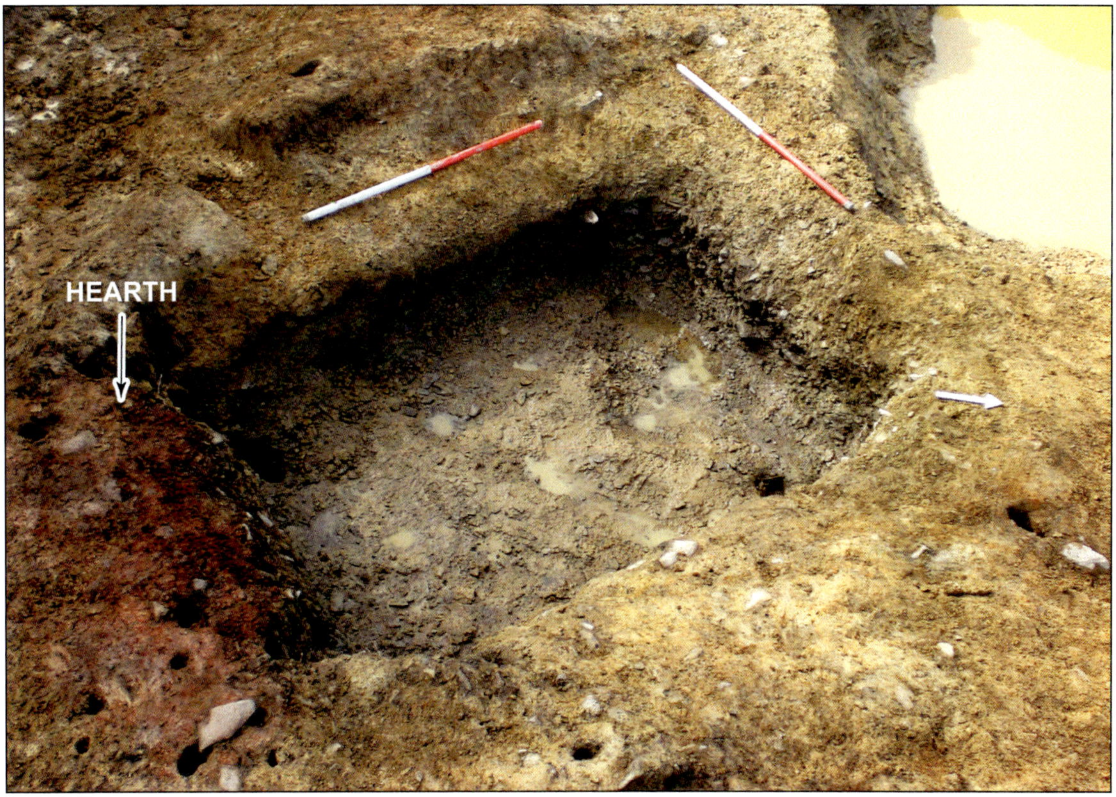

Illus. 5.16—Lismore 2. Hearth on the south-eastern edge of a rectangular trough, view to south-west (Rubicon Heritage Services Ltd).

burnt mounds excavated in advance of the gas pipeline between Dublin and Limerick were dated to between 1700 and 1000 BC, though a significant number were also dated to between 2500 and 1700 BC (Grogan et al. 2007, 96; see also Brindley & Lanting 1990 for an earlier dataset), with only a small number dating from the later Bronze Age. A recent review records that 838 out of 1,165 excavated burnt mounds and related sites dated from the Copper Age or Bronze Age (Hawkes 2018, 125).

Twenty-four dates were returned from 15 of the bypass sites (the site at Gortbrack East 2 had no material from a secure context that was suitable for dating). Twenty-two dates were obtained from charcoal samples of hazel, alder or blackthorn and two from oak (a less desirable sample material, as the heartwood may already have been very old when burnt). The samples were from various contexts, including mound deposits, trough fills and trough lining (with the latter two being preferred where available). Where a site showed evidence of multiple phases of use, an attempt was made to date each phase. Three sites produced dates in more than one major period—Ballinorig West 1, Camp 1 and Camp 2.

The earliest burnt mound identified (Caherleheen 1) was Late Neolithic in date, while four other sites (Ballindooganig 1 [oak charcoal], Camp 4, Ballinorig South 1 and Ballinorig West 1) produced dates in the Late Neolithic/Copper Age. These dates are early in the known period of use of hot-stone technology and add to a growing corpus of sites dated to this period, including Killaspy B, Co. Waterford (Pollock & Halpin 2011, 156), Ballycorick and Ballyleaan, Co. Clare (Grogan et al. 2007, 87), and Mullamast, Co. Kildare (Clark 2010). Evidently hot-stone technology was well established by the beginning of the Bronze Age, having its roots in the Neolithic period. Fourteen of the excavated burnt mound sites on the bypass route produced dates in the Bronze Age, while Camp 5 dated from the Late Bronze Age/Early Iron Age transition period. This fits with the general nationwide picture of burnt mounds being predominantly of Early and Middle Bronze Age date.

Reuse of the burnt mound sites

Burnt mounds were often reused, sometimes in multiple phases of activity separated by long periods of time. Identifying the number of phases of use on a site is often difficult owing to natural slumping of the mound and the spreading and/or partial removal of it by subsequent ploughing or land improvements. Nevertheless, based on radiocarbon dates or the layering of mound deposits or both, it was possible to determine that eight sites had only one phase of use, whereas five others had evidence of at least two phases—Ballindooganig 1, Ballinorig South 1, Knockawaddra West 1, Camp 2 and Camp 5. Three phases were distinguishable at Camp 1, each represented by a distinct mound, while three mounds and six troughs attested to at least four episodes of activity at Ballinorig West 1, spanning the Late Neolithic/Copper Age transition through to the Middle Bronze Age.

In most cases, multiple phases of use coincided with multiple troughs and/or mounds. At Camp 2, however, two phases were indicated by the presence of two distinct layers of heat-shattered stone within the same mound, separated by a layer of silt. This was confirmed by radiocarbon dating, which indicated that the phases were separated by a period of at least 700 years.

The reuse of sites over such long time-spans suggests that they held some significance for the communities in question or at the very least that knowledge of them passed down through the generations, aided perhaps by the fact that many mounds retained a prominent surface expression and almost all were located on a spring or wetland margin or some similarly reliable water source. Roving hunting groups may have returned to particular locations on a seasonal basis. There are also suggestions that some of these sites may have had a more spiritual aspect which would have encouraged repeated visits. It may have been in this context that human bones were deposited on burnt mound sites at Grange, Co. Tyrone (Site 1) (Masser & Bailey 2008), and at Busherstown 8, Co. Carlow (Baker et al. 2015).

Positioning burnt mounds in the landscape

Burnt mounds are almost invariably located close to a water source. This was well demonstrated during a study of the later prehistoric landscape of North Munster—encompassing counties Clare and Limerick and portions of Kerry and Tipperary—during which burnt mounds were consistently identified along the margins of wetlands, small lakes, turloughs, river estuaries and on the banks of rivers and streams (Grogan 2005). On the present project, 12 sites were within 60 m of a water source (stream, floodplain or marshland).

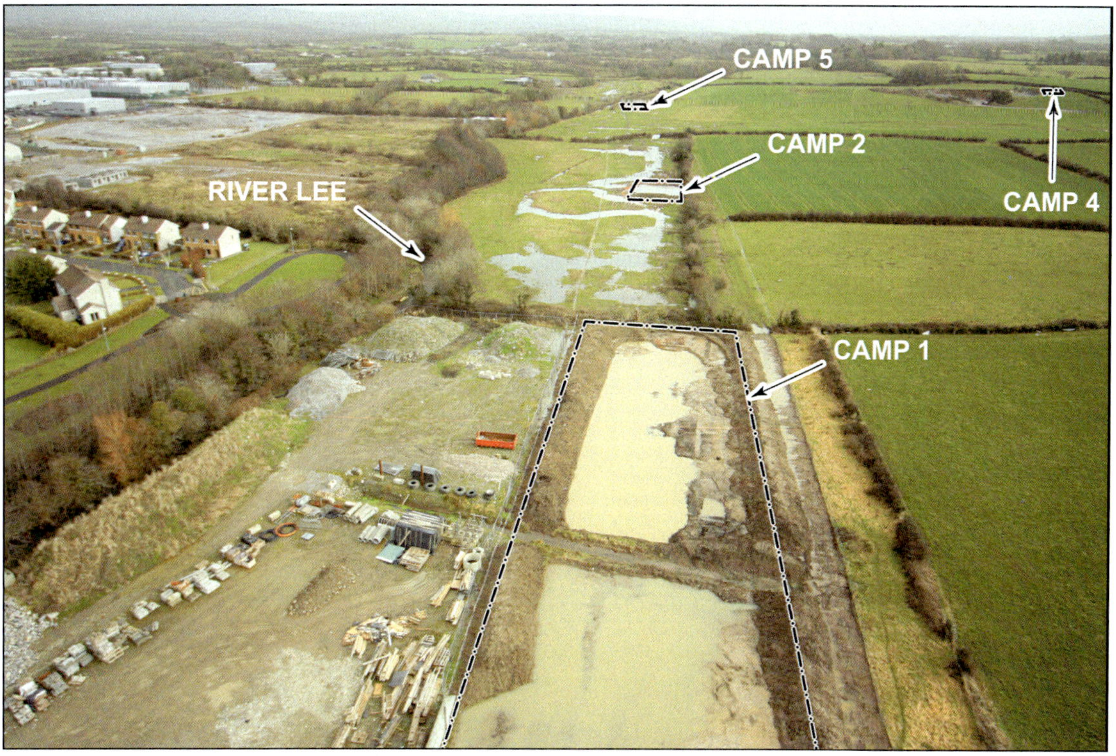

Illus. 5.17—Aerial view of construction work on the N22 Tralee Bypass, showing a cluster of burnt mound sites in the River Lee floodplain at Camp 1, 2, 4 and 5, view to east (Aerialphoto.ie).

A degree of clustering sometimes occurs in areas suited to the use of hot-stone technology. The southern floodplain of the River Lee appears to have been just such a locale, with a string of four sites—Camp 1, Camp 2, Camp 4 and Camp 5—excavated within a 500 m stretch, parallel to the river (Illus. 5.17). Similar clustering in the Tralee area is evident from the group of five burnt mounds (KE029-306–8, 215–16) recorded just east of a tributary of the River Lee in Ballingowan, as well as by the group of four excavated by Dunne & Buckley (2011) in Caherleaheen.

Dealing with the dead

The discussion thus far has focused on how people lived and worked in the Bronze Age. Here we look at the treatment of the dead and what this can tell us about beliefs and religious practices at this time.

Prior to the bypass excavations, evidence for Bronze Age funerary activity in the Lee Valley consisted of a cist burial in Carrigeendaniel (KE029-208002), 19 undated possible barrows at various locations in the landscape identified in the Sites and Monuments Record, and eight sites containing human remains and/or formal burials which were discovered during the course of development-led archaeological investigations (Illus. 5.18).

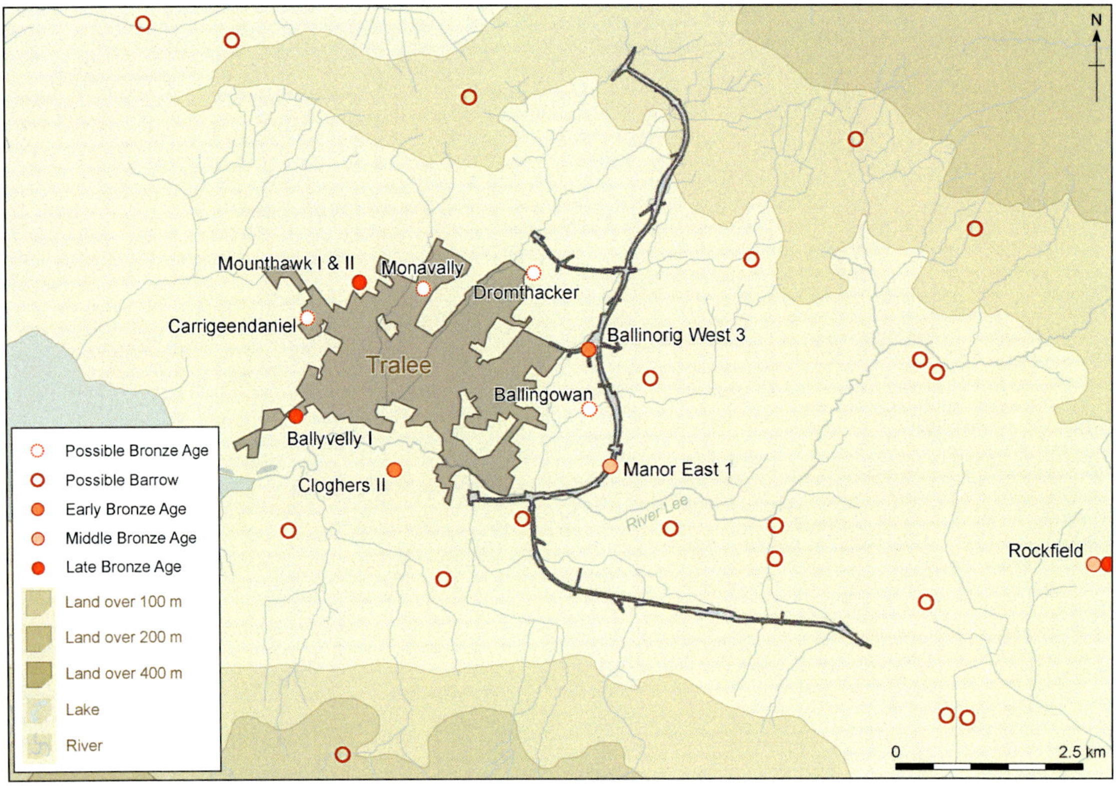

Illus. 5.18—Known Bronze Age burial sites and possible barrows in the Lee Valley and wider environs, including Bronze Age burials excavated on the N22 Tralee Bypass.

During excavation at Cloghers II, cremated human bone was recovered from a pit and post-hole of Structure D, one of four Early Bronze Age circular structures excavated at the site (Dunne & Kiely 2005). This building was interpreted as a domestic dwelling rather than a funerary monument, but it is not uncommon in the Bronze Age to find human remains deliberately deposited in a domestic context. Cleary (2005, 28) suggests that these were 'foundation deposits' placed before or during the construction of a house to ensure good fortune for the inhabitants.

Two cremation pit burials at Mounthawk I, each containing the remains of an adult, were dated to the Late Bronze Age on the basis of pottery sherds found in one of the pits (Dunne & Kiely 2005). Very small quantities (0.1 g and 0.09 g) of cremated human bone were also recovered from two pits at the adjacent site of Mounthawk II. These pits also contained animal bone, charcoal and barley grains, suggesting that they were domestic waste pits rather than formal burials. Small quantities of bone, possibly human, were also found in two post-holes. As at Cloghers II, at Mounthawk I and II there seemed to be deliberate deposition of cremated human remains in domestic spaces.

At Ballyvelly I, to the east of Tralee, elongated pits containing charcoal, cremated bone and heat-shattered stone were interpreted as the under-pyre draught pits of a late prehistoric crematorium (ibid., 43). A number of surrounding pits also contained cremated remains.

Radiocarbon dating suggests that this activity occurred in the Late Bronze Age and Iron Age (ibid.).

A similar interpretation was proposed for a pyre pit at Rockfield, which had two flues and was only 6 m from a cremation pit burial (Collins 2000). Another pyre pit was subsequently discovered in the same townland, a short distance to the south-west (Connolly 2002) (see Chapter 8 for a discussion on the similarity of these pyre pits to limekilns excavated on the bypass). Closer to Tralee, a cremation pit of possible Bronze Age date in Dromthacker contained the partial remains of at least one individual (ibid., 54). Two further undated pit burials were excavated in Ballingowan (Dunne & Buckley 2010), while a flat cemetery of eight pit burials was identified by test excavations in Carrigeendaniel but does not appear to have been subsequently excavated (Dunne & Buckley 2009).

In addition, while the bone was too small to identify as human, it is likely that a series of seven pits identified at Monavally, on the north side of Tralee, represent a series of cremation pits of possible Late Bronze Age date (Connolly 2008, 168).

Cremation burials on the bypass

Carmelita Troy

Bronze Age cremation burials were found on two sites on the bypass—Ballinorig West 3 and Manor East 1 (Illus. 5.19; Table 5.2). Even though all of the cremated bone from the three burials was identifiable as human, just 14.3% could be identified to skeletal element and most of this came from the skull and lower limbs (Table 5.3). This does not necessarily mean that only certain body parts were selected for burial: the identifiable bones were those that have a better chance of surviving, and skull fragments are among the easiest to identify.

Although there is some clustering of Early Bronze Age cremation sites, such as in the Emly area of west Tipperary or around Cush, Co. Limerick, the current pattern suggests that burial took place in discrete individual sites, possibly representing dispersed communities. The burials from Glenatlucky (Hegarty & Kiely 2019) and Ballynacarriga, Co. Cork, as well as a possible disturbed burial from Caherdrinny, Co. Cork, tend to confirm this pattern (Grogan & Roche 2009b, 292–9).

The quantity of cremated human bone in the Ballinorig West 3 burial is significantly less than what would be expected for two individuals. A whole adult cremation deposited in antiquity would have ranged from 350 g to 2,270 g (McKinley 1997; Troy 2015). As the burial had been truncated by plough disturbance, it is impossible to state whether the full remains were interred or only a selected portion.

Both the adult and the sub-adult remains at Ballinorig West 3 were identified throughout the burial deposit, suggesting that they had become mixed when gathered from the funerary pyre before being interred within the urn. It is unlikely that the two individuals became mixed as a result of the plough truncation, as this action would have removed the bone from the feature rather than mixing it within the context of the urn deposit. The presence of adult remains was determined by the size of a number of long bone fragments and the thickness of skull fragments. The sub-adult was identified from fragments of the skull and finger bones.

The presence of two individuals in one burial raises the question of relationship. It is tempting when faced with the burial of a sub-adult and adult to ascribe a familial relationship to the pair,

Illus. 5.19—Manor East 1. Bronze Age cremation burials, one prior to excavation and the other prior to being block-lifted for excavation under laboratory conditions (Rubicon Heritage Services Ltd).

such as that of parent and child or of extended family members. It is, of course, equally possible that the only connection between them was that they belonged to the same community, died around the same time and were cremated together. The tradition of double burial is not uncommon in Irish prehistory. For example, an isolated Early Bronze Age double cremation burial from Screggan 1, Co. Offaly (dated to 1776–1601 BC), contained a possible female and a child (6–8 years) (Troy & Lalonde 2011), while a double burial at Ask, Co. Wexford (dated to 1890–1690 BC), contained a child (<14 years of age) and a possible female adult (Troy 2011).

Two Middle Bronze Age cremation burials were identified at Manor East 1. One was contained in a coarse, apparently inverted, domestic vessel; the other was a simple unaccompanied pit burial. The degree of fragmentation was noted to be higher within the pit burial, where 30.2% of the bone was greater than 10 mm in size, compared to the burial in the inverted vessel, where the rate was 51.2%, possibly because the pottery vessel offered more protection to the cremated remains after deposition.

During the Middle Bronze Age a preference for 'token' burials developed, whereby the deceased was represented by the interment of only a small portion of the cremated remains (ibid., 136). At Manor East 1, the burial that included the pottery may have been truncated and so we do not know how much of the original deposit survives and whether it could have been a token burial.

Table 5.2—Bronze Age burials discovered on the N22 Tralee Bypass.

Site	Description	Weight of bone (g)	Radiocarbon date
Ballinorig West 3	Subcircular pit (086; 0.4 m by 0.3 m) containing the cremated remains of an adult and sub-adult (sex unidentifiable) within an inverted encrusted urn, of which only part of the rim survived. Oak and non-oak charcoal also present.	519	1928–1752 BC (SUERC-37086)
	Thin spread (0.46 m by 0.37 m by 0.04 m deep) adjacent to the urn burial.	1.6	Not dated
Manor East 1	Circular pit (965; 0.42 m in diameter by 0.38 m deep) containing the cremated remains of an adult (sex unidentifiable), sherds of an inverted plain ware vessel and oak charcoal.	167.7	1436–1296 BC (SUERC-37088)
	Circular pit (108; 0.4 m in diameter by 0.51 m deep) containing the cremated remains of an adult (sex unidentifiable), along with oak, ash and blackthorn charcoal, fragments of burnt clay, a naked barley grain, a fumitory fruit, a convex end scraper and two undiagnostic fragments of metallurgical waste.	448.2	1450–1309 BC (SUERC-37087)

Table 5.3—Distribution and weight of identifiable skeletal elements.

Site	Skull (g)	Axial (g)	Upper limb (g)	Lower limb (g)	Total (g)	Unidentifiable to element (g)
Ballinorig West 3	95.5	1.8	0.4	–	97.7	422.9
Manor East 1, pit with pottery	–	–	–	11.8	11.8	155.9
Manor East 1, simple pit	47.5	0.5	4.5	0.3	52.7	395.5
Total	**143.0**		**4.9**	**12.1**	**162.2**	**974.3**

.0The simple pit burial, however, showed less signs of disturbance and contained enough bone to possibly represent a full cremation.

Bronze Age funerary pottery on the bypass

Eoin Grogan

The single Early Bronze Age pottery vessel from the bypass—an inverted encrusted urn of the Vase Tradition—came from Ballinorig West 3. This represents the first classic Early Bronze Age burial discovered in County Kerry and, as such, is a find of considerable interest. The poorly preserved material represents a vessel with a rim diameter of c. 295 mm, with faint oblique incised lines on the rim and two applied strips forming an inverted V-shape on the exterior surface. The returned radiocarbon date places the vessel late in the encrusted urn series (c. 2000–1800 BC; Brindley 2007, 274).

Classic Early Bronze Age burials are rare elsewhere in the south-west but include encrusted urn burials, for example, at Coolnahane, Liscahane (Waddell 1990, 60–1) and Gortavehy East (Kavanagh 1973, 536) in West Cork, with Gortavehy East and Liscahane just 16 km and 22 km to the east of Killarney respectively. To the north and east of the region, however, encompassing north Cork and the adjacent areas of south-east Limerick and south-west Tipperary, extensive evidence for Early Bronze Age funerary activity has been uncovered (Grogan & Roche 2010).

The vessel from Manor East 1 was similar to pottery found at Ballinorig West 2, Ballingowan 1 and Ballynabrennagh Lower 1. It was a coarse, apparently inverted, domestic vessel. This had a rim diameter of about 180 mm, which indicates a small pot, perhaps 190–200 mm in height, with a flat, inward-sloping rim. A similar simple pit cremation at Mounthawk I, to the north-west of Tralee, was accompanied by sherds from a similar vessel (Dunne 1998; Roche 1998). Urned burials, simple cremation pits with broken sherds and unaccompanied cremation pits (i.e. with no pottery)—represented at both Manor East 1 and Mounthawk I—are recognised features of the Irish Middle Bronze Age (Grogan 2004).

Conclusions

The round-houses discovered on the bypass are a significant addition to our knowledge of Bronze Age settlement in the Lee Valley, complementing the previous discoveries at Cloghers, Killierisk and Ballingowan. Infrastructural developments nationally have resulted in a huge increase in the number of known Bronze Age settlements. Doody's (2000) study of Bronze Age house shape and construction was based on the 78 examples then known. Within only six years the number of excavated houses had at least doubled (Carlin 2006), and many more have been identified since. The general characteristics of the Tralee Bypass round-houses are in keeping with what is seen

Illus. 5.20—This Early Bronze Age flat axe (CPM holding no. 1777.2077) was found in Ballyard on the south side of the River Lee estuary, between Tralee and Blennerville. Possession of an axe like this may have been an indicator of power or status at a time when metallurgy was in its infancy. It is mounted here in a modern replica wooden handle (Dara McGrath, Cork Public Museum).

Illus. 5.21—In 1875 a hoard of five Late Bronze Age horns was found in Clogherclemin bog beside the River Lee, 2 km east of the N22 Tralee Bypass. Ger O'Neill's sculpture in the Garden of the Senses in Tralee Town Park represents Sound. It was inspired by the Bronze Age horns from Clogherclemin (James Eogan, TII).

elsewhere in the country, though overall there is a great deal of variety in this house type. The rectangular building at Manor East 1 is less typical and there is insufficient evidence to interpret it as a house, though the surrounding features do indicate that it was the focus of domestic activity.

The possible enclosure at Ballingowan 1 and the scattered, unenclosed domestic features at this site, as well as at Manor East 1 and 4 and Clashedmond 1, attest to the fact that a recognisable house is not the only indicator of domestic occupation. The possible enclosure seemed to be a defined space but offered little evidence of functionality in terms of shelter, defence or containment. We can only assume that defining the area was somehow important, even if the boundary features were not in themselves substantial barriers.

While a significant number of Bronze Age sites were identified on the bypass, the number of artefacts recovered was conspicuously low. This paucity of artefacts is also seen on sites previously excavated in the area. At Cloghers II, for example, where settlement evidence included four round-houses, only a small assemblage of Beaker pottery, a rubbing stone and a flint flake were found (Dunne & Kiely 2005, 53). A cluster of three artefact-rich pits 20 m north of the houses suggests, however, that the removal of objects from the settlement area was deliberate, perhaps carried out as part of a ritual 'cleansing' of the domestic site after it went out of use. If this was a widespread practice in the area, it may explain the dearth of material in the houses on the bypass route. A more mundane possibility is that the scarcity of artefacts reflects a preference for fashioning tools from wood and other organic materials which do not generally survive, in tandem with the careful retention of stone tools, owing to the difficulty of acquiring good-quality raw material such as flint in the south-west of the country.

The scarcity of metal artefacts is perhaps less surprising, as these tend to be rare finds on sites of this period. On the N25 Waterford Bypass, for example, no metal artefacts were found on any of the 52 excavated Bronze Age sites (Eogan 2011, 256), yet we know from stray artefacts such as the bronze axes from Kilmore, Ballyard (Illus. 5.20) and Parkearagh that metal objects were either manufactured in or imported into the area. Indeed, a very high level of skilled craftsmanship is evident in the hoard of Late Bronze Age horns discovered in Clogherclemin in 1875, just 2 km east of the bypass ((Illus. 5.21; Eogan 1983, 91). A similar find was made in 1835 near Killarney (Waddell 2010, 136). Gold-working is also in evidence, with the discovery of gold ornaments in a wooden box in Kilmoyly North in 1940, about 10 km north-west of Tralee (Eogan 1983, 93).

In general, the evidence from the bypass excavations shows that the Bronze Age communities of the Lee Valley were aware of, and had adopted, countrywide trends in pottery, domestic architecture, farming (increasing levels of grain production) and hot-stone technology. It confirms for the first time that classic Early Bronze Age burials in inverted encrusted urns of the Vase Tradition were taking place in the Kerry area. There are also unusually early dates for a cereal-drying kiln and a cattle droveway, which may indicate that these communities were open to innovation.

The identification of settlement and burial sites on the bypass complements the discovery of similar sites during development-led excavations in and around Tralee town. Inevitably, however, the close association between development and archaeological discovery has introduced a bias to the record, resulting in an apparent concentration of activity in the western end of the Lee Valley. That said, as a generally north/south transect across the valley, the bypass has highlighted a marked concentration of settlement and burial sites on the valley floor, with some burnt mounds also occurring on its lower slopes.

6

THE IRON AGE: GRAIN, ORE AND DEATH

James Hession
with a contribution by Carmelita Troy

The Iron Age is still an enigmatic period in Irish archaeology, but 'the invisible people' described by Raftery (1994, 112) are finally starting to reveal themselves. Archaeological discoveries in advance of major infrastructural projects (e.g. roads, gas pipelines, main drainage schemes), coupled with research programmes funded by the Heritage Council (Becker et al. 2008a and 2008b) and the Discovery Programme (Cahill Wilson 2014), have shown that the invisible people were hiding in plain sight after all. The apparent gaps in the archaeological record were due more to the

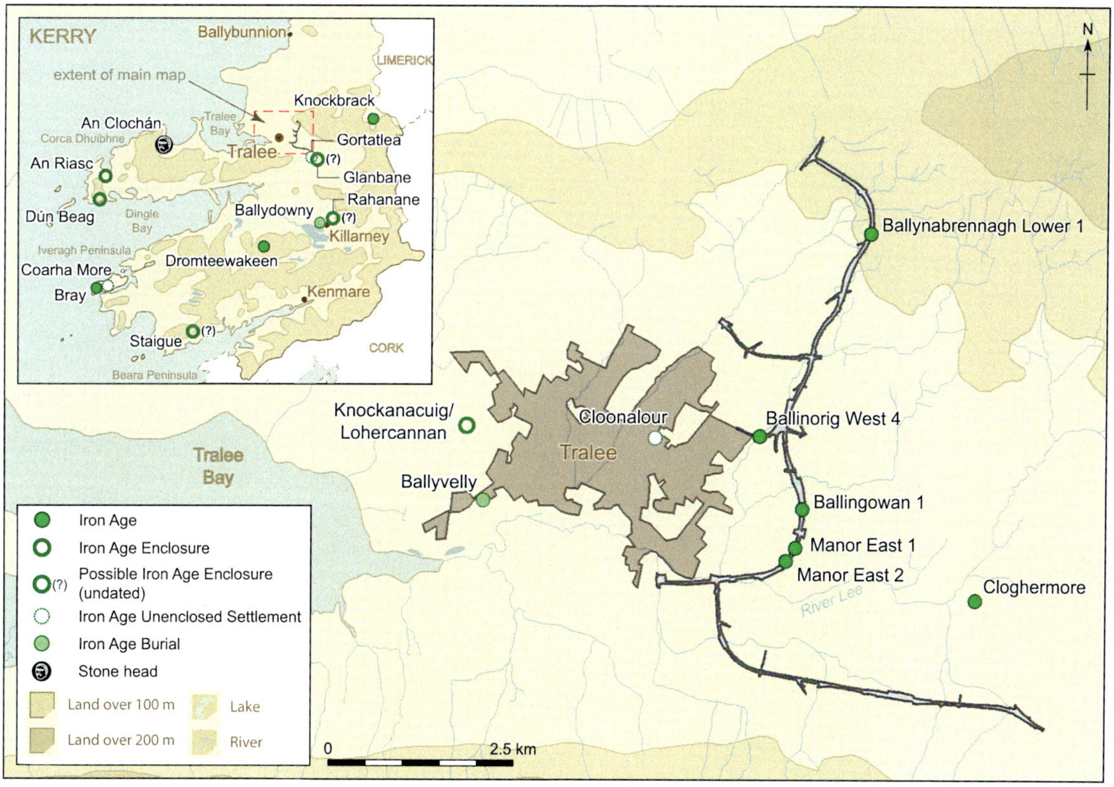

Illus. 6.1—Locations (mentioned in the text) where signs of Iron Age activity have been identified in County Kerry, including sites excavated on the N22 Tralee Bypass.

difficulty of identifying sites of this period rather than to an outright absence of sites. This was compounded by the fact that pottery, a key indicator of domestic activity on prehistoric sites, was no longer being produced on the scale witnessed in earlier periods. Becker (2012, 5) suggests that Iron Age occupation sites have only come to light because of systematic radiocarbon dating on infrastructure projects. This is the case not only for post-hole and pit scatterings but also for large multi-period settlements.

Although the majority of recent excavations of Iron Age sites recorded evidence of occupation (burials, pit clusters and scatterings of pits and post-holes), more substantial evidence of settlement, such as enclosures, farmsteads and houses, is still quite rare. Despite this, the transition from the prehistoric to the historic period is finally beginning to take shape in the archaeological record, often characterised by a continuity in the locations of burial, ritual and settlement sites from the Late Bronze Age through to the early medieval period.

Prior to the excavations on the Tralee Bypass, evidence for the Iron Age in the Lee Valley, and in Kerry in general, was quite sparse (Illus. 6.1). The discovery of Iron Age remains at five sites on the bypass route—Ballynabrennagh Lower 1, Ballinorig West 4, Ballingowan 1, Manor East 1 and Manor East 2—is very significant, therefore, for the study of this period in the region. A Late Bronze Age/Early Iron Age date was also obtained for a burnt mound at Camp 5 (see Chapter 5).

Some of the known coastal/inland promontory forts may date from this period. The only excavated example, at An Dún Beag (KE052-270001) in the townland of Fán on the Dingle Peninsula, returned a date of c. 580 BC from one of its enclosing ditches, though activity here extended into the early medieval period (Barry 1981, 307; Cuppage & Bennett 1986, 94). Closer to Tralee, test excavations at a hillfort in Knockanacuig/Lohercannan (KE029-112) confirmed an Iron Age date (Dunne & Bartlett 2009), while Bennett (1987, 48) has tentatively suggested similar origins for Staigue stone fort on the Iveragh Peninsula. Two other hillforts, at Glanbane and Rahanane (KE039-065 and KE059-091), are potentially Iron Age but are yet to be scientifically dated. It is worth noting here, however, that the hillforts at Rathgall, Co. Wicklow, and Haughey's Fort, Co. Armagh, were originally believed to be Iron Age but upon excavation proved to be earlier in date (Becker 2012, 5). Conversely, some sites for which the evidence is predominantly early medieval have been found to have had Iron Age origins, including the excavated settlement cemetery at An Riasc (Reask) in west Kerry (Fanning 1981).

Excavated examples of unenclosed Iron Age settlement include a cluster of five pits and two stake-holes at Cloonalour (Ó Faoláin 2004) and a polygonal stone hut at Coarha More, Valentia Island (Becker et al. 2008b). There was evidence for Iron Age activity at an enclosure in Gortatlea, where significant Bronze Age and early medieval occupation phases were also recorded (Connolly 2003). Iron Age timber trackways have been found at Bray, on Valentia Island (O'Sullivan & Sheehan 1996), and Dromteewakeen (Becker et al. 2008b).

Evidence for Iron Age funerary activity is particularly rare in the south of the country but was detected at Ballyvelly (approximately 1 km south of the hillfort at Knockanacuig/Lohercannan), where a possible crematorium and associated burials were found to have Late Iron Age phases, though with Late Bronze Age origins (Dunne & Kiely 2005). A Developed Iron Age date was also returned from a cremation pit associated with a ring-ditch at Ballydowny, near Killarney (Kiely 2004). It is probable that some of the funerary monuments in the area, such as barrows and cairns, which have been tentatively assigned to the Bronze Age may in fact date from the Iron Age, though this has yet to be confirmed through excavation.

Iron Age metal-working sites have been found in Kerry. At Cloghermore, c. 6 km east of the bypass, a number of bowl furnaces and pits containing iron-smelting waste were dated to between the second and fifth centuries AD (Coyne 1999a and 1999b; Frank Coyne, pers. comm.). Similar small-scale metal-working, including an iron-smelting furnace, was identified at Knockbrack, c. 12.5 km north-west of Castleisland (Hull et al. 2006), and a bowl furnace and two crucible fragments were identified at Settlement G, An Riasc (Reask), on the Dingle Peninsula (Becker et al. 2008b).

Finally, more enigmatic evidence is represented by the stone head on the 13th-century church at An Clochán (Cloghane), near Brandon Bay, which may be a reused Iron Age sculpture (Bennett 1987, 48; Cuppage & Bennett 1986, 367).

Cereal processing

The majority of excavated Irish cereal-drying kilns date from the Late Iron Age (AD 1–400) and early medieval period (AD 400–1169), when they were a vital component of the agrarian economy (Moriarty 2011; Monk & Power 2014). Although no Iron Age cereal-drying kilns were identified on the bypass, a small amount of hulled barley was recovered from an Early Iron Age pit in Ballinorig West 4, and a series of four-post and six-post structures of contemporary date—interpreted as elevated grain/hay stores—were excavated at Ballingowan 1 (Illus. 6.2). Cereal grain and straw (indeterminate species) were recovered from a post-hole of one of the four-post structures, and a date of 780–417 BC (SUERC-37302) was returned from a charcoal sample (alder) from one of the corner post-holes. The construction of grain stores implies a focus on cultivation that is at odds with the regional shift towards pastoralism suggested by Raftery (1994, 122). The recovery of (probable) cattle bone from one of the grain stores is a reminder, however, that a mixed farming regime would have been normal in the Lee Valley in most periods, including the Iron Age. The remains of the settlements/farmsteads associated with these grain stores are probably nearby, lying undiscovered beyond the road footprint. Similar four-post structures were interpreted as elevated grain stores at Tober, Co. Offaly, although these were Middle to Late Bronze Age in date (Walsh 2009). Other examples at Knockgraffon, Co. Tipperary (McQuade et al. 2009, 77), and Sallymount, Co. Limerick (Clark & Long 2011), were dated to the Late Bronze Age and early medieval period respectively. The current evidence suggests that this method of storing grain was in use for several millennia.

Iron-working

Prior to Carlin's (2008) work on the excavation results from the M4 motorway in counties Meath and Kildare only a handful of publications described the process of early iron-working in Ireland,

Illus. 6.2—Ballingowan 1, Area 1b. Artist's impression of Iron Age elevated grain stores (Jonathan Millar).

with the majority of scholars relying on the pioneering work of O'Kelly (1952; 1961; 1963) and, later, Scott (1990) and Mytum (1992, 229–35). Further development-led excavations have added to the number of known iron-working sites and, consequently, to the number of relevant publications (e.g. Becker et al. 2008a and 2008b; Delaney et al. 2012a; Gillespie & Kerrigan 2012; Kenny 2010; Wallace & Anguilano 2010). The majority of excavated iron-working sites date from the early medieval period, with those of Iron Age date remaining quite rare. Published examples include Developed Iron Age furnaces excavated at Rathwilladoon 5, Co. Galway, and Derrygarriff 2, Co. Clare (Delaney et al. 2012b, 148–51); Tonybaun, Co. Mayo (Nolan 2006, 98–9); Knockcommane, Co. Limerick (McQuade et al. 2009, 151–3); Hardwood 3, Johnstown 3 and Rossan 6, Co. Meath, and Kinnegad 2, Co. Westmeath (Carlin 2008, 104).

Only three iron-working sites of this period had previously been identified in the Kerry region—Cloghermore, Knockbrack and An Riasc (Reask). The evidence from Ballinorig West 4 (charcoal-production pit and hearths) and Ballingowan 1 (rock-cut smelting furnace and associated features) on the present project therefore represents an important contribution to the archaeological record. The dates place this activity in the Developed Iron Age, with further metal-working taking place at Ballinorig West 4 during the early medieval period. This reuse of the same location some 600 years later suggests that it remained as attractive to early medieval metal-workers as it had been to their Iron Age predecessors, most likely because the necessary raw materials were available locally. While the charcoal assemblage confirms that oak, which was the preferred wood for charcoal production, was growing here in both periods, no local source of iron ore has been identified. Taken with the evidence for cereal cultivation, the occurrence of metal-working strongly suggests the existence of associated Iron Age and early medieval settlements in the wider area.

The iron-working process

Until the late 16th century, iron was produced in smelting furnaces using the bloomery process. This involved first crushing the ore to increase its exposed surface area and then roasting it in an oxygen-rich atmosphere. As well as drying the ore, roasting also removed some highly reactive impurities such as sulphur (Cosham 2012, 1). The ore was then added to the furnace along with charcoal, while a continuous 'forced draught' was provided by one or more sets of bellows. The result was a reducing atmosphere which changed the iron compounds in the ore to iron metal (ibid.). The furnace temperatures (1,100–1,200°C) were not hot enough to melt the iron itself (approximately 1,500°C) but were sufficient to cause the impurities to liquefy and separate from the iron in the form of slag (a waste product that formed on the base of the furnace), leaving a spongiform lump of iron and slag called 'the bloom' within the furnace (Scott 1990, 155–6).

The bloom underwent further refinement by heating and hammering (primary smithing) to expel the remaining slag impurities and form a 'billet' of iron. Secondary smithing was then required to transform the billet into a usable bar of iron (Henderson 2000; McDonnell 2001). Analysis of iron objects can identify minute pieces of slag that remained in the billet after smithing, and from these we can determine whether an object was produced using the bloomery process, as well as indicating the source of the ore (Carlin 2008, 89).

There were two main furnace types: the bowl furnace and the shaft furnace. Shaft furnaces can be further divided into two subtypes: slag-tapping and non-slag-tapping (also known as a slag-pit furnace). There is much debate as to the form of each furnace type because they generally survive as shallow, heat-scorched, bowl-shaped depressions containing slag, charcoal and vitrified clay fragments and as such can be difficult to differentiate from one another. Bowl furnaces are thought to have consisted of simple, open-air pits with provision made for the attachment of a bellows (Raftery 1994; Pleiner 2000), but experimental archaeology using open bowl furnaces showed them to be inefficient at best, if not completely flawed (Tylecote 1986, cited in Carlin 2008, 91–2), suggesting that they must have had a superstructure or shaft component in order to produce the reducing conditions necessary for smelting. This could mean that the 'bowl furnace' of our archaeological typology is merely the base of a larger shaft furnace, with the superstructure having been truncated or removed in antiquity (Mytum 1992; Crew & Rehren 2002).

Shaft furnaces, as the name suggests, had a cylindrical, chimney-like clay superstructure, needed for producing better reducing conditions (Carlin 2008, 92). The excavated evidence

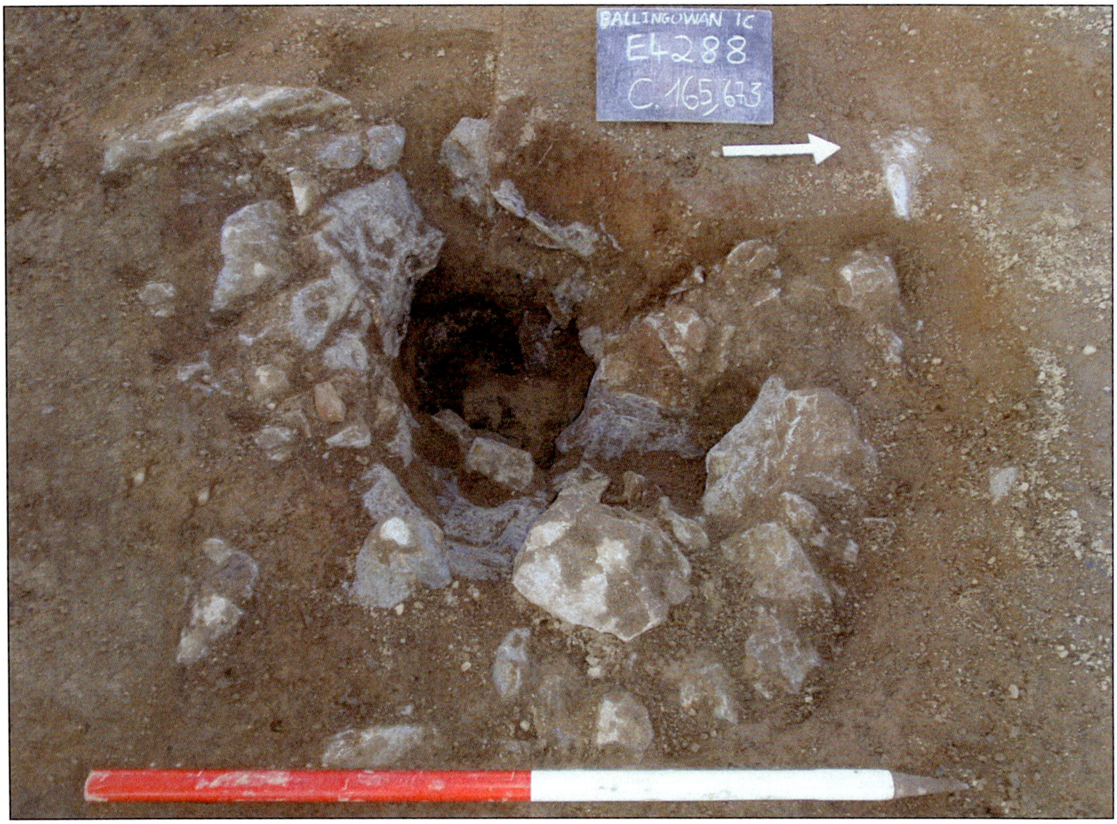

Illus. 6.3—Ballingowan 1, Area 1c. Developed Iron Age rock-cut iron-smelting furnace (673), view to west (Rubicon Heritage Services Ltd).

suggests that both subtypes (slag-tapping and non-slag-tapping or slag-pit furnaces) essentially worked in the same way, the only difference being that slag-tapping shaft furnaces were not always dug into the ground. Slag-tapping simply refers to the provision for removing (tapping) slag during the operation of the furnace. Tapping slag is beneficial because it allows the furnace to continue operating for longer periods of time without clogging up, thus potentially forming bigger blooms. Slag-tapping furnaces are common finds in Britain and appear to have been the dominant type from the Iron Age to the mid-18th century (Cosham 2012, 3). Conversely, no Iron Age slag-tapping furnaces have been definitively recorded in Ireland, with all known examples dating from the medieval period, such as Farranastack, Co. Kerry (Dowd & Fairburn 2005), Ballydowny, Co. Kerry (Fairburn 2003a), Shandon, Co. Waterford (Fairburn 2003b), and Ballinorig West 2 on the present project (Chapter 7).

Non-slag-tapping furnaces, as the name implies, do not have provision for slag removal. Theoretically, this would make them less efficient than their tapping counterparts, although digging a pit below the furnace would have had the same effect as tapping, as the slag would have drained into it. Such furnaces are commonly referred to as slag-pit furnaces but are essentially a version of the shaft furnace (Cosham 2012, 3). Slag-pit furnaces dating from the Iron Age are commonly found in Eastern Europe (Pleiner 2000), with only a few examples from Britain.

The rock-cut smelting furnace identified at Ballingowan 1 is the first Iron Age slag-pit furnace to have been discovered in the county (Illus. 6.3). It was dated to 382–186 BC (SUERC-37313) using oak charcoal from one of its basal fills, while smithing slag in its upper fills suggests that it may have been reused as a smithing hearth. What little settlement evidence was uncovered most likely represents temporary shelters to accommodate the iron-workers and/or windbreaks. This fits with the common perception that iron-working was carried out close to the source of the raw materials, away from settlements, in areas close to bogs, lakes and rock outcrops for the sources of ore, and in the vicinity of oak woodlands for the production of charcoal. It is possible, therefore, that a more substantial Iron Age settlement is lying undiscovered beyond the road footprint.

Charcoal production

Charcoal was integral to the metallurgical process, with large quantities being required for both the smelting and smithing stages. It was produced by slowly roasting the wood and carefully controlling the oxygen content during burning. It is not surprising, therefore, that charcoal-production pits are commonly found in association with iron-smelting and iron-smithing sites (Henderson 2000, 211; Carlin 2008; Delaney et al. 2012b); indeed, the presence of a charcoal-production pit alone can hint at nearby metal-working. The quantities of charcoal involved and the difficulties of transporting it meant that both charcoal production and iron-working were usually undertaken close to woodlands. Oak was particularly sought after because it burns at high temperatures for longer periods compared to other wood species. Locating these industries at a remove from settlements minimised the fire risk to dwellings and farm buildings, and distanced them from unpleasant smells and smoke (Delaney et al. 2012b). The two charcoal-production pits identified at Ballinorig West 4 were subcircular, with evidence of *in situ* burning on the base and sides. Only one of these was dated, indicating that it was in use during the Developed Iron Age (397–207 BC; SUERC-37251). Both contained large amounts of charcoal and the dated example also contained tiny fragments of a smithing-hearth bottom (slag that accumulates near the hearth blow-hole during the smithing process), undiagnostic slag and fragments of slagged ceramic (slag that settles on the clay walls of the hearth, causing them to melt). This represents waste material dumped into the charcoal-production pit, with the charcoal itself most likely having been used for smelting and smithing. The undated charcoal-production pit was truncated by a later hearth or waste pit (Illus. 6.4). No *in situ* smithing hearths were identified, but a possible metal-working hearth dated to 202–2 BC (SUERC-37243) was recorded in the north-west part of the excavated area, in addition to a cluster of undated hearths, pits, post-holes and stake-holes, which may also relate to this activity. Tapped slag was recovered from the upper fill of this hearth, which suggests that the smithing process must have occurred somewhere beyond the road footprint.

Illus. 6.4—Ballinorig West 4. Developed Iron Age charcoal-production pit (left) cut by later hearth/waste pit (right), view to north-east (Rubicon Heritage Services Ltd).

Identifying Iron Age settlement

Evidence for Early, Developed and Late Iron Age settlement was uncovered at Ballynabrennagh Lower 1, Ballingowan 1 and Manor East 1 and 2 (Table 6.1). All of this activity was unenclosed and consisted of groups of pits and/or post-holes and stake-holes with no discernible houses and no artefacts. This corresponds with recent research on the Irish Iron Age, which identifies this kind of patchy, patternless evidence as characteristic of the period (Becker 2009, 354). This type of

Table 6.1—Summary of Iron Age occupation evidence.

Site	Description	Radiocarbon date
Ballynabrennagh Lower 1	Three pits and two clusters of four stake-holes.	355–53 BC (SUERC-37258), 350–45 BC (SUERC-37254)
Ballingowan 1	Pit, post-hole and stake-hole cluster south-west of grain/hay stores.	790–421 BC (SUERC-37310)
	Two dense clusters of pits, stake-holes and post-holes.	166 BC–AD 50 (SUERC-37309), AD 65–232 (SUERC-37301)
Manor East 1	Two pits and eight stake-holes.	370–115 BC (SUERC-37320), 44 BC–AD 122 (SUERC-37329)
Manor East 2	Cluster of four post-holes, four pits and eight stake-holes.	355–53 BC (SUERC-37299)

occupation evidence is also typical of the Late Bronze Age and it is only in recent years, through systematic programmes of radiocarbon dating, that it has begun to be recognised as such. The scarcity of identifiable houses in the Iron Age may represent a society that was relatively mobile and a shift towards a pastoral economy linked to an improving climate (ibid., 356), though evidence of grain storage suggests that tillage formed part of the Iron Age agricultural economy in the Tralee area.

Monuments to the dead

Funerary ritual is less well defined in the Iron Age than in other periods of Irish prehistory, but recent excavations have greatly increased the number of known sites. While burial in the Iron Age could take various forms, including flat cemeteries, isolated pits, mounds and cairns, the emerging picture is one of continuity in burial traditions from the Middle to Late Bronze Age into the Iron Age, most notably in the persistence of cremation as the main burial rite, the practice of token burial and the continued use of barrows and ring-ditches (Cooney & Grogan 1999, 199; McGarry 2009, 413, 415, 421).

The clearest changes, on the other hand, were the near-complete absence of pottery in Iron Age burials, suggesting that it was no longer being produced, and the amount of bone recovered from cremation burials. The quantity of bone found in Iron Age cremation burials, including token burials, is very variable but is generally less than in the Middle to Late Bronze Age; rarely, if ever, is all the bone included (Troy 2015).

A ring-ditch typically comprised a circular ditch, enclosing an average area of 8 m in diameter, with an east-facing entrance (Eogan 2007). The earliest known ring-ditches were constructed in the Neolithic, and although they were most common during the Bronze Age they continued to be built and reused throughout the Iron Age, and even into the early years of the early medieval period. They were often used repeatedly, over a long period of time, with the burials themselves found not only in the centre of the monument but also within the ditch and in nearby external pits, leading some commentators to suggest that ring-ditches were family or tribal burial places (Raftery 2005, 172).

A burial place of this type was recorded at Ballinorig West 4, in the form of a penannular ring-ditch with an internal diameter of 4.25 m and a causewayed entrance on its eastern side (Illus. 6.5). Evidence for an external bank, consisting of an intermittent layer of redeposited soil, was identified along the base and outer edge of the ditch. A stone deposit in the lower and middle ditch fills is interpreted as slippage of a cairn/mound that originally covered the interior. The use of this monument spanned the Developed Iron Age and the early Late Iron Age period (355–46 BC), with 10 cremation burial deposits recovered from the fills of the ring-ditch, five cremation burials located within the interior, and three pit burials and one deposit/spread identified in the surrounding area. The total weight of cremated bone was 3,454.7 g, which ranged from token deposits of 1.1 g to more substantial deposits of 1,287.7 g (Illus. 6.6).

Analysis of the five radiocarbon dates obtained from the cremation deposits not only suggests that a number of individuals were interred around the same time but also indicates that there were

Illus. 6.5—Ballinorig West 4. Excavation in progress around the Developed Iron Age ring-ditch and associated cremation burials, with the ditch fills still *in situ*, view to north-west (Rubicon Heritage Services Ltd).

two clear phases of burial activity at this monument. The first phase spans the Developed Iron Age and early Late Iron Age period (mid-fourth to mid-first centuries BC) with the second phase occurring slightly later, in the latter half of the Developed Iron Age and early part of the Late Iron Age period (late second to mid-first centuries BC). The central cremation pit (355–57 BC; SUERC-37096) is contemporary with a satellite cremation pit (353–56 BC; SUERC-37092), and at a slightly later date a burial deposit (336–47 BC; SUERC-37090) was interred within the ring-ditch itself. This burial was dug into material that had accumulated within the ditch, which suggests that the monument had changed in appearance over the intervening period but was still held to be significant and was being reused. This pattern of interment seems to be repeated at a later period, when one burial (198–46 BC; SUERC-37089) was inserted into the upper fills of the ditch, while a satellite burial (191–47 BC; SUERC-37091) was also interred at this time. The repeated reuse of this monument over a period of c. 300 years certainly supports Raftery's (2005) proposal that ring-ditches were family or tribal burial places used by communities to bury their dead near tribal ancestors or revered leaders already interred there. The later remains were perhaps buried by people with a folk memory of the significance of the monument and who chose to bury their own relatives in the same space, although they had no direct connection with those who created it.

Illus. 6.6—Ballinorig West 4. Pre-excavation view of two cremation burials within the interior of the ring-ditch, view to north-west (Rubicon Heritage Services Ltd).

We know from other excavated cemeteries that only a small proportion of the population received the type of formal burial that would leave such a recognisable archaeological trace (Cooney & Grogan 1999, 132). It seems likely, given the small number of interments, that only selected members of the community were honoured at Ballinorig West. These, however, were not necessarily the burials of high-status or wealthy individuals. They may instead have been respected persons selected to interact with the ancestors on behalf of the community and over time became revered themselves by future generations (Thomas 1999, 162).

What the bones tell us

Carmelita Troy

Analysis of the cremated material indicates that the pyre technology at Ballinorig West 4 was well developed, as 97% of the bone from the assemblage was completely oxidised. Oxidation is the complete burning of the organic element of the bone and only takes place at temperatures above 800°C over a sustained period. The high temperatures caused the Ballinorig West bones to crack, twist and warp, resulting in splitting and fragmentation. Characteristic dehydration patterns such as horizontal, longitudinal and U-shaped fissuring were also present on the bone, which indicates that there was still flesh, and particularly fat, attached to the bone when the bodies were being cremated, as this sort of fissuring does not occur when burning defleshed or excarnated bones.

In total, 83.4% of the recovered bone fragments were under 10 mm in size. The highly fragmented nature of the remains, as well as the token nature of some of the burials, meant that it was possible to identify just 9.7% of the assemblage to specific skeletal elements. In all but one case (Burial 626, an adult male) it was not possible to determine the age and sex of those interred. The most identifiable elements were skull fragments, which represent 97% of the identifiable bone. This may be because the skull is one of the most recognisable body parts, though it is also possible that it was ascribed a special significance and that skull fragments were therefore specifically selected for inclusion in the burials.

Going by McKinley's (1997) criteria, only two of the Ballinorig West burials were deemed to be whole cremation burials. The largest of these (Burial 626) was interred in the upper fill of the ditch; it contained 1,287.7 g of bone and represented the remains of a probable male adult. The other whole burial was found in the upper fill of a cremation pit in the ring-ditch interior and contained 361.7 g of cremated bone. The lower fill of the same pit contained a further discrete deposit of bone, but owing to the fragmentary nature of the remains it could not be established whether this represented a second individual. The remaining 17 cremated bone deposits were token cremations, of which nine weighed less than 100 g. Token deposits are thought to have served as a representation of the whole individual (Cooney & Grogan 1999, 136).

The presence of 10 cremation deposits within the ditch fills leaves little doubt that these were deposited as deliberate ritual acts, albeit at different times. McGarry's (2009, 418) synthesis of Late Bronze Age and Iron Age ring-ditches noted that almost as many sites had cremation burials in the ditch fills as in central contexts. The ditch, bank and mound/cairn would have clearly signalled the special nature of the site. Indeed, the scarcity of non-funerary features and the lack of disturbance to existing burials within ring-ditches suggests that they were normally well respected, or perhaps even feared (ibid., 420).

Grave-goods

Six cobalt-blue glass beads (2–2.5 mm in diameter) were recovered from one of the internal burial pits (Illus. 2.18). The beads were likely once worn in a necklace, bracelet or perhaps around the ankles (Raftery 2005, 150). They were pock-marked or otherwise heat-affected, with some accretions, indicating that the deceased was wearing them when cremated (Cropper 2012). This type of tiny bead is among the most common of Iron Age types and is found in cremation burials such as those at Knockcommane, Co. Limerick (McQuade et al. 2009), Marlhill and Knockgraffon, Co. Tipperary (ibid.), and Ballyboy 1 and 2, Co. Galway (Delaney et al. 2012c). Tiny blue beads were also recovered from around the wrists of a female inhumation burial (No. 13) at Knowth, Co. Meath (Eogan 1974, 81–2). A larger blue glass bead was found in topsoil at Lismore 1 on the present project, but it remains undated (Illus. 6.7).

Illus. 6.7—Lismore 1. Translucent, annular, blue glass bead found in topsoil. Beads like this are often found on Irish Iron Age and early medieval sites. It may have been strung with other glass beads to form a necklace or could have been sewn onto clothing (Rubicon Heritage Services).

Regional tradition

Cremation burials of similar date to those at Ballinorig West in the south-west of the country include Ballyvelly (Dunne 1999) and Ballydowny (Kiely & O'Callaghan 2010), Co. Kerry, and Bruff (O'Connell 2010), Knockcommane (McQuade et al. 2009) and Ballybronoge South (Eogan 2012), Co. Limerick. The Ballinorig West ring-ditch, at 6.34 m in external diameter (max.), falls within the same range as those recorded at Ballydowny, Knockcommane and Ballybronoge South, which were all 5.55 m to 7 m in diameter. Like Ballinorig West 4, these other ring-ditches also contained cremated bone deposits within the ditches themselves, though Ballinorig West 4, with 10 deposits in the ditch, appears at the higher end of the scale in terms of the number of deposits, being second only to the Ballybronoge South ditch, with 14 deposits. By comparison, the ditches at Bruff, Knockcommane and Ballydowny only contained four, three and one deposit respectively. Cremation burials within the ring-ditch interior were also identified at Bruff and Knockcommane.

Overall, the Iron Age funerary ring-ditches of the south-west seem to be typical of the period, with no distinctive regional trends or variations. In terms of size, they are in line with McGarry's (2009, 415) observation that 'a considerable number measured less than 7 m', though with an average of 11 m. They also correspond in general with his other characteristics of such monuments: the entrances most likely at the east; little evidence for substantial, related structures of any kind; more likely to be associated with cremated burials than with inhumations; cremated individuals almost always placed within the footprint of the monument and never only externally; and generally small cemetery populations, probably representing a local group rather than a substantial community or large territory.

Conclusion

The five Iron Age sites identified along the route of the bypass are significant, as they add to the growing corpus of known Iron Age sites in the region and confirm that Iron Age activity in this part of Kerry was at a level comparable with the rest of the country.

The sites identified ranged from unenclosed settlement, comprising pits and associated post-hole and stake-hole clusters, to evidence for cereal processing/storage, iron-working and burial. The location of the identified sites is also interesting. Although they were all found north of the River Lee, they were located across a varied landscape, situated not only on the valley floor (Manor East 1 and 2) but also on the lower hillslopes at the northern valley edge (Ballynabrennagh Lower 1). As such, they indicate that there was a substantial Iron Age population living, working and burying their dead throughout this part of County Kerry.

The location of the excavated sites also reflects national trends. They were all located in areas with evidence for multi-period occupation, dating from the Bronze Age to the early medieval period. Unfortunately, the results mirror findings from elsewhere in the country in that we have significant evidence for a settled population but did not discover the houses, farmsteads, larger settlements and enclosures where people were actually living. Perhaps, in some way, Raftery's (1994) 'invisible people' have not yet fully revealed themselves but are still waiting to be discovered beyond the footprint of the bypass.

7

THE LEE VALLEY IN EARLY MEDIEVAL TIMES

James Hession

Ireland has one of the best-preserved early medieval settlement landscapes in Europe, with approximately 50,000 raths (ringforts), cashels, crannogs and other settlement enclosures dotted across the country. The landscape was rural, with numerous scattered farmsteads, and no villages or towns. Irish society was roughly divided into three main classes—the semi-free, the free and the noble, with landownership the determining factor of wealth and status. Initially landownership passed along male kinship lines of those who shared a common great-grandfather, and later in the period of those who shared a common grandfather. Members of a kin-group jointly controlled the land and were responsible for the behaviour of those within their group. The slow rise of Christianity in the fifth century and the first half of the sixth century was accelerated by the rapid spread of monasticism from the later sixth century. By the later eighth century some of the larger ecclesiastical foundations supported diverse populations of clergy, craftsmen, labourers and their families. A few had become proto-urban centres, with streets lined by houses and workshops, as well as the several churches that were typical of the largest sites (Edwards 1990; O'Sullivan et al. 2014; Bolger 2014).

There is ample evidence for early medieval settlement in the mid-Kerry area in this period, with numerous settlement enclosures and ecclesiastical sites. It is perhaps surprising, then, that only 10 sites dating from between the fifth and seventh centuries AD were discovered along the bypass (Illus. 7.1). A previously unknown bivallate enclosure was identified at Ballinorig West 2, although the evidence for occupation here was very limited. The only possible early medieval buildings recorded by our excavations were subcircular structures at Knockawaddra Middle 2 and Ballingowan 1. There were cereal-drying kilns at Ballinorig West 3 (Illus. 7.2) and Ballinorig West 4 (two kilns) (Illus. 7.3), and another possible kiln at Ballingowan 1c. Metal-working was identified in the same area as the cereal kilns at Ballinorig West 4, in what appeared to be a designated industrial area, and iron slag fragments were recovered from a sink-hole in Knockawaddra West 2. This site also produced a high-quality early medieval glass bead (Illus. 7.4). There was a charcoal-production pit at Gortbrack East 1 and a hearth at Dromthacker 2. At Manor East 1, one of a small cluster of pits yielded a fragment of an early medieval bone needle or weaving tool. Further west, at Manor East 7, stone, timber and cobble deposits formed crossing points over a former stream channel.

The only evidence on the bypass route for later medieval activity was found at Manor East 4, where two cut and trimmed alder branches and stakes from a peat-filled channel were dated to AD 1403–1441 (UBA-17592) and AD 1413–1469 (UBA-18518) (Delaney 2012, 2).

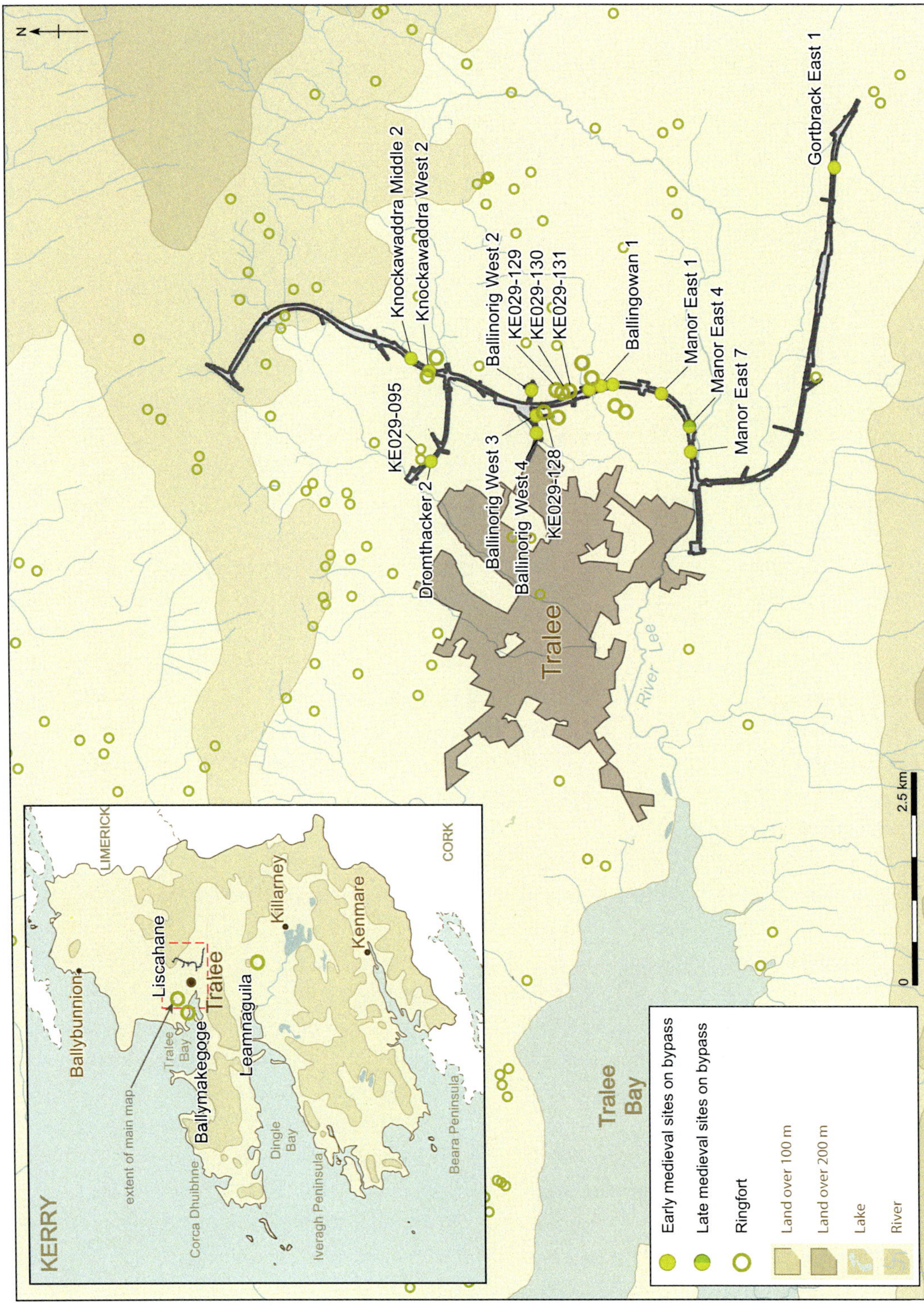

Illus. 7.1—Early medieval settlement in the Lee Valley, including those sites found on the N22 Tralee Bypass (non-bypass sites are based on RMP classification as 'Ringfort' and do not include undated enclosures).

Illus. 7.2—Ballinorig West 3. Excavation in progress of an unlined cereal-drying kiln with a high degree of *in situ* burning along the base, view to west (Rubicon Heritage Services Ltd).

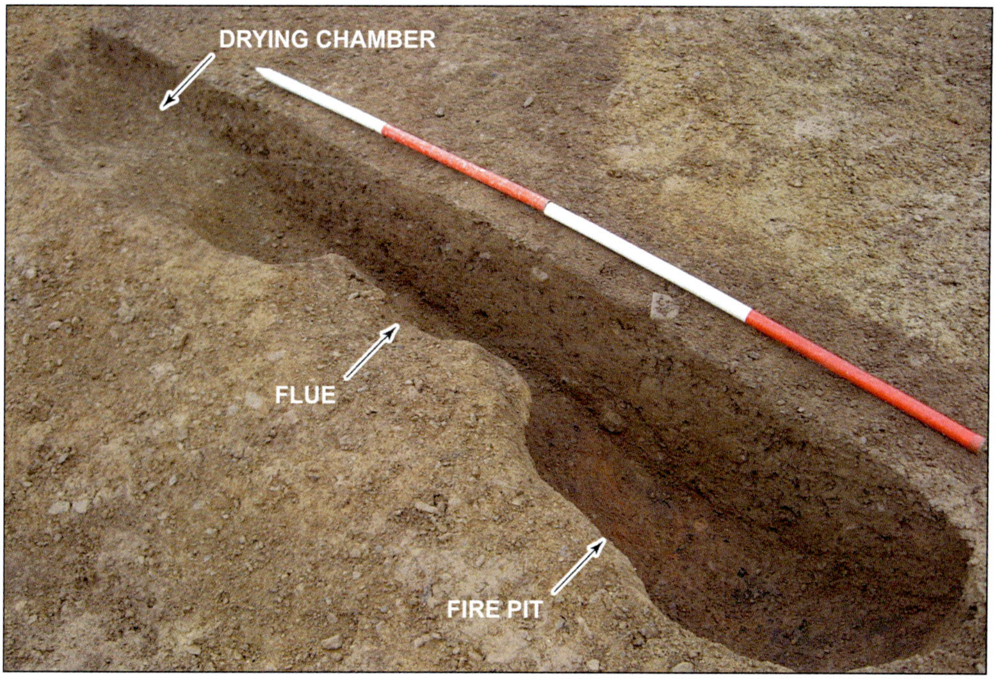

Illus. 7.3—Ballinorig West 4. Excavation in progress of a cereal-drying kiln (654) with the main elements indicated, view to west (Rubicon Heritage Services Ltd).

Illus. 7.4 (left)—Knockawaddra West 2. Translucent glass bead (Hannah Sims).

Illus. 7.5 (below)—Ballingowan 1, Area 1a. Post-excavation view of possible early medieval house, view to west (Aerialphoto.ie).

Unenclosed settlement

Two unenclosed possible domestic buildings were discovered along the route of the bypass. At Ballingowan 1a an oval building was identified, measuring 7.7 m long by 5.2 m wide, with an internal area of c. 32 m^2 (Illus. 7.5). It comprised six pits/post-holes and an internal pit/post-hole. Willow charcoal from one of the pits was radiocarbon-dated to AD 903–1154 (SUERC-37308). Other than a single pit/post-hole, there were no internal features and no artefacts were recovered from this building, casting some doubt on its interpretation as a domestic building. Elsewhere, at Ballingowan 1c, a dense cluster of post-holes and stake-holes, a number of scattered pits, two hearths and other undated features were identified at the north end of the site. No clear patterns or functions could be defined for these features, but an early medieval spindle-whorl was recovered from the topsoil in this area and a charred oat grain from one of the pits was dated to AD 419–574 (SUERC-37319).

At Knockawaddra Middle 2 a suboval building (Structure 2) measured 4.8 m long by 4 m wide, with an internal area of 15 m^2 (Illus. 7.6). The evidence consisted of eight post-holes and an

Illus. 7.6—Artist's impression of an early medieval house at Knockawaddra Middle 2 (Jonathan Millar).

external slot-trench or drip-gully on the south-east side. A sample of hazel charcoal from one of the post-holes was dated to AD 441–646 (SUERC-37289).

The shape and dimensions of these buildings, and the fact that they were most likely of post-and-wattle construction, meant that they are comparable to numerous domestic buildings identified within enclosed settlements elsewhere in Ireland. The early Irish law tract *Críth Gablach* prescribes that the house of the lowest grade of free farmer (the *ócaire*) was between 6 m and 8 m in diameter, and that there was a direct correlation between house size and social ranking (Binchy 1941, 4 and 103; Kelly 1997, 362). However, the data coming from archaeological excavations show that most houses were 5–6 m in diameter (O'Sullivan et al. 2014, 90). The buildings recorded at Ballingowan 1a and Knockawaddra Middle 2 lie close to this range. The legal texts also indicate that the houses within enclosed homesteads represented dwelling places of the free classes—*bóaire*, *ócaire* and *fer midboth*—whilst the unfree and semi-free classes of *bothach*, *fuidir* and *sen-chleithe* (hereditary serfs) lived outside the homesteads (O'Sullivan 2011, 26), presumably in unenclosed houses of the sort described here.

O'Sullivan & Nicholl (2010, 73) suggest that the construction, occupation and abandonment of most early medieval houses took place over the course of a single generation and, therefore, they should occur frequently in the archaeological record. However, there is comparatively little evidence for isolated, unenclosed, early medieval buildings in the Irish archaeological record. This is something of a mystery as it is likely that both house types (enclosed and unenclosed) were constructed in a similar manner and from comparable materials. As such, there is no readily identifiable explanation as to why more of them are not identified, as they should leave the same imprint in the archaeological record.

Examining the wider area, we can see that there are two ringforts and eight other enclosures of possible early medieval date within c. 1 km of the possible domestic buildings at Knockawaddra Middle 2, and seven ringforts and 10 enclosures within c. 1 km of the building at Ballingowan 1a (Illus. 7.1). Although the enclosures are undated and only a portion may be early medieval, this nevertheless suggests that the excavated buildings were part of an extensively settled landscape and supports the evidence of the law tracts regarding different classes of society living in proximity to one another in a complex social mosaic.

Further evidence for unenclosed, seemingly isolated activity of fifth- to seventh-century date was uncovered at three other sites along the bypass. This consisted of a hearth at Dromthacker 2 (AD 436–643; SUERC-37278) and a small cluster of pits at Manor East 1 (AD 441–646; SUERC-37324), as well as one stone and two timber-and-cobble deposits that formed crossing points over a former stream channel at Manor East 7 (AD 428–571; UBA-17593). The pits at Manor East 1 contained charred cereal grain and burnt animal bone, as well as a poorly preserved fragment of a bone needle or weaving tool.

Crop processing

Cereal production played an essential role in the early medieval Irish economy. According to eighth-century law texts such as the *Bretha Déin Chécht* (cited in Kelly 1997, 219), bread wheat was considered the most valued cultivar, followed by rye, while emmer wheat, barley and oats were more often associated with the small to medium-sized grades of farmer.

Cereal-drying kilns dating from between the fifth and ninth centuries were excavated at Ballinorig West 3 (one suboval kiln) and Ballinorig West 4 (two keyhole-shaped kilns). A further, undated, figure-of-eight-shaped kiln identified at Ballingowan 1c is also thought to be early medieval, though it was not scientifically dated.

Kilns are classified according to their shape in plan, with figure-of-eight, dumb-bell and keyhole-shaped kilns being some of the most common. At their simplest, they consisted of an earth-cut fire-pit connected via a linear flue to a roofed or covered drying chamber. The grain was placed in the drying chamber, probably spread out on wicker matting known as a *cliath* (hurdle), and was dried by hot air channelled from the fire-pit via the flue (Monk & Kelleher 2005, 93; Gibson 1989) (Illus. 7.7). The covering or roof of the drying chamber rarely leaves any archaeological traces, and such was the case with the kilns excavated on the bypass.

The main cereal recovered from the Ballinorig West kilns was hulled barley. This corresponds with the findings from excavated kilns across the island, which consistently show that hulled barley

Illus. 7.7—Artist's impression of an early medieval cereal-drying kiln, cut away to show the internal details of the drying chamber (Jonathan Millar).

and oats were the main crops being grown at this time (Timpany et al. 2011; O'Sullivan et al. 2014). Cereal-drying kilns are listed among the possessions of the *bóaire* in the eighth-century law tract *Críth Gablach*, but a share of the kiln would also have been afforded to those of lower social status to enable them to dry their own grain (cited in Kelly 1997, 241). The economic value of cereal grain meant that drying kilns were an essential part of Irish agriculture, fulfilling two basic purposes: to dry and harden the grain prior to grinding and to kill off the shoots of germinating grains in the malting process (Johnston 2003, 3; Monk 1981, 217–18). Most importantly, this process helped to prevent the grain from becoming rancid once stored, which it was prone to do once the chaff was removed (Monk & Power 2012).

The law tracts also indicate that, because of the fire risk they posed to thatched wooden buildings, kilns were not built within the main settlement area but within the *airlise* of the settlement—an area in its immediate environs used for grazing and cultivation (Kelly 1997, 368–9). The absence of any domestic evidence at Ballinorig West 3 and Ballinorig West 4 suggests that the most likely candidate for the associated settlement was a nearby ringfort (KE029-128), situated c. 145 m and 220 m respectively from the kilns (Illus. 7.1).

The time required for the drying process depended on such factors as the weather conditions, the intended use of the grain, the temperature of the kiln, the strength of the draught and how well it was controlled, the quantity and moisture content of the grain and the depth to which it was spread on the drying floor. Drying a 'loaded' kiln could have taken from six to 24 hours (Fenton 1978; Knox 1907, 270). Once dried, the grain could probably have been stored for about 4–5 months when kept at approximately 10°C, and the law tracts indicate that it was stored in wicker baskets. One such wicker basket was identified during an excavation at Drumadoon, Co. Antrim, while other excavations have identified four- and nine-post structures that have been interpreted as elevated grain stores (McSparron & Williams 2009, 122–3; O'Sullivan et al. 2014, 199). Similar structures were uncovered on the bypass at Ballingowan 1, though these were of Iron Age date.

Craftwork

The recovery of iron slag from numerous sites excavated across the country indicates that small-scale iron-working was a common aspect of early medieval life. High-quality products like swords may have been made by specialist smiths, but it seems that ordinary farmers had enough knowledge and skill to forge simple tools (O'Sullivan & Nicholl 2010, 83). An excavation at Dromthacker ringfort (Cleary et al. 2008), for instance, recovered 24 kg of iron slag from a pit within the ringfort, indicating that small-scale iron-working was being undertaken, most likely to meet the domestic needs of the occupants.

At Knockawaddra West 2, deposits within a sink-hole included iron slag fragments and a translucent, amber-coloured glass bead. The recovered slag—a by-product of iron-smelting—was most likely produced in a furnace located just outside the road footprint but was disposed of in the sink-hole.

The bead is of annular shape and is decorated with six regularly spaced opaque dots along its circumference. Mannion (2012, 1) points out that, while the Knockawaddra West bead has no exact parallels, it compares favourably in colour, form and size with beads from Lagore, Co. Meath (Hencken 1950), and from the ringforts of Garranes (Ó Ríordáin 1942) and Garryduff (O'Kelly 1963), Co. Cork. A dark, spiralling line is visible within the interior of the beads from both Knockawaddra West and Garryduff. Beads of comparable colour and form decorated with trailing bands of opaque white glass are also known from the Knowles collection (1908), and there are many more examples among the unprovenanced beads in the National Museum of Ireland, with one (No. 63:1920) comparing favourably to the Knockawaddra West bead (Mannion 2012, 1).

More direct evidence of small-scale iron-working was identified at Ballinorig West 4, in the form of a slag-tapping shaft furnace and several waste pits and hearths containing iron-working debris (Illus. 7.8; see also Illus. 2.20). The metal-working process (described in Chapter 6) changed very little from the Iron Age to the early medieval period, so that there are no diagnostic differences between late prehistoric and medieval furnaces. In fact, it is common to find evidence of both Iron Age and early medieval iron-working on the same site, conveniently located near the available raw materials. This was evident at Ballinorig West 4 and also at sites such as Johnstown 1

Illus. 7.8—Ballinorig West 4. Artist's impression of the slag-tapping shaft furnace in operation (Jonathan Millar).

and Hardwood 3, Co. Meath (Carlin 2008), where the iron-working remains of each period could only be distinguished through radiocarbon dating.

The slag-tapping shaft furnace at Ballinorig West 4 was dated to the beginning of the early medieval period, AD 396–547 (SUERC-37249). Unusually, enough of the clay superstructure of the furnace survived for some accurate measurements to be taken: the internal diameter was between 0.3 m and 0.4 m and the minimum wall thickness was 0.12 m. Evidence of slag-tapping shaft furnaces is very rare in Ireland. Carlin (2008, 93) has suggested that they were used where smelting relied on solid rock ores, with non-slag-tapping furnaces/slag-pit furnaces associated with bog ores. Ballinorig West 4 was located near a limestone ridge that could have been the source of rock ore, though no obvious seam of iron ore was observed during our fieldwork for the present project.

Indirect evidence of possible metal-working was recorded at Gortbrack East 1, where a charcoal-production pit dated to AD 441–646 (SUERC-37282) was excavated. An undated charcoal-production pit at Manor East 1 is also likely to be early medieval in date. The production of charcoal did not involve any specialist tools and so could have been carried out by local farmers with access to woodland and knowledge of the process (Kenny 2010, 113). While charcoal could have been used as a domestic fuel, the effort that went into its production points to a specific need, most likely metal-working and/or other high-temperature crafts like glass- or enamel-making. The *Críth Gablach* lists 'a sack of charcoal for the irons' among the household possessions of the *mruigfer* (strong farmer), suggesting that farmsteads of the period kept a ready supply of charcoal for metal-working (ibid., 114).

Ballinorig West 2: defended farmstead?

A previously unknown bivallate enclosure (i.e. having two concentric enclosing banks and ditches) was identified at Ballinorig West 2 (Illus. 7.9). Enclosed settlements were the main foci of early medieval Irish society and were mostly built and occupied from c. AD 600 to 850 (Kerr 2007, 98–9). Their earthen banks and ditches (ringforts or raths) or drystone walls (cashels or cahers) encompassed the living spaces and stockyards of extended farming families, complete with houses, barns, storage and work areas.

The settlement at Ballinorig West 2 was situated on a small rise in relatively flat terrain (approximately 28–32 m OD) which afforded good views of the surrounding landscape, particularly towards the Slieve Mish Mountains to the south-west and the Dingle Peninsula and

Illus. 7.9—Ballinorig West 2. Aerial view of the bivallate enclosure, view to south-east (Aerialphoto.ie).

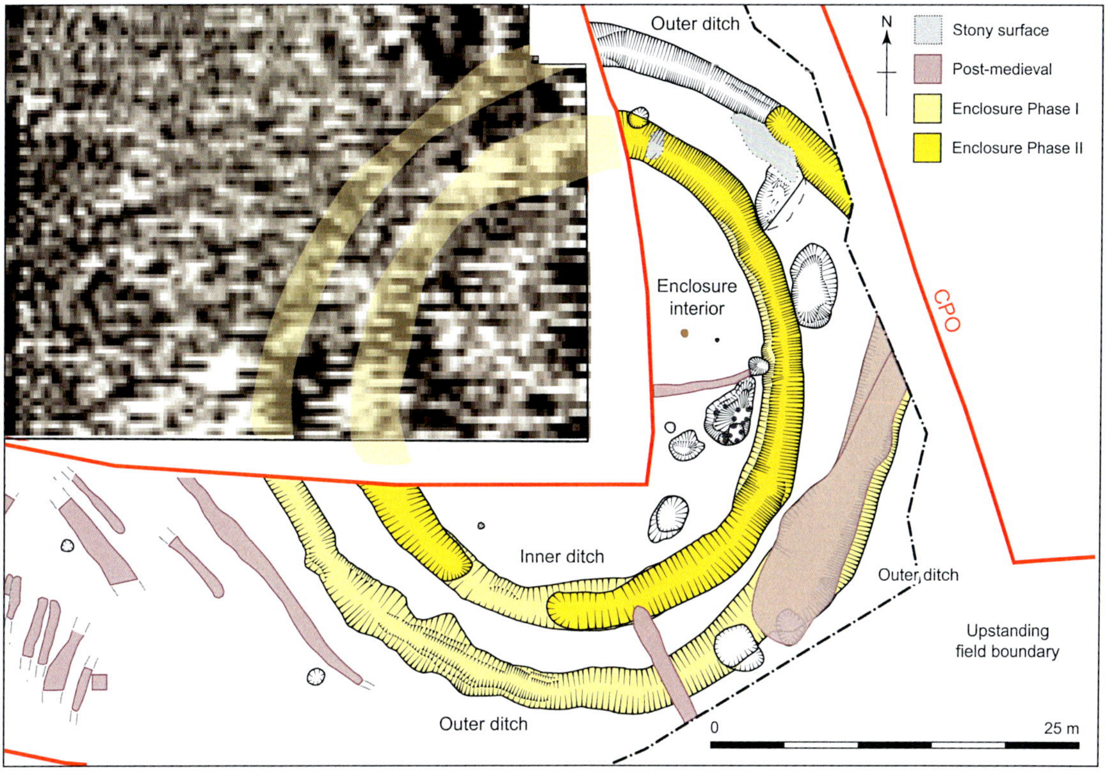

Illus. 7.10—Ballinorig West 2. Results of geophysical survey (recorded using magnetic gradiometer method) undertaken on the portion of the enclosure that lay beyond the road footprint (after Bonsall 2011).

Mount Brandon to the west. With an internal diameter of 28 m, the Ballinorig West enclosure is approximately the same size as the average ringfort on the Dingle Peninsula (30 m; Stout 1997, 16) and about a third of those in the north Kerry region (27–30 m; Toal 1995, 82). Stout (1997, 18) observed that multivallate ringforts tended not to have larger living spaces than their average univallate counterparts and this certainly seems to apply to Ballinorig West 2. Given that 88% of ringforts in north Kerry are univallate (ibid., 17), it is reasonable to assume that the Ballinorig West enclosure was a residence of some importance.

The inner enclosing ditch was dated to AD 655–779 (SUERC-37238), although, as the dated charcoal (alder) was taken from a middle fill of the ditch owing to a lack of suitable material in the basal fills, it is likely that the ditch was dug some years prior to this. Though it contained no datable material, the outer enclosing ditch is thought to have been contemporary with the inner ditch. As such, this initial settlement at Ballinorig West falls within the peak period of the construction and use of settlement enclosures, as defined by Stout (1997) and more recently by Kerr (2007).

The entrances to early medieval enclosures were typically on the east or south-east side, but there is evidence for other entrance points (Stout 1997, 18). As no entrance was identified within the excavation area at Ballinorig West 2, it was presumably located on the unexcavated north-western side of the enclosure, which lay beyond the road footprint. This unexcavated portion was subject to geophysical survey, but difficult ground conditions made for poor results overall (Bonsall 2011; Illus. 7.10). Similarly, there was no definite evidence for enclosing banks, but it can be assumed that such banks were built using the upcast material from the excavation of the ditches. They were most likely levelled by later agricultural activity.

There is evidence for a second period of occupation at Ballinorig West, when the earthworks were recut. The recutting and modification of enclosing elements was a common occurrence on early medieval settlement enclosures (O'Sullivan et al. 2010, 92), and a date of AD 893–1019 (SUERC-37242) was obtained from a charcoal sample (hazel) from the recut section of the inner ditch. This places the activity within the ninth to 11th centuries, which is within the acceptable chronology of these enclosures in the western half of Ireland. The dated material came from a middle fill of the ditch and so the recutting probably took place some years before this.

The later activity involved the creation of a new causewayed entrance over a section of the inner ditch that had been deliberately backfilled, as well as the recutting of the remaining part of the inner ditch, which had largely silted up by this time. The new entrance was located in the SSW side of the enclosure and was formed from a deposit of boulder clay that created an earthen causeway 1.2 m in width. There was no evidence for a corresponding causewayed entrance in the outer ditch, though part of this was recut on the ESE side. It is unlikely that this evidence represents a 'staggered' entrance. No multivallate enclosures with misaligned entrances were identified by O'Sullivan et al. (2010; 2014) in their review of all excavated early medieval settlement sites. It is more likely that the outer ditch was filled in, or was crossed by a wooden gangway, to give access to the new earthen causeway in the inner ditch.

How was Ballinorig West 2 used?

Bivallate enclosures are generally classified as settlement enclosures. That said, no domestic features such as houses, hearths, barns, workshops or pathways were identified within the enclosure, though it is possible that these exist within the part of the interior (c. 50%) that was beyond the excavated portion of the site. Notably, however, no early medieval artefacts were recovered, and very little palaeoenvironmental material.

The only evidence of domestic activity associated with the first phase of occupation consisted of a small quantity of animal bone fragments recovered from fills of the enclosing ditches. That this was mostly cattle bone is not surprising, as cattle formed the basis of what was then a predominantly pastoral economy, providing meat, milk, draught power (traction) and leather. The domestic evidence associated with the later occupation of the enclosure was also scant, comprising charred plant remains, a limestone rubbing stone and two smithing hearth bases (one partial) from the recut inner ditch. The plant remains included a hazelnut shell fragment and single grains of oats, indeterminate cereals and wild seed species. Oats are strongly associated with the early medieval period in Ireland (Monk 1986). The wild plants included ruderals such as nipplewort, which are found on broken and trampled ground (i.e. on the margins of cultivated ground).

Some excavated earthen enclosures are found to be lacking internal features and these are thought to have served as the livestock enclosures or *bódúine* mentioned in the law tracts (Kelly 1997, 366). At 1.2 m wide, the causewayed entrance at Ballinorig West could have accommodated cattle and so its use as a *bódún* is a possibility. A review of the archaeology of early medieval farming did not, however, identify any bivallate enclosures that were interpreted as livestock pens (McCormick et al. 2011), and thus we should assume that the enclosure at Ballinorig West 2 is more likely to have been a homestead, even in the absence of strong evidence for this.

Archaeological excavations at Baronstown (Linnane & Kinsella 2009) and Raystown (Seaver 2006), Co. Meath, and Glebe, Co. Dublin (Seaver 2011), have shown that the lands surrounding enclosed settlements were sometimes organised into field enclosures of various shapes and sizes, allowing a better archaeological understanding of the complex and highly evolved settlement landscape suggested by the medieval Irish law tracts (Bolger 2011, 1). Unfortunately, the road footprint at Ballinorig West was very limited and therefore no evidence for land organisation in the immediate area could be established, in contrast with the extensive open-area excavations carried out at Baronstown and Raystown.

An early medieval landscape

The North Kerry Archaeological Survey lists 39 bivallate ringforts north of the barony of Trughanacmy (Toal 1995, 82–206), while three further examples were investigated during pre-development work—in Ballymakegoge (O'Callaghan 2009) and Liscahane (Bartlett 2011) (both in Trughanacmy) and in Leamnaguila (Bennett 1996), to the south of Farranfore, in the barony of Magunihy. In common with Ballinorig West, none of these excavations produced diagnostic artefacts or material suitable for radiocarbon dating, though this comes with the caveat that two of them were limited in scale (i.e. partial excavations of the sites). In contrast, a ringfort enclosed by a single ditch at Dromthacker was found to contain direct evidence of occupation, which included remains of two circular houses; here, however, the north-western and central parts of the ringfort were almost devoid of features (Cleary et al. 2008).

In the immediate vicinity (1 km) of Ballinorig West 2 there are eight known ringforts and nine enclosures of possible early medieval date, representing a high density of settlement in the area (Illus. 7.11). Many of these sites were intervisible and at least some were presumably contemporary. This type of interrelated settlement pattern may have facilitated 'defence in depth', whereby neighbouring settlements could come to one another's aid or, indeed, to the aid of the local lord or king. Thus, while the banks and ditches of individual enclosures provided some security for their inhabitants, the real defensive strength of settlement enclosures may have been in their numbers and distribution within a given territory (O'Sullivan & Nicholl 2010, 65).

Social order

The following summary description of early medieval social organisation is based on publications by Bolger (2011, 4–7), Charles-Edwards (1972, 29; 1992, 63), O'Sullivan and Nicholl (2010, 61) and O'Sullivan et al. (2014, 179).

Illus. 7.11—Aerial view of the enclosure at Ballinorig West 2, showing also the locations of four of the eight recorded ringforts within 1 km of the site, view to east (Aerialphoto.ie).

The archaeological remains uncovered on the bypass are limited in what they can tell us about social organisation in the early medieval period, but we do have an amount of knowledge from historical sources. The early law tracts describe a complex system of social status based on family, land and cattle. Essentially, each household group or *muintir* belonged to a distinct kin-group or *fine*, defined along patrilineal descent, with each *fine* divided into a number of subgroups. The *derbfine* (common great-grandfather) and the *gelfine* (common grandfather) comprised the two most important divisions, with the landholdings themselves under the control of the wider *fine*. This kin-land or *finitu* was the hereditary property of the patrilineal line of each *fine* and as such was passed on to the male descendants of a family upon the death of the patriarch. A simplistic view of the archaeological landscape would be to see individual settlement enclosures as the household groups, while the *derbfine* and *gelfine* were in turn nested within the *túath*, or kingdom, of the extended *fine*, containing a whole settlement landscape of dispersed enclosed settlements.

Internally, the population of the *túath* was organised on a hierarchical basis in accordance with the three grades of social status described in the law tracts: the noble grades such as *rí* (king) and *aire* (lord), free commoners, and the unfree and semi-free grades. The members of the *fine* were bound not only by blood ties but also by social obligations to provide co-operative labour. Clientship contracts, whether *sóerchéile* (free clientship) or *dóerchéile* (base clientship), between a lord and client farmer involved the granting of fiefs of land, livestock or farming equipment in return for a *bés tige* (annual food rent) of calves, meat, grain and dairy produce. The unfree and semi-free grades worked their lord's land in return for goods and protection. Finally, there were probably large numbers of male and female slaves, who possessed no property and who, along with the semi-free grades, undertook most of the physical labour on the land or the menial tasks within the households.

The law tracts indicate that when a man died his land (*finitu*) and movable property were divided equally among his male heirs. In the absence of male heirs, his daughters were entitled to hold the land for life, after which time it reverted to the kin-group. This process undoubtedly created new landholdings and new social grades within the kin-group. It has been argued that it would have created a somewhat nucleated or clustering effect among kin-group settlements, forming, in effect, a compact, contiguous system of landholdings across the early medieval landscape.

In this social scheme there was a correlation between multivallate sites and people of high status. It is tempting, therefore, to look at the bivallate enclosure at Ballinorig West as the residence of a lord or wealthy farmer, though the lack of artefacts and paucity of habitation debris do not support this. Whatever their status, the inhabitants were probably affiliated with the *Ciaraige Luchra*, a subordinate branch of the *Eóghanacht Locha Léin*, whose territory encompassed the baronies or *túatha* of Trughanacmy, Clanmaurice and Iraghticonnor (Ó Corráin 1972, 7).

Conclusion

The settlement evidence from the bypass appears to reflect the hierarchical nature of early medieval society. The unenclosed homesteads or hut sites at Ballingowan 1a and Knockawaddra Middle 2 are in marked contrast to the more impressive bivallate enclosure at Ballinorig West 2. These humble, unenclosed abodes of the lower classes are comparatively rare discoveries and thus the two examples on the bypass make a significant contribution to the archaeological record.

In contrast, the discovery of levelled, previously unrecorded settlement enclosures is a common occurrence on development-led excavations throughout the country, which highlights the fact that our recorded upstanding monuments represent only a portion of Ireland's relict early medieval settlement landscape. Most likely the residence of a lord or wealthy farmer, the Ballinorig West enclosure can be interpreted as a manifestation of the clientship system, its double ditches and banks no doubt constructed by those obliged by client-based contracts to provide labour and other services to the occupants.

The cereal-drying kilns show that tillage played an important role in the economy and point towards an organised local population coming together to sow, harvest, thresh and dry the grain. This communal activity was undertaken at least partly in fulfilment of clientship duties. The same can probably be said of charcoal production, but iron-working, however small-scale, required particular expertise and is more likely to have been the domain of a few skilled practitioners. What is clear is that these industrial activities were undertaken outside of the settlements, possibly in designated areas.

The recovered artefacts, although few, provide a tangible link to the daily lives of these farmers. The bone needle fragment from Manor East 1, for instance, was probably used to make textile and hide garments, as well as footwear. The high-quality amber-coloured glass bead from Knockawaddra West 2, on the other hand, was a luxury item of personal decoration that provides a glimpse of individual style but also hints at the wider trade networks that connected communities.

Overall, the results reflect the lives of a wealthy farmer or lord and those of the lower social classes within the extended kin-group. They point to a complex, integrated landscape based on a mixed farming economy centred on cattle and tillage, which is consistent with what is currently known about settlement and industry in the early medieval period.

8

CREATING A MODERN LANDSCAPE, 1540–1900

Enda O'Flaherty and Louise Baker

The post-medieval and early modern periods in Ireland were characterised by great social change, witnessing the fall of the old Gaelic order and the transformation of Irish society to a centralised state, more like those found elsewhere in Europe. The Tudor conquest in the 16th century and the subsequent conflicts of the 17th century were followed by a period known as 'the long peace' (O'Flaherty 2009) and, indeed, for over 100 years (1691–1798) there was little political violence in the country relative to the preceding centuries. This period was partly characterised by the sweeping changes in landownership that resulted from the Cromwellian conquest (1649–53) and the War of the Two Kings (1688–91), and, in turn, by significant changes to the organisation and appearance of the Irish rural landscape.

A new social organisation founded on landed estates, the dominance of the Protestant Ascendancy and tenant farming greatly affected the use and enclosure of land. The steady growth in population, which began in the late 17th century, was accompanied by a proliferation of rural tenants' houses, designed landscapes (mansions and their demesnes) and planned villages, as well as major innovations in transport, agriculture and industry. Landlords were frequently the primary agents of change, with an insistent emphasis on technological innovations in farming practices, including liming, draining and enclosure of lands. This impetus for improvement was continued by larger tenant farmers (in effect a new rural middle class) after the Great Famine (1845–9). New technologies in industry were also developed at this time, along with improvements in transport infrastructure, such as the Cork–Tralee turnpike road, which was completed in 1748 and superseded in 1812 by the opening of the Cork to Tralee mail-coach road (Barrington 1999, 190–1). The railway network extended to Kerry in the second half of the 19th century, with Tralee Railway Station opening in 1859.[1] New lines were subsequently built, connecting Tralee to Dingle, Fenit, Castleisland, Valentia Harbour and Listowel (and onwards to Limerick), opening up the west and north Kerry regions to trade and commerce (Barrington 1999, 192). The construction of the Blennerville windmill by order of Sir Rowland Blennerhassett c. 1800 and the adjacent Tralee Ship Canal, which was completed in 1846 (Cox & Gould 1998), further reflect the changes in the industrial and economic landscape during this time. It would be remiss, however, not to note the devastating social impact of the Great Famine, when the population of the county was reduced by over 20% between 1845 and 1852 (MacMahon 2017).

---

[1] Irish Railway Station Dates (https://www.railscot.co.uk/articles/Irish_Railway_Station_Dates, accessed May 2019).

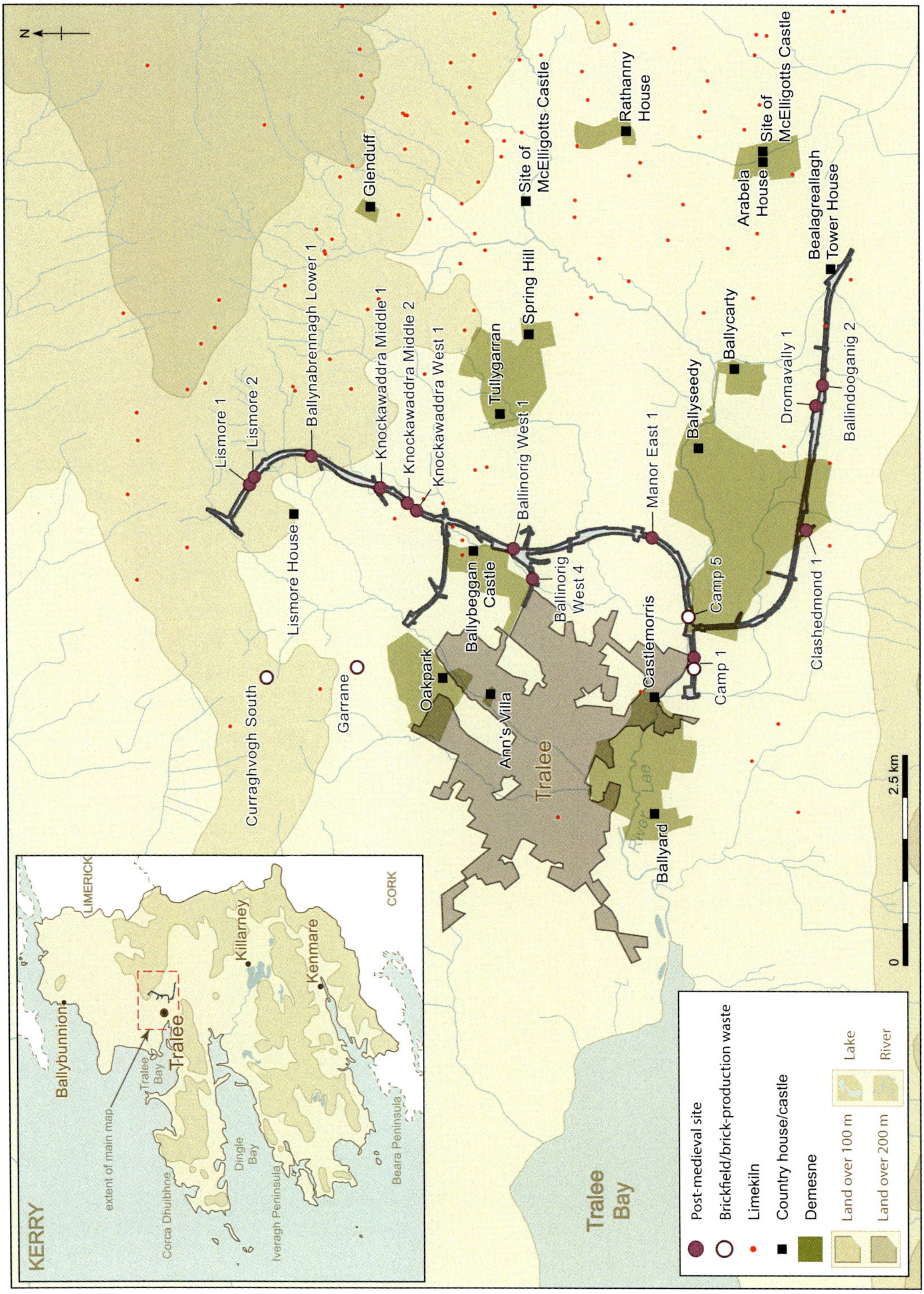

Illus. 8.1—Post-medieval sites excavated on the N22 Tralee Bypass, showing the Ordnance Survey distribution of limekilns, country houses, castle sites and landed estates in the Lee Valley (based on the 25-inch map, published 1899).

Illus. 8.2—Ruins of Castlemorris tower house at Ballymullen (RMP KE029-163), view to south-west (Rubicon Heritage Services Ltd).

It is in this context that much of the agricultural landscape of small fields and hedgerows that we see around Tralee today was formed. Unsurprisingly, the changes to landownership, agricultural practices and industry that occurred during this period are reflected in the archaeological discoveries on the bypass (Illus. 8.1).

Lordly homes and farmers' fields: settlement evidence

At the beginning of the post-medieval period (c. 1540), the town of Tralee and its environs were part of the Fitzgerald earldom of Desmond. A number of castles helped to control the territory, including a tower house at Ballybeggan (KE029-123), which was besieged in the 1640s, another at Castlemorris in the townland of Ballymullen (Illus. 8.2; KE029-163), and two castles associated with the McElligott family in Carrignafeela (KE030-016) and Arabela (KE039-001) (both now levelled). The latter was reputedly destroyed by Cromwellian forces (Ruvigny et Raineval 1904, 2–3; Crane 1907, 190).

Bealagrellagh tower house (KE039-004) is located immediately adjacent to the new bypass. Little is known of its history, beyond an association with the McElligott family (Atkins 2008, 239). As part of the present project, geophysical survey and test excavations were undertaken beside the castle ruins. These investigations identified several linear features—two courses of a narrow wall overlying alluvium deposits and a network of stone drains—but these are not thought to be associated with the castle (Bartlett et al. 2010, 104–5). Desmond hegemony over the town and county ended with the defeat and subsequent execution of the 15th earl in the Second Desmond Rebellion (1579–83). In the Munster Plantation that followed, a large part of the county was granted to Sir Edward Denny, whose family eventually rebuilt much of Tralee in the 17th century, following the destruction wrought during the rebellion (O'Carroll 2009, 38). Tralee and its environs saw further upheaval with the onset of the Confederate War and much of the town was again burned in 1642 (ibid., 43). Following the Cromwellian conquest, much of the land of north Kerry was redistributed to merchant adventurers and English soldiers. This did not have as great an impact in north Kerry as it did in some parts of Ireland, however, as for over half a century much of the land had already been owned by Protestants, who were less likely to be displaced by Cromwellian confiscations. Furthermore, many of the new landowners sublet the land to the former owners (ibid., 46).

With new land organisation and continuing rapid population growth throughout the 18th and early 19th centuries, County Kerry became increasingly populated by poor tenant farmers who relied on the potato as their main food. As a result, when the potato crop failed in 1845 the county was particularly badly hit by famine, with many thousands of poor farmers and their families either starving, succumbing to disease or emigrating to seek a better life elsewhere.

At the time of the first-edition Ordnance Survey six-inch map (surveyed 1841, published 1846), a number of country houses and demesnes are shown in our study area (i.e. in the environs of the bypass). Many of these remained in the hands of families who were granted land under the Acts of Settlement in the 1660s, such as the Blennerhassetts of Ballyseedy and the Chutes of Chute Hall (also known as Tullygarren) and Spring Hill.[2] The boundaries of their demesnes were planted with trees both to provide shelter and for aesthetic purposes. There were also initiatives at this time to replant land in an attempt to redress the extensive deforestation of the 16th and 17th centuries, when ancient native woodlands were commercially exploited for industry, housing and fuel (Mitchell & Ryan 1997, 300). These landscaped, planted demesnes and their mansion houses were in marked contrast to the landscape that surrounded them, which was dotted with the clustered habitations of tenants (clachans) and remained largely bare of trees. In time, however, hedgerows would develop along the field boundaries with which tillage and pasture lands were now being enclosed.

The homes of the ordinary people in this period were 'vernacular' buildings, designed and constructed not by architects but by those living in them, with no formal plans and using only local materials.

Vernacular dwellings on the bypass

A group of three vernacular houses was excavated on the bypass route in the townland of Lismore (Illus. 8.3). The houses correspond to buildings depicted on the first-edition Ordnance Survey six-inch map as a settlement cluster surrounded by a network of small, regular fields (Illus. 8.4). The map shows several buildings as well as two limekilns, and a road leading north from Lismore House.

2 Landed Estates Database (http://landedestates.nuigalway.ie:8080/LandedEstates/jsp/, accessed January 2019).

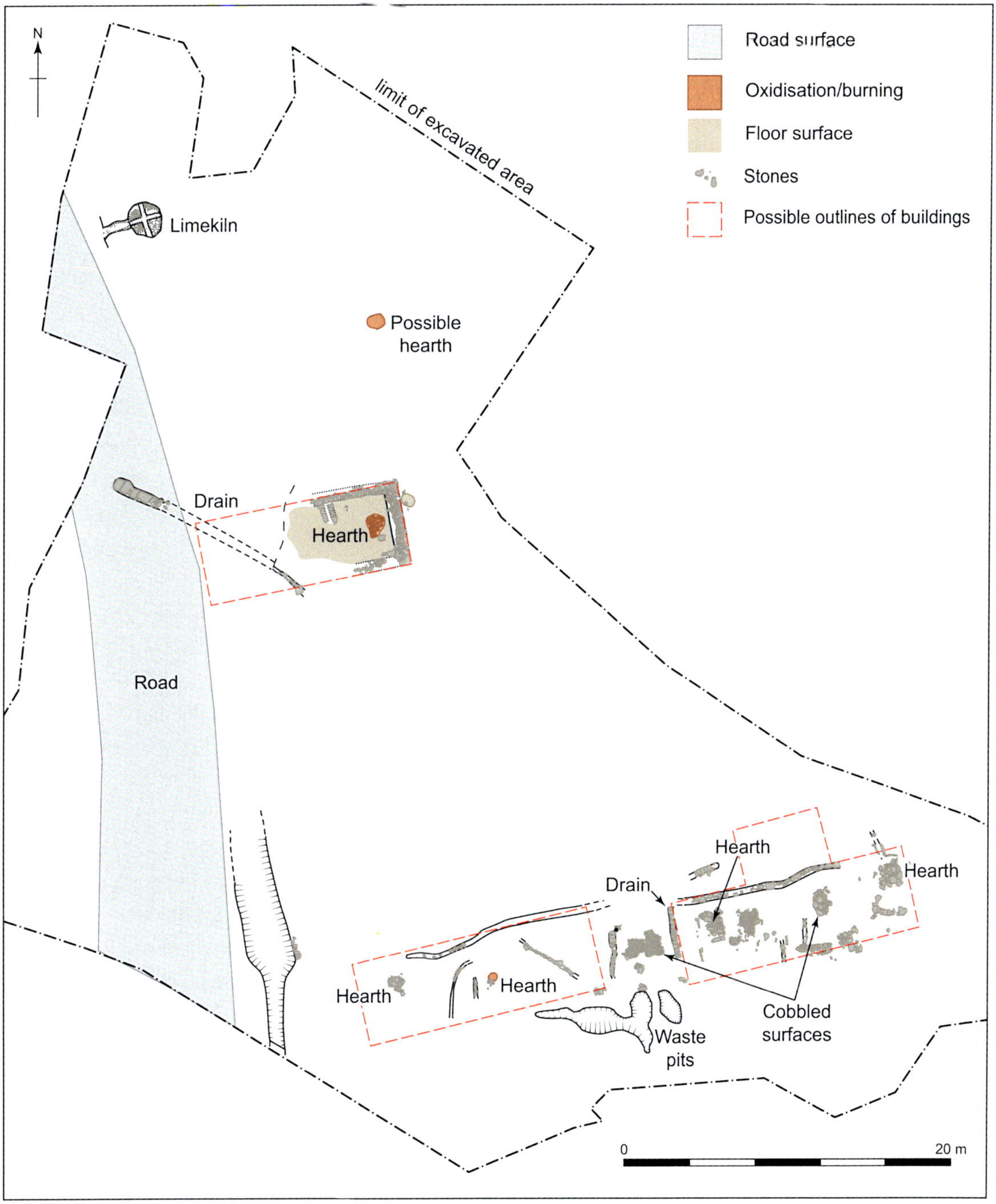

Illus. 8.3—Lismore 1. Vernacular buildings and limekiln.

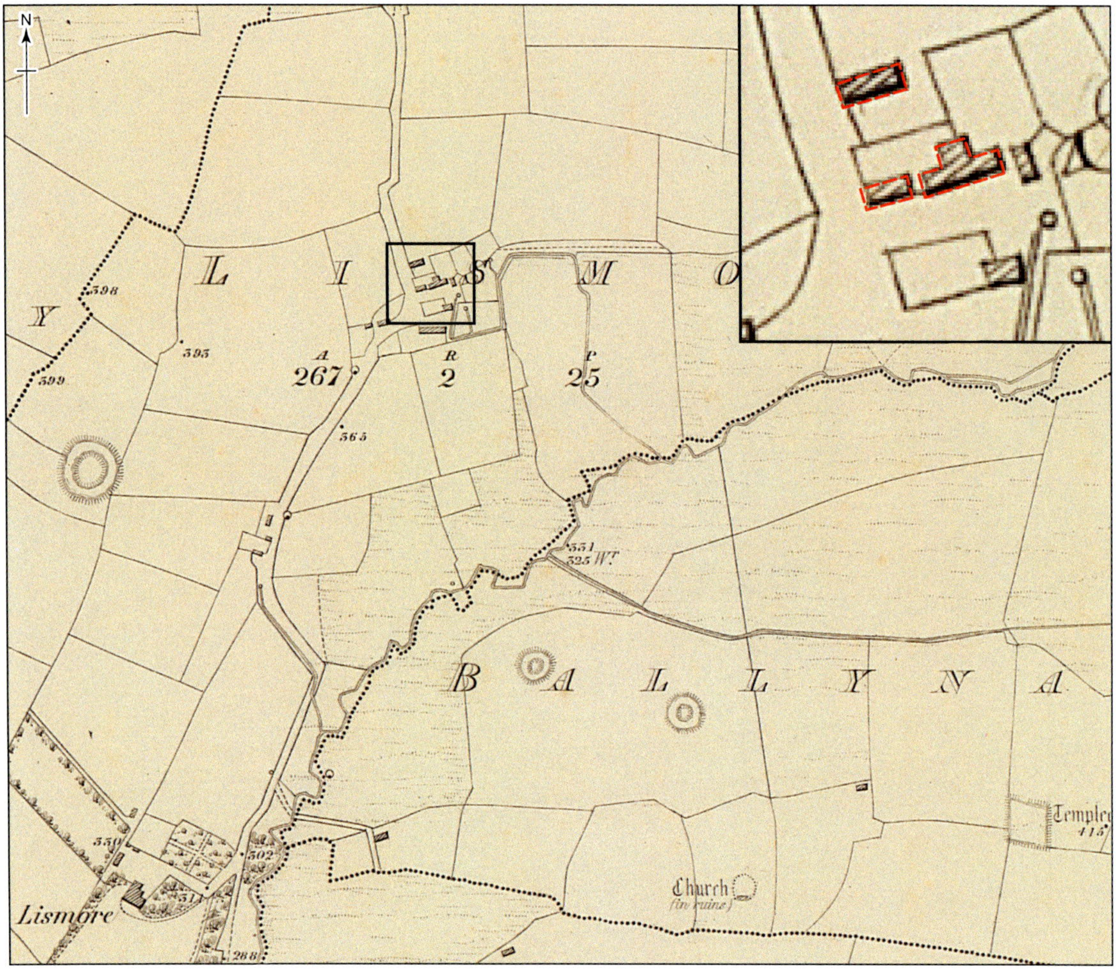

Illus. 8.4—The first-edition Ordnance Survey six-inch map, showing settlement at Lismore 1 (excavated buildings outlined in red) (Kerry Sheet 029; surveyed 1841, published 1846).

The northernmost of the excavated houses was rectangular in plan, with its long axis aligned ENE/WSW. Its size and construction were in keeping with other vernacular buildings of this time (Ó Danachair 1972). The excavated portion of the building was 6.8 m long by 5 m wide (Illus. 8.5) and the full length is estimated to have been c. 12 m, with its west end directly adjacent to the road. No entrance to the house was identified, but the main (front) elevation probably faced SSE in order to maximise its exposure to sunlight, an orientation typical of such buildings. Only the eastern end survived to be excavated. The building was one room wide internally (c. 3.4 m). The walls were built with sandstone rubble, with no evidence for mortar bonding. In places two courses of stonework survived, up to 0.2 m high and 0.85 m wide. The remains of an internal wall appeared to divide the building into two rooms. The eastern room was 3 m long and contained the partial remains of a hearth, comprised of a subrectangular setting of flagstones and bricks at

Illus. 8.5—Lismore 1. Northernmost vernacular building, view to east. Only the east end survived on plan, with a hearth by the end wall. Part of a transverse partition wall can be seen in the foreground (left) (Rubicon Heritage Services Ltd).

the centre of the eastern wall. There was no evidence for a chimney-breast. The internal floor surface was compacted clay with stone and pebble inclusions. A stone drain extended from the interior of the building as far as the road to the west. This internal drain and the division into two rooms suggest that this building was probably a 'byre house'—a dwelling that accommodated both people and their livestock. The adjacent road comprised a slightly raised area of heavily compacted yellowish brown gravelly clay and varied in width between 6.5 m and 8 m.

Approximately 45 m to the south were the remains of two stone buildings, each measuring c. 16 m long by 4.5 m wide. The remains comprised foundations, drains, hearths and cobbled surfaces. The buildings were again aligned ENE/WSW and were of similar construction to the house to the north. The presence of a hearth in each indicates that these also were dwellings. Artefacts recovered from the houses and nearby waste pits included sherds of pottery of 18th- to 20th-century date, a whetstone, a highly corroded piece of iron which may have been an agricultural tool, a 19th-century copper-alloy button and a translucent annular blue bead. The pottery sherds represent a minimum of 10 vessels and include creamware, which was a cheaper, more durable alternative to porcelain. Overall, the artefacts indicate the use of everyday items in a domestic setting.

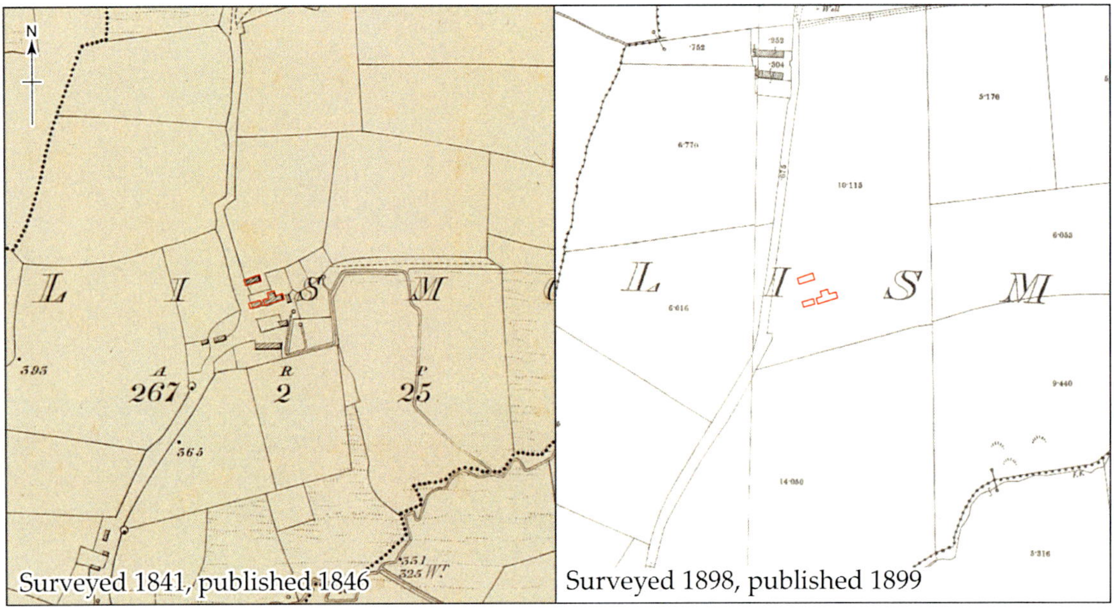

Illus. 8.6—Extracts from the six-inch (left) and 25-inch (right) Ordnance Survey maps, showing settlement at Lismore 1 (excavated buildings outlined in red) (Kerry Sheet 029).

In the *Tithe Applotment Books* of 1824 seven names (Savage, Scotland, Duncan, Prindable, Collins, Moore and Ahern) are listed in the townland of Lismore.[3] These books recorded a survey of agricultural land, detailing the names of those occupying the land and the tithes due to the Church of Ireland for returns from the land. A further survey, in this case for secular taxation purposes, was carried out in 1848–64 under the supervision of Sir Richard Griffith and is colloquially known as 'Griffith's Valuation'. The volume for Kerry was published in 1852. In this survey, only two names are connected to the townland of Lismore, in the parish of Ratass: Edward Day Stokes of Lismore House and Laurence Sullivan, who is listed as having a house but no land (Griffith 1847–64). Neither of these is listed in the *Tithe Applotment Books*. It is likely that the inhabitants of the vernacular buildings had perished or emigrated during the Great Famine and that the land was now being farmed as part of a larger estate. This pattern of population decrease is reflected in statistics for the parish of Ratass (including Lismore), where the number of inhabited houses fell from 175 to 133 between 1841 and 1851.[4] There were no uninhabited houses listed in the parish in 1841 and only five in 1851, which suggests that up to 37 of the 42 abandoned houses had either been demolished or become ruinous in the intervening decade.

The short-lived nature of the excavated settlement is confirmed by cartographic sources, as the houses were no longer present by the time the 25-inch Ordnance Survey map was published in 1899 (Illus. 8.6).

[3] Tithe Applotment Books 1823–37 (http://titheapplotmentbooks.nationalarchives.ie/search/tab/home.jsp, accessed January 2019).

[4] All-Island Research Observatory, *Historic Population Data for the 1841 and 1851 census* (http://airo.maynoothuniversity.ie, accessed March 2016).

Limekilns

With the growing emphasis on land management, improvement and drainage from the 18th century onwards, 'liming' became common practice, especially in peaty areas with acidic soil and readily available limestone (i.e. in poorly drained soil on limestone bedrock) (O'Sullivan & Downey 2005). As a result, limekilns remain one of Ireland's most numerous and widely distributed industrial monuments (Rynne 2006, 157).

Limekilns were used to convert limestone into calcium oxide, or 'quicklime', by heating it to a temperature of at least 900°C. The process was often referred to as 'burning the lime' and took a number of days. Quicklime could be spread on land as a fertiliser. Slaked with water to form hydrated

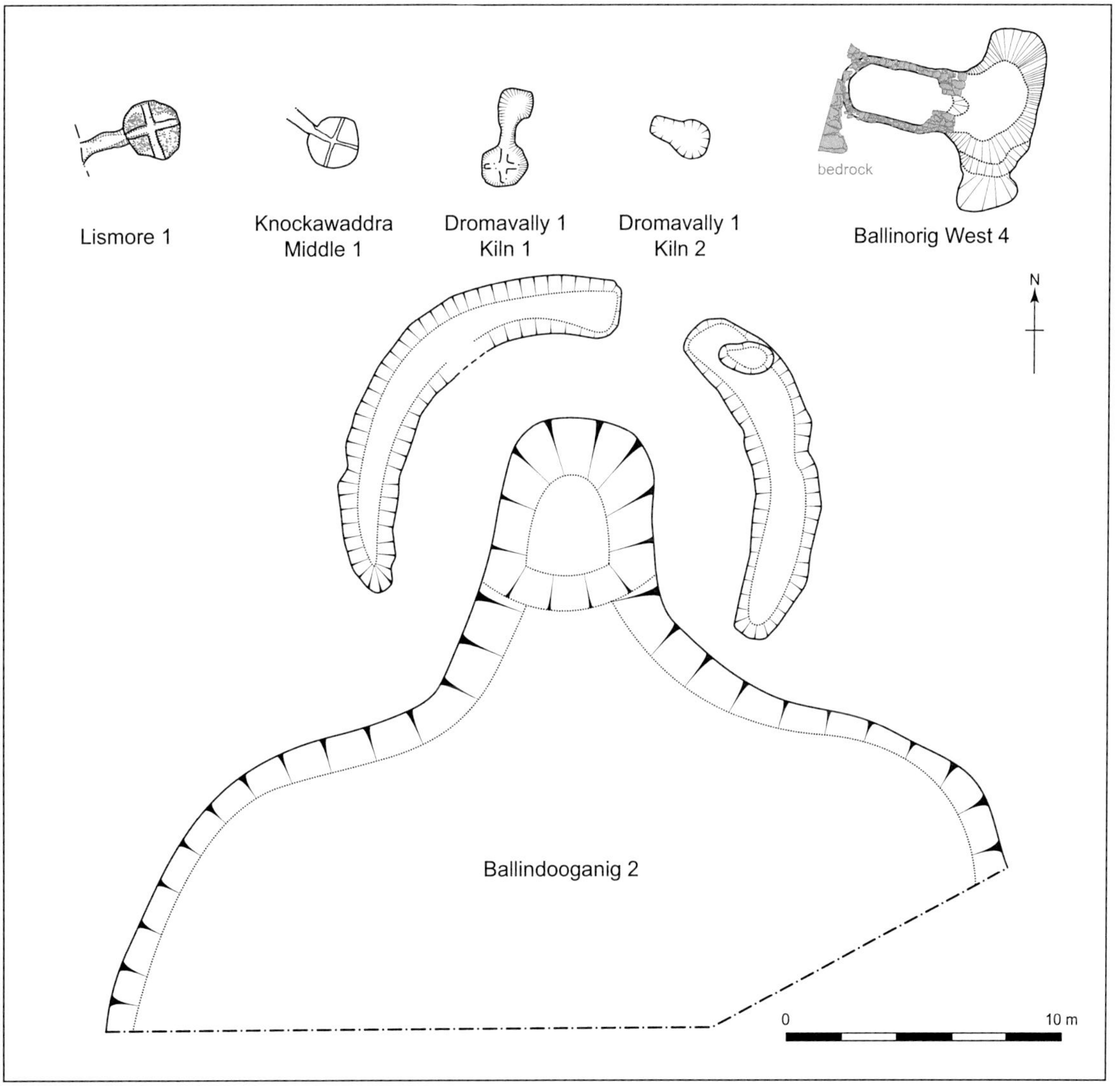

Illus. 8.7—Comparative plans of limekilns excavated on the N22 Tralee Bypass.

lime, it could be used in mortar, plaster and as a limewash. Agricultural land was improved with the application of lime from at least the mid-17th century in Ireland (Ó Drisceoil 2005).

Six previously unknown limekilns were excavated as part of the present project, in the townlands of Lismore, Knockawaddra Middle, Ballinorig West, Dromavally (two kilns) and Ballindooganig (Illus. 8.7). Given the prevalence of limestone in the area and the local soil quality, the presence of these kilns is not surprising. The surrounding landscape comprises acidic surface-water gley soils and, although relatively productive, these soils can benefit greatly from liming. There are two basic types of kiln, the flare kiln and the draw kiln, and examples of both were encountered on the bypass.

Flare kilns

In rural areas, such as the Tralee hinterland, many limekilns were temporary structures used intermittently, with the need for small quantities of quicklime tying into the agricultural cycle (Rynne 2006, 159). For these purposes flare kilns were the most practical kiln type. The chamber held the limestone charge, which was separated from the fuel by a crude arch or vault of limestone blocks. The fire was kept stoked for several days until all the limestone had been calcined. The kiln was then unloaded and the process repeated with the next batch of limestone. Often the kilns were either left to collapse after use or were dismantled.

The kilns at Lismore 1, Knockawaddra Middle 1 and Dromavally 1 (Kiln 1) were probably all flare kilns. They consisted of simple, earth-cut pits with a circular firing bowl, 1.6–2.1 m in diameter and 0.4–0.6 m in depth, with an elongated flue 1–2 m long, which at Dromavally widened out at the end. Ventilation channels cut into the base of the bowls ensured that air circulated evenly throughout. This was crucial in producing evenly burnt lime (Bick 1984). In each case the sides of the firing bowls were heavily oxidised, indicating that they had not been lined with stone. There was no above-ground trace of these kilns and it is likely that their use was intermittent and/or short-lived. Very large pits were found in association with the kilns at Knockawaddra Middle 1 and Dromavally Kiln 1, which contained waste material such as lime residue, charcoal and heat-affected stone. A 17th- or early 18th-century glass bottle was recovered from the Knockawaddra Middle 1 kiln, but no radiocarbon date could be obtained. The example at Lismore 1 returned a radiocarbon date of AD 1681–1938 (SUERC-37293) and appeared to have been associated with the post-medieval vernacular buildings at this location. Kiln 1 at Dromavally included minute amounts of burnt bone and charcoal as well as burnt limestone residue in the fill. Charcoal from this feature returned a date of AD 1492–1953 (SUERC-37280). A second limekiln and rectangular structure (described below) were found in the immediate vicinity of this kiln at Dromavally 1. It appears that this was a small-scale post-medieval industrial site. Very similar limekilns have previously been excavated at Dromthacker, Co. Kerry (Cleary et al. 2008, 47–9), and at Bricketstown, Co. Wexford, where one of the kilns was radiocarbon-dated to AD 1450–1660 (Noonan & Johnston 2009).

Almost identical features consisting of heavily oxidised circular pits with cruciform channels at the bases, and flues extending from the pits, were identified in the townland of Rockfield, 8 km to the south-east of Tralee (Collins 2000; Connolly 2002). These have been interpreted as Late Bronze Age/Iron Age cremation pyre pits (Collins & Lynch 2001). One of these pits was found close to a cremation burial but contained no burnt material, while the other contained cremated bone and charcoal. They were radiocarbon-dated to 780–380 BC and 390–60 BC. The similarity of the Rockfield pits to the features excavated on the bypass route is striking. Nevertheless, the absence of significant amounts of cremated bone and the presence of the glass, the lime residue in the waste pits and the post-medieval radiocarbon dates support their interpretation as limekilns.

A second, keyhole-shaped kiln with the remains of a stone lining was identified at Dromavally 1 (Kiln 2) and is thought to have been slightly later in date than Kiln 1. Overall it measured 2.4 m in length, 0.65 m in width and 0.7 m in depth. This kiln did not include ventilation channels but may have also functioned as a flare kiln. A nearby subrectangular post-built structure (6.2 m by 3.8 m) with a hearth and compacted clay floor may have been used by the workers tending the two kilns. The hearth returned a radiocarbon date of AD 1679–1940 (SUERC-37279).

Draw kilns

During the latter part of the 18th century, improved agricultural techniques, including new crops and machinery, were introduced into Ireland. This led to an increased demand for quicklime as fertiliser, resulting in the construction of larger, continuous draw kilns (Rynne 2006, 158). In a draw kiln the limestone and fuel were built up in alternating layers. As it burnt through, the lime was extracted from the bottom of the kiln and further layers of limestone and fuel were added through the opening at the top.

The largest kiln excavated on the bypass was a probable draw kiln at Ballindooganig 2. Excavation revealed a substantial kiln with a roughly rectangular chamber (7 m north/south by 6 m with an excavated depth of 2 m) that opened out from the draw-hole onto a large apron, some 30 m wide, which would have facilitated access by horse and cart to the base of the kiln. The stone lining of the chamber had been robbed out. The kiln was partly enclosed by a discontinuous curvilinear ditch at its northern end. The form of the kiln, together with a small assemblage of ceramic, glass and metal objects, dates the activity here to the late 18th or 19th century.

A stone, keyhole-shaped limekiln of 19th- or 20th-century date was identified at Ballinorig West 4 (Illus. 8.8). It was constructed adjacent to a rock outcrop and was a typical draw kiln, consisting of a drystone subrectangular chamber (4.2 m long by 2.23 m wide and 0.85 m deep), a short flue (0.84 m long by 1.23 m wide) and a rake-out pit (6.5 m long by 2.8 m wide and 0.83 m deep).

The 25-inch Ordnance Survey map (surveyed 1898, published 1899) shows a dense distribution of limekilns in the Tralee area (some marked 'disused'). Particular concentrations occur in the foothills of the Stack's Mountains (Illus. 8.1). Only three of the 161 limekilns identified on the map are located within demesne landscapes. The building of limekilns and the use of their products for soil improvement are likely to have been carried out by tenant farmers, and the construction of a kiln was often a condition of their tenancy. Much of the produce grown here was consumed as part of a subsistence diet by the families who farmed the land, though

Illus. 8.8—Ballinorig West 4. Excavation in progress on the limekiln, view to west (Aerialphoto.ie).

undoubtedly the area also served as Tralee's 'bread-basket' to some degree, supplying produce to the townspeople.

Other agricultural improvements

As part of the overall drive for improvement, the process of liming was frequently accompanied by attempts to drain land that was formerly unproductive. Much of this post-medieval drainage network remains in use today. Our excavations revealed simple, earth-cut field drains at Lismore 2 and Manor East 1. At Knockawaddra Middle 2, a free-standing double span culvert of rubble-stone construction, built c. 1820, was identified during the architectural survey carried out as part of the bypass investigations at EIS stage (Yates 2010).

Horse-power and simple horse-drawn machinery were essential for carrying out improvement works, and the smithy was a pivotal feature of the Irish landscape. During the architectural survey, a former forge/smithy was identified in the townland of Dromthacker (ibid.). It is depicted on both the six-inch and 25-inch Ordnance Survey maps and is shown with a small yard to the front. The forge comprised a detached, two-bay, two-storey building dating from c.

1840, though little or nothing remained of its workings at the time of the survey.

Much of the countryside that we see around us was shaped during the early modern period, and it forms a distinct and highly visible part of our cultural heritage. Population growth and the social upheavals mentioned at the beginning of this chapter provided the background to changing settlement forms and the drainage, enclosure and improvement of lands. The process of land improvement began late in much of Ireland compared to many other parts of Europe. The draining of extensive tracts of bog and marginal land commenced in the first half of the 19th century in many parts of the country but continued throughout the Victorian period. The population pressures of the 18th and early 19th centuries and the desire to improve marginal lands to facilitate (and profit from) the rising population were the strongest driving forces in the landscape management of this period.

Local brick production

The earliest known use of brick in Ireland is from high-status buildings of 16th-century date, such as Carrickfergus Castle, Co. Antrim, and Bunratty Castle, Co. Clare (Pavia & Bolton 2000, 177). Brick was used in some vernacular buildings in Ulster in the late 1600s but was not widely used in Ireland until the early 18th century (Lynch & Roundtree 2009).

Evidence of small-scale brick-making during the 18th and 19th centuries was uncovered at Camp 1 and Camp 5. The remains of two brick clamp kilns were excavated at Camp 1, c. 1.75 km south-east of Tralee. Situated 80 m south of the River Lee, the clamps are likely to have used clay extracted from the floodplain as the raw material for the bricks, while the finished products could be easily transported by boat or barge. One of the clamps (Illus. 8.9) was roughly rectangular in plan. The surviving remains measured 8.07 m by 6.2 m. The other clamp was subrectangular in plan, measuring 3.1 m north/south by 1.85 m. The remains of both clamps comprised alternate lines of heat-fused brick/clay and charcoal. These were 0.75 m and 0.45 m wide respectively in the bigger clamp, and a uniform 0.4 m wide in the smaller clamp. Peat appears to have been the main fuel. The brick fragments that were present were handmade and showed no evidence of burning or frogging (a brick frog was an indentation that reduced the amount of clay used per brick and speeded up the drying process, often also the location of the maker's mark). The fragments consisted of fired clay with inclusions of grit and were orange-red in colour.

Brick-production waste, comprising fragments of fired bricks, was found in a large pit (5.2 m long by 1.8 m wide by 0.32 m deep) at Camp 5, approximately 500 m east of Camp 1. The brick fragments here were similar in colour and fabric to those at Camp 1 and indicate the presence of a further brick clamp in this area.

Clamp kilns were an early method of production, and brick-making using this technique was a seasonal activity often carried out by casual workers and farmers. These were temporary, single-use kilns which were dismantled to access the bricks. Clay for brick-making was extracted by hand, following which any stones were removed and the clay was mixed with water and left for some time. It was then pressed by hand into rectangular wooden moulds to produce bricks of a

Illus. 8.9—Camp 1. Basal remnants of a simple brick clamp kiln, view to north. The dark bands represent the fuel that was piled between brick 'benches' in the kiln (Rubicon Heritage Services Ltd).

standard size and left to air-dry before being arranged into 'benches' for firing. A clamp kiln could take up to two weeks to construct and consisted of parallel rows of fire-hardened bricks (the benches), on top of which were placed air-dried 'green' bricks, with rows of fuel (peat, wood, coal or culm) packed in between. The sides of the completed clamp were battered (sloped) inwards. The rows of bricks were laid in alternate courses of headers and stretchers and were sometimes built into arches. An outer casing of fired bricks, turf or clay was sometimes added before the fuel was set alight (Lynch & Roundtree 2009). The clamp burned for a number of days or weeks and needed constant observation and tending, with the fuel being intermittently stoked. The bricks produced were inconsistent in terms of quality and colour. They were often charred where they had come into contact with the flame and were fired to variable degrees, depending on where in the clamp they were situated. They were used internally in buildings or, if used externally, were most likely rendered to produce a better finish. Brick for building façades was often imported to ensure the required uniformity in colour and shape. The bricks used in the vernacular houses at Lismore 1 were probably of local origin.

On the first-edition Ordnance Survey six-inch map, an 'Old Brick Field' is noted in Garrane and a 'Brick Field' is noted in Curravogh South (Illus. 8.10). In both instances a regular array of rectangular features is depicted. These are likely to indicate clamps but it is not known whether

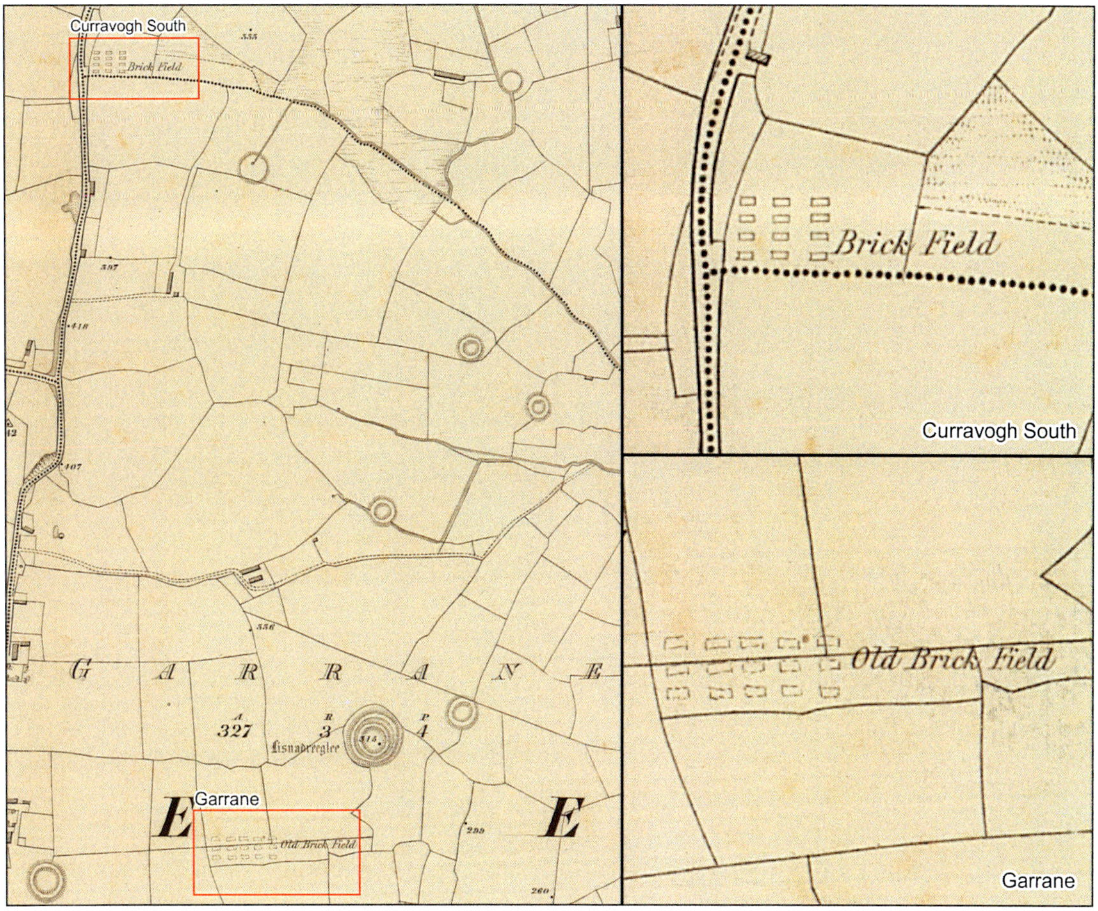

Illus. 8.10—Extracts from the first-edition Ordnance Survey six-inch map, showing brickfields in Garrane and Curravogh South townlands (Kerry Sheet 029; surveyed 1841, published 1846).

they are an accurate depiction or merely a cartographic convention. The clamp kilns excavated at Camp 1 were not marked on this map or on any subsequent editions, suggesting that they were either on such a small scale as to have escaped notice or that they pre-dated the first-edition map. By the middle of the 19th century brick-making was becoming mechanised, and bricks of higher and more consistent quality were being produced. The excavated clamp kilns probably represent a short-lived, small-scale, local industry where bricks were produced for use in vernacular buildings.

Conclusion

The remains of vernacular houses, limekilns and brick clamps uncovered on the bypass route are reflective both of landowners' drive for agricultural improvement and economic development in the early modern period and of the often precarious existence of the ordinary families who laboured to deliver it. At Lismore 1, we see a small, clustered settlement of at least three houses, set perpendicular to the road in a loose courtyard arrangement. On the first-edition Ordnance Survey six-inch map, the settlement is no more than three fields away from large tracts of rough pasture to the north, south and east. This suggests that it was at the forefront of efforts to bring marginal land on the lower foothills of the Stack's Mountains into productive agricultural use. This is supported by the discovery of an associated limekiln during the bypass investigations, additional to the three shown in this townland on the six-inch map. The abandonment of this settlement during or shortly after the Famine, and the consolidation of the small farms in Lismore into larger holdings, mirrors trends observed throughout the county at this time. That the process of improvement continued unabated is clear from the 25-inch map of 1899, where the largely unenclosed rough pasture of the six-inch map had been replaced by a regular array of enclosed fields.

It would be wrong to assume, however, that the inhabitants of Lismore 1 were the poorest of society. The stone houses here were considerably larger and more comfortable than the one-roomed mud cabins occupied by a large proportion of Kerry people at this time (O'Hare 1993, cited in Fleming 2016, 33). The ceramic assemblage of plates, bowls, cups and jars, while not high-end tableware, was certainly beyond the reach of many. And yet by 1852, only 11 years after their homes were surveyed for the six-inch map, these people had either perished or emigrated, and by 1899 all traces of their homestead had vanished entirely.

The archaeological investigations on the bypass have provided glimpses of the lives of these people, and of their contemporaries in Knockawaddra Middle, Ballinorig West, Dromavally, Ballindooganig and Camp, as they harvested turf to fuel their landlords' brick clamps, quarried limestone for their kilns and toiled to expand the boundaries of cultivated land. Their labours, though difficult, allowed them to subsist rather than prosper, the precarious nature of their existence exemplified by the abandonment of the settlement at Lismore 1 in the years surrounding the Famine.

Appendix 1
Radiocarbon dates

All dates are AMS (Accelerator Mass Spectrometry) dates. Dates obtained from the Scottish Universities Environmental Research Centre (SUERC lab code) were calibrated using datasets from Reimer et al. (2009) and the OxCal4 calibration program (Bronk Ramsey et al. 2010). Dates obtained from Queen's University Belfast (UBA lab code) were calibrated with the CALIB REV6.0.0 calibration programme, using the IntCal09.14c calibration curve (Reimer et al. 2009).

Lab code	Dated material and context	Years BP	$\delta^{13}C$ ‰	Calibrated date range
Ballindooganig 1				
SUERC-37223	Oak charcoal from primary burnt mound deposit (007)	3950±35	–25.0	2563–2350 BC (1σ) 2570–2310 BC (2σ)
Ballingowan 1				
SUERC-37300	Charred barley grain from basal fill (219) of post-hole (221)	3600±30	–25.0	2018–1910 BC (1σ) 2116–1881 BC (2σ)
SUERC-37301	Blackthorn charcoal from single fill (049) of pit (050)	1875±35	–24.8	AD 78–210 (1σ) AD 65–232 (2σ)
SUERC-37302	Alder charcoal from single fill (314) of post-hole (313)	2490±35	–26.5	763–542 BC (1σ) 780–417 BC (2σ)
SUERC-37303	Hazel charcoal from single fill (125) of curvilinear ditch (114)	2635±35	–25.5	826–792 BC (1σ) 895–770 BC (2σ)
SUERC-37304	Hazel charcoal from basal fill (076) of post-hole (198)	2560±35	–26.6	801–596 BC (1σ) 806–547 BC (2σ)
SUERC-37308	Willow charcoal from middle fill (437) of pit (439)	1010±35	–27.7	AD 986–1116 (1σ) AD 903–1154 (2σ)
SUERC-37309	Hazel charcoal from basal fill (012) of pit (203)	2040±35	–25.7	99 BC–AD 5 (1σ) 166 BC–AD 50 (2σ)
SUERC-37310	Charred barley grain from upper fill (111) of post-hole (290)	2500±35	–23.6	767–545 BC (1σ) 790–421 BC (2σ)
SUERC-37311	Hazel charcoal from upper fill (089) of pit (090)	3045±35	–25.7	1382–1268 BC (1σ) 1411–1212 BC (2σ)
SUERC-37312	Charred barley grain from charcoal-rich hearth deposit (054)	3300±35	–24.5	1617–1527 BC (1σ) 1678–1499 BC (2σ)
SUERC-37313	Oak charcoal from a basal fill (675) of furnace (673)	2205±35	–27.8	359–205 BC (1σ) 382–186 BC (2σ)
SUERC-37314	Alder charcoal from upper fill (207) of pit (488)	3095±35	–25.6	1418–1316 BC (1σ) 1436–1269 BC (2σ)
SUERC-37318	Charred barley grain from lower fill (689) of kiln (082)	3315±35	–25.8	1629–1531 BC (1σ) 1687–1513 BC (2σ)
SUERC-37319	Charred oat grain from single fill (029) of pit (555)	1560±35	–23.7	434–543 BC (1σ) 419–574 BC (2σ)
SUERC-37678	Sample of probable cattle bone from single fill (066) of post-hole (067)	2385±30	–23.0	508–399 BC (1σ) 723–393 BC (2σ)

Lab code	Dated material and context	Years BP	δ13C ‰	Calibrated date range
Ballinorig South 1				
SUERC-37228	Alder charcoal from basal fill (043) of pit (005)	3840±35	–24.5	2399–2206 BC (1σ) 2460–2201 BC (2σ)
SUERC-37229	Alder charcoal from middle fill (054) of trough (056)	3875±35	–24.9	2456–2297 BC (1σ) 2468–2210 BC (2σ)
Ballinorig West 1				
SUERC-37230	Hazel charcoal from burnt mound deposit (003)	3065±35	–23.9	1396–1302 BC (1σ) 1420–1220 BC (2σ)
SUERC-37231	Alder charcoal from single fill (064) of trough (024)	3055±35	–26.4	1390–1293 BC (1σ) 1415–1215 BC (2σ)
SUERC-37232	Alder charcoal from basal fill (034) of trough (021)	3565±35	–26.5	1972–1832 BC (1σ) 2023–1776 BC (2σ)
SUERC-37233	Alder charcoal from basal fill (039) of trough (019)	3970±35	–26.5	2566–2464 BC (1σ) 2577–2348 BC (2σ)
SUERC-37234	Alder charcoal from upper fill (015) of trough (008)	3365±35	–26.5	1731–1616 BC (1σ) 1743–1535 BC (2σ)
Ballinorig West 2				
SUERC-37238	Alder charcoal from middle fill (204) of inner enclosing ditch (003)	1295±35	–24.4	AD 670–768 (1σ) AD 655–779 (2σ)
SUERC-37239	Hazel charcoal from lower fill (270) of sink-hole (291)	3475±35	–27.1	1877–1746 BC (1σ) 1890–1692 BC (2σ)
SUERC-37240	Alder charcoal from basal fill (512) of trough (008)	2905±35	–27.1	1188–1020 BC (1σ) 1257–999 BC (2σ)
SUERC-37241	Hazel charcoal from middle fill (118) of sink-hole (292)	3070±35	–26.3	1400–1309 BC (1σ) 1424–1261 BC (2σ)
SUERC-37242	Hazel charcoal from middle fill (141) of the recut inner enclosing ditch (439)	1080±35	–27.4	AD 899–1012 (1σ) AD 893–1019 (2σ)
Ballinorig West 3				
SUERC-37086	Cremated human bone from single fill (003) of urned burial (086)	3520±30	–24.8	1894–1775 BC (1σ) 1928–1752 BC (2σ)
SUERC-37224	Charred oat grain from basal fill (074) of cereal-drying kiln (051)	1265±35	–23.6	AD 686–774 (1σ) AD 665–866 (2σ)
Ballinorig West 4				
SUERC-37089	Cremated human bone from bone deposit (626) within fill (183) of ring-ditch (522)	2100±30	–22.4	170–70 BC (1σ) 198–46 BC (2σ)
SUERC-37090	Cremated human bone from bone deposit (737) within fill (523) of ring-ditch (522)	2110±30	–22.1	181–61 BC (1σ) 336–47 BC (2σ)
SUERC-37091	Cremated human bone from token deposit (767)	2095±25	–25.8	166–60 BC (1σ) 191–47 BC (2σ)
SUERC-37092	Cremated human bone from bone deposit (584) within upper fill (193) of cremation pit burial (581)	2140±30	–22.8	346–111 BC (1σ) 353–56 BC (2σ)
SUERC-37096	Cremated human bone from upper fill (187) of cremation pit burial (548)	2145±30	–23.4	348–115 BC (1σ) 355–57 BC (2σ)
SUERC-37243	Oak charcoal from upper fill (410) of possible metal-working hearth (010)	2090±35	–24.1	166–54 BC (1σ) 202–2 BC (2σ)
SUERC-37244	Blackthorn charcoal from basal fill (534) of rake-out pit (535) of limekiln (793)	145±35	–27.5	AD 1674–1942 (1σ) AD 1667–1950 (2σ)

Lab code	Dated material and context	Years BP	δ^{13}C ‰	Calibrated date range
SUERC-37248	Hazel charcoal from basal fill (488) of pit (489)	2455±35	−25.5	748–417 BC (1σ) 756–411 BC (2σ)
SUERC-37249	Charred barley grain from basal fill (679) of rake-out pit (617) of shaft furnace (561)	1595±35	−23.5	AD 423–533 (1σ) AD 396–547 (2σ)
SUERC-37250	Hazel charcoal from middle fill (403) of hearth (404)	1715±35	−27	AD 259–383 (1σ) AD 245–406 (2σ)
SUERC-37251	Alder charcoal from basal fill (682) of charcoal-production pit (681)	2260±35	−25.6	390–234 BC (1σ) 397–207 BC (2σ)
SUERC-37252	Charred barley grain from lower fill (736) of fire-pit (653), part of cereal-drying kiln (654)	1580±35	−23.9	AD 432–535 (1σ) AD 410–559 (2σ)
SUERC-37253	Alder charcoal from single fill (276) of pit (557)	2850±35	−26.5	1056–933 BC (1σ) 1124– 918 BC (2σ)
Ballynabrennagh Lower 1				
SUERC-37254	Hazel nutshell from basal fill (024) of pit (013)	2120±35	−25.7	199–94 BC (1σ) 350–45 BC (2σ)
SUERC-37258	Hazel nutshell from single fill (043) of pit (030)	2140±35	−25.1	346–111 BC (1σ) 355–53 BC (2σ)
SUERC-37259	Alder charcoal from single fill (060) of pit (061)	3885±35	−26.0	2458–2311 BC (1σ) 2471–2213 BC (2σ)
Caherleheen 1				
SUERC-37260	Oak charcoal from burnt spread deposit (004)	4050±35	−24.4	2828–2492 BC (1σ) 2840–2473 BC (2σ)
Camp 1				
SUERC-37261	Alder charcoal from upper fill (035) of trough (004)	2635±35	−25.2	826–792 BC (1σ) 895–770 BC (2σ)
SUERC-37262	Alder charcoal from burnt mound deposit (016)	2945±35	−24.1	1258–1114 BC (1σ) 1289–1026 BC (2σ)
SUERC-37263	Alder charcoal from single fill (034) of pit (033)	3060±35	−23.9	1392–1298 BC (1σ) 1417–1217 BC (2σ)
Camp 2				
SUERC-37264	Alder charcoal from basal deposit (006) of burnt mound	3675±35	−26.1	2134–1981 BC (1σ) 2192–1952 BC (2σ)
SUERC-37268	Blackthorn charcoal from upper deposit (008) of burnt mound	2895±35	−26.3	1127–1014 BC (1σ) 1249–949 BC (2σ)
Camp 4				
SUERC-37269	Hazel charcoal from basal fill (007) of pit (003)	3890±35	−25.2	2461–2341 BC (1σ) 2471–2235 BC (2σ)
Camp 5				
SUERC-37270	Alder charcoal from burnt mound deposit (004)	2840±30	−28.3	1044–936 BC (1σ) 1114–916 BC (2σ)
SUERC-38049	Waterlogged alder stake (053; Wood no. 4) from north-east corner of trough (005)	2610±35	−27.8	812–780 BC (1σ) 839–601 BC (2σ)
Clashedmond 1				
SUERC-37271	Charred barley grain from lower fill (088) of enclosing ditch (003)	2710±35	−24.1	896–823 BC (1σ) 919–805 BC (2σ)
SUERC-37272	Alder charcoal from single fill (052) of pit (051)	3060±35	−25.8	1392–1298 BC (1σ) 1417–1217 BC (2σ)

Lab code	Dated material and context	Years BP	δ^{13}C ‰	Calibrated date range
SUERC-37273	Hazel charcoal from single fill (043) of pit (044)	2905±35	–26.0	1188–1020 BC (1σ) 1257–999 BC (2σ)
Dromthacker 1				
SUERC-37274	Hazel charcoal from basal fill (010) of possible trough (008)	3465±30	–25.9	1877–1741 BC (1σ) 1883–1693 BC (2σ)
Dromthacker 2				
SUERC-37278	Charred oat grain from middle fill (005) of isolated hearth (003)	1500±35	–24.4	AD 441–646 (1σ) AD 436–643 (2σ)
Dromavally 1				
SUERC-37279	Willow charcoal from basal fill (031) of shallow hearth (008)	115±35	–26.7	AD 1689–1926 (1σ) AD 1679–1940 (2σ)
SUERC-37280	Indeterminate charcoal from basal fill (071) of Kiln 1 (084)	270±35	–25.7	AD 1524–1794 (1σ) AD 1492–1953 (2σ)
Dromavally 2				
SUERC-37281	Hazel charcoal from basal fill (011) of trough (010)	3780±30	–24.7	2282–2141 BC (1σ) 2336–2046 BC (2σ)
Gortbrack East 1				
SUERC-37282	Charred oat grain from basal fill (004) of charcoal-production pit (003)	1490±35	–24.8	AD 545–609 (1σ) AD 441–646 (2σ)
Gortbrack East 3				
SUERC-37283	Alder charcoal from basal fill (008) of pit (007)	3435±35	–25.9	1866–1688 BC (1σ) 1880–1641 BC (2σ)
Knockawaddra Middle 1				
SUERC-37284	Alder charcoal from basal fill (028) of trough (027)	3300±35	–25.1	1617–1527 BC (1σ) 1678–1499 BC (2σ)
Knockawaddra Middle 2				
SUERC-37288	Willow charcoal from single fill (009) of post-hole (030) (Structure 1)	2820±35	–25.0	1011–921 BC (1σ) 1114–896 BC (2σ)
SUERC-37289	Hazel charcoal from post-pipe fill (047) of post-hole (097) (Structure 2)	1490±35	–26.0	AD 545–609 (1σ) AD 441–646 (2σ)
SUERC-37290	Alder charcoal from single fill (276) of post-hole (279) (Structure 3)	2895±30	–26.2	1123–1023 BC (1σ) 1211–981 BC (2σ)
Knockawaddra West 1				
SUERC-37291	Blackthorn charcoal from single fill (032) of stake-hole (033)	2875±35	–26.2	1116–1006 BC (1σ) 1193–930 BC (2σ)
Knockawaddra West 2				
SUERC-37292	Alder charcoal from basal fill (020) of sink-hole (015)	3215±35	–26.4	1512–1444 BC (1σ) 1605–1415 BC (2σ)
Lismore 1				
SUERC-37293	Charred oat grain from basal fill (055) of limekiln (045)	95±35	–23.2	AD 1695–1918 (1σ) AD 1681–1938 (2σ)
Lismore 2				
SUERC-37294	Alder charcoal from secondary fill (034) of pit (025)	2675±35	–27.5	891–801 BC (1σ) 900–797 BC (2σ)

Lab code	Dated material and context	Years BP	δ^{13}C ‰	Calibrated date range
SUERC-37298	Hazel charcoal from basal fill (024) of trough (017)	2730±35	–25.2	904–833 BC (1σ) 971–809 BC (2σ)
Manor East 1				
SUERC-37087	Cremated human bone from basal fill (139) of cremation pit burial (108)	3115±30	–24.6	1431–1323 BC (1σ) 1450–1309 BC (2σ)
SUERC-37088	Cremated human bone from fill (966) of cremation pit burial (965)	3100±30	–24.0	1420–1318 BC (1σ) 1436–1296 BC (2σ)
SUERC-37320	Hazel charcoal from single fill (116) of pit (117)	2175±35	–26.8	354–176 BC (1σ) 370–115 BC (2σ)
SUERC-37321	Hazel charcoal from single fill (215) of post-hole (214)	4955±35	–25.9	3775–3695 BC (1σ) 3798–3653 BC (2σ)
SUERC-37322	Alder charcoal from single fill (457) of pit (458)	3125±35	–27.3	1441–1322 BC (1σ) 1493–1311 BC (2σ)
SUERC-37323	Oak charcoal from single fill (730) of pit (729)	5165±35	–24.2	4037–3955 BC (1σ) 4045–3817 BC (2σ)
SUERC-37324	Charred barley grain from basal fill (710) of pit (711)	1490±35	–24.3	AD 545–609 (1σ) AD 441–646 (2σ)
SUERC-37328	Oak charcoal from basal fill (868) of post-hole (870)	2630±35	–23.9	822–791 BC (1σ) 894–767 BC (2σ)
SUERC-37329	Alder charcoal from basal fill (706) of pit (705)	1965±35	–26.6	AD 1–75 (1σ) 44 BC–AD 122 (2σ)
Manor East 2				
SUERC-37299	Hazel nutshell from single fill (089) of pit (088)	2140±35	–23.4	346–111 BC (1σ) 355–53 BC (2σ)
Manor East 4				
UBA-17592	Alder wood from peat (004) from infilled water channel	510±23	–30.1	AD 1413–1431 (1σ) AD 1403–1441 (2σ)
UBA-18057	Sample of peat (004) from top of soil monolith from infilled water channel, at a depth of 0.3 m	1136±24	–29.3	AD 887–966 (1σ) AD 784–983 (2σ)
UBA-18058	Sample of peat (004) from base of soil monolith from infilled water channel, at a depth of 1.06 m	1776±25	–28.4	AD 225–323 (1σ) AD 139–337 (2σ)
UBA-18362	Hazel charcoal from upper fill (017) of hearth (006)	3543±29	–25.1	1936–1783 BC (1σ) 1955–1770 BC (2σ)
UBA-18517	Sample of peat (004) from soil monolith from infilled water channel, at a depth of 0.81 m	1424±38	–26.2	AD 604–652 (1σ) AD 566–663 (2σ)
UBA-18518	Alder wood from peat (004) from infilled water channel	458±30	–29.7	AD 1427–1449 (1σ) AD 1413–1469 (2σ)
Manor East 7				
UBA-17593	Hazel wood from peat (005) from infilled water channel	1549±27	–32.0	AD 436–553 (1σ) AD 428–571 (2σ)
UBA-18055	Sample of peat 0.1 m from the top of peat deposit (005/007)	1679±26	–27.9	AD 343–407 (1σ) AD 259–423 (2σ)
UBA-18056	Sample of peat from base of peat deposit (005/007)	2116±27	–28.9	191–105 BC (1σ) 203–51 BC (2σ)

Bibliography

Ainsworth, S 2009 *Prehistoric Embanked Pit Alignments on Ebberston Low Moor.* English Heritage, York.

Allen, D 1994 'Hot water and plenty of it', *Archaeology Ireland*, Vol. 8, No. 1, 8–9.

Anderson, E, Harrison, S, Passmore, D G, Mighall, T M & Wathan, S 2004 'Late Quaternary river terrace development in the Macgillycuddy's Reeks, southwest Ireland', *Quaternary Science Reviews*, Vol. 23, 1785–801.

Atkins (compilers) 2008 *N22 Tralee Bypass/Tralee to Bealagrellagh: environmental impact statement* (4 vols). Kerry County Council (http://ciarrai.ie/en/allservices/roads/n22traleebypass/, accessed May 2019).

Baker, L, Bolger, T & Clark, L 2015 'Busherstown 8: Middle/Late Bronze Age to Early Iron Age *fulacht fiadh*', *in* T Bolger, C Moloney & D Shiels (eds), *A Journey Along the Carlow Corridor. The archaeology of the M9 Carlow Bypass*, 40–1. NRA Scheme Monographs 16. National Roads Authority, Dublin.

Bamforth, M, Gray, L & Taylor, M 2009 *Waterlogged Wood Analysis Report; A4/A5 corridor improvements (Dungannon–Ballygawley).* Unpublished report to the Northern Ireland Environment Agency on behalf of L-P Archaeology.

Barfield, L & Hodder, M 1987 'Burnt mounds as saunas and the prehistory of bathing', *Antiquity*, Vol. 61, 370–9.

Barnosky, C W 1988 'A late-glacial and post-glacial pollen record from the Dingle Peninsula, County Kerry', *Proceedings of the Royal Irish Academy*, Vol. 88B, 23–37.

Barrington, T J 1999 *Discovering Kerry* (reprinted 2004). Collins Press, Cork.

Barry, T B 1981 'Archaeological excavations at Dunbeg Promontory Fort, County Kerry, 1977', *Proceedings of the Royal Irish Academy*, Vol. 81C, 295–329.

Bartlett, T 2011 'Liscahane', *in* I Bennett (ed.), *Excavations 2008: summary accounts of archaeological excavations in Ireland*, 188. Wordwell, Dublin.

Bartlett, T, Hession, J & Long, P 2010 *N22 Tralee Bypass/Tralee to Bealagrellagh, Co. Kerry. Archaeological services contract, Stage (i) and Stage (ii)—standard test excavation and pre-excavation services (including townland boundary survey and architectural/built heritage survey). Final test excavation report, under Ministerial Directions Number A056 (E4149).* Unpublished report to Kerry County Council on behalf of Headland Archaeology (Ireland) Ltd.

Becker, K 2009 'Iron Age Ireland—finding an invisible people', *in* G Cooney, K Becker, J Coles, M Ryan & S Sievers (eds), *Relics of Old Decency: archaeological studies in later prehistory: festschrift for Barry Raftery*, 351–61. Wordwell, Dublin.

Becker, K 2012 'Redefining the Irish Iron Age', *in* C Corlett & M Potterton (eds), *Life and Death in Iron Age Ireland*, 1–14. Wordwell, Dublin.

Becker, K, Ó Néill, J & O'Flynn, L 2008a 'Iron Age Ireland: finding an invisible people', *Archaeology Ireland*, Vol. 22, No. 3, 5–8.

Becker, K, Ó Néill, J & O'Flynn, L 2008b *Iron Age Ireland: finding an invisible people.* University College Dublin (https://www.ucd.ie/t4cms/iron_age_ireland_project_16365_pilotweb.pdf, accessed May 2019).

Bennett, I 1987 'The archaeology of County Kerry', *Archaeology Ireland*, Vol. 1, No. 2, 48–51.

Bennett, I 1996 'Leamnaguila', *in* I Bennett (ed.), *Excavations 1995: summary accounts of archaeological excavations in Ireland*, 42. Wordwell, Bray.

Bick, D 1984 'Limekiln on the Gloucestershire–Herefordshire border', *Industrial Archaeology Review*, Vol. 7, 85–93.

Binchy, D A 1941 *Críth Gablach.* The Stationery Office, Dublin.

Bolger, T 2011 'Status, inheritance and land tenure: some thoughts on early medieval settlement in the light of recent archaeological excavations', *in* C Corlett & M Potterton (eds), *Settlement in Early Medieval Ireland in the Light of Recent Archaeological Excavations*, 1–10. Wordwell, Dublin.

Bolger, T 2014 'The metal-working evidence from Kilgobbin, Co. Dublin', *in* C Corlett & M Potterton (eds), *The Church in Early Medieval Ireland in the Light of Recent Archaeological Excavations*, 1–12. Wordwell, Dublin.

Bonsall, J 2011 *Novel Methods Testing 2011: Ballingowan 4 & Ballinorig West 2, N22 Tralee Bypass, County Kerry. Archaeological geophysical survey (11R33).* Unpublished report to the National Roads Authority as part of an NRA-funded research fellowship at the University of Bradford.

Boyd, W E 1988 'Methodological problems in the analysis of fossil non-artifactual wood assemblages from archaeological sites', *Journal of Archaeological Science*, Vol. 15, 603–19.

Bradley, J 1986 'The medieval towns of Kerry', *North Munster Antiquarian Journal*, Vol. 28, 28–39.

Bradley, J, Halpin, A & King, H 1985 *The Urban Archaeological Survey Part XIV—County Kerry.* Unpublished report for the Office of Public Works.

Bradshaw, R W & Browne, P 1987 'Changing patterns in *Pinus sylvestris* in Ireland', *Journal of Biogeography*, Vol. 14, 237–48.

Brindley, A L 2007 *The Dating of Food Vessels and Urns in Ireland.* Bronze Age Studies 7. NUI Galway, Galway.

Brindley, A L & Lanting, J 1990 'The dating of *fulachta fiadh*', *in* V Buckley (ed.), *Burnt Offerings: international contributions to burnt mound archaeology*, 55–6. Wordwell, Bray.

Brindley, A L, Lanting, J N & Mook, W G 1990 'Radiocarbon dates from Irish fulachta fiadh and other burnt mounds', *Journal of Irish Archaeology*, Vol. 5 [1989/90], 25–33.

Bronk Ramsey, C, Dee, M, Lee, S, Nakagawa, T & Staff, R 2010 'Developments in the calibration and modelling of radiocarbon dates', *Radiocarbon*, Vol. 52, No. 3, 953–61.

Brown, T G, Davis, S R, Hatton, J, O'Brien, C, Reilly, F, Taylor, K, Dennehy, E, O'Donnell, L, Birmingham, N, Mighall, T M, Timpany, S, Tetlow, E, Wheeler, J & Wynne, S 2016 'The environmental context and function of burnt-mounds: palaeoenvironmental studies of Irish fulacht fiadh', *Proceedings of the Prehistoric Society*, Vol. 82, 259–90.

Cahill Wilson, J (ed.) 2014 *Late Iron Age and 'Roman' Ireland*. Discovery Programme Reports 8. Wordwell, Dublin.

Carlin, N 2006 *M3 Research Report on Bronze Age Houses in Ireland*. Unpublished report to the National Roads Authority on behalf of Archaeological Consultancy Services Ltd.

Carlin, N 2008 'Ironworking and production', *in* N Carlin, L Clarke & F Walsh, *The Archaeology of Life and Death in the Boyne Floodplain: the linear landscape of the M4*, 87–112. NRA Scheme Monographs 2. National Roads Authority, Dublin.

Carlin, N & Brück, J 2012 'Searching for the Chalcolithic: continuity and change in the Irish Final Neolithic/Early Bronze Age', *in* M Allen, A Sheridan & D McOmish (eds), *The British Chalcolithic: people, place and polity in the later third millennium*, 193–210. Prehistoric Society/Oxbow, Oxford.

Charles-Edwards, T 1972 'Kinship, status and the origins of the hide', *Past and Present*, Vol. 56, 3–33.

Charles-Edwards, T 1992 'The pastoral role of the church in early Irish laws', *in* J Blair & R Sharpe (eds), *Pastoral Care Before the Parish*, 63–109. Leicester University Press, Leicester.

Charman, D J 2010 'Centennial climate variability in the British Isles during the mid–late Holocene', *Quaternary Science Reviews*, Vol. 29, 1539–54.

Clapham, A R, Tutin, T G & Warburg, E F 1962 *Flora of the British Isles* (2nd edn). Cambridge University Press, Cambridge.

Clark, L 2010 *N9/N10 Kilcullen to Waterford Scheme: Phase 3, Kilcullen to Carlow. Archaeological services contract no. 5—resolution, Kilcullen to Moone and Athy link road. Final report on archaeological investigations at Site E2858, in the townland of Mullamast, Co. Kildare.* Report to Kildare County Council on behalf of Headland Archaeology (Ireland) Ltd. TII Digital Heritage Collections, Digital Repository of Ireland (https://doi.org/10.7486/DRI.6w92ht34k, accessed May 2019).

Clark, L & Long, P 2011 *N7 Limerick to Nenagh High Quality Dual Carriageway. Archaeological resolution project. Sallymount Site 1, E3420, Co. Limerick, final excavation report.* Report to Limerick County Council on behalf of Headland Archaeology (Ireland) Ltd. TII Digital Heritage Collections, Digital Repository of Ireland (https://doi.org/10.7486/DRI.66839j81x, accessed May 2019).

Cleary, K 2005 'Skeletons in the closet: the dead among the living on Irish Bronze Age settlements', *Journal of Irish Archaeology*, Vol. 14, 23–42.

Cleary, R, McClatchie, M & McKeown, S A 2008 'Excavations of an early medieval settlement and other sites at Dromthacker, Tralee, Co. Kerry', *Proceedings of the Royal Irish Academy*, Vol. 108C, 19–64.

Cole, E E & Mitchell, F J G 2003 'Human impact on the Irish landscape during the late Holocene inferred from palynological studies at three peatland sites', *The Holocene*, Vol. 13, No. 4, 507–15.

Collins, T 2000 'Rockfield', *in* I Bennett (ed.), *Excavations 1999: summary accounts of archaeological excavations in Ireland*, 115. Wordwell, Bray.

Collins, T & Lynch, L 2001 'Prehistoric burial and ritual in southwest Ireland', *Antiquity*, Vol. 75, 493–4.

Connell, K H 1962 'The potato in Ireland', *Past & Present*, Vol. 23, 57 71.

Connolly, M 1999 *Discovering the Neolithic in County Kerry: a passage tomb at Ballycarty*. Wordwell, Bray.

Connolly, M 2002 'Rockfield', *in* I Bennett (ed.), *Excavations 2000: summary accounts of archaeological excavations in Ireland*, 148. Wordwell, Bray.

Connolly, M 2003 'Gortatlea', *in* I Bennett (ed.), *Excavations 2001: summary accounts of archaeological excavations in Ireland*, 166–7. Wordwell, Bray.

Connolly, M 2008 *The Prehistoric Settlement of the Lee Valley, County Kerry: a landscape perspective*. Unpublished PhD thesis, University College Cork, Cork.

Connolly, M 2010 'Variable rate deposits: Beaker and Early Bronze Age finds from Tralee', *Kerry Archaeological Magazine*, Issue 20, 12–13.

Connolly, M 2012 'A parable of parabolas: graveyards with evidence for early enclosure', *in* M Connolly (ed.), *The Unquiet Grave: the development of Kerry's burial grounds through the ages*, 146–80. Kerry County Council, Tralee.

Connolly, M 2015 'Killaclohane, Co. Kerry' (https://excavations.ie/report/2015/Kerry/0024117, accessed January 2019).

Connolly, M 2017 'Killaclohane II, Co. Kerry' (https://excavations.ie/report/2015/Kerry/0024117, accessed January 2019).

Connolly, M 2018 'Killaclohane II, Co. Kerry' (https://excavations.ie/report/2015/Kerry/0024117, accessed January 2019).

Cooney, G 2000 *Landscapes of Neolithic Ireland*. Routledge, London.

Cooney, G & Grogan, E 1999 *Irish Prehistory: a social perspective*. Wordwell, Bray.

Cooney, G & Mandal, S 1998 *The Irish Stone Axe Project*, Monograph 1. Wordwell, Bray.

Cooney, G, Bayliss, A, Healy, F, Whittle, A, Danaher, E, Cagney, L, Mallory, J, Smyth, J, Kador, T & O'Sullivan, M 2011 'Ireland', *in* A Whittle, F Healy & A Bayliss (eds), *Gathering Time: dating the early Neolithic enclosures of southern Britain and Ireland*, 562–669. Oxbow Books, Oxford.

Cooney, T 1996 'Vegetation changes associated with Late-Neolithic copper mining in Killarney', *in* C Delaney & P Coxon (eds), *Central Kerry Field Guide*, No. 20, 28–32. Irish Association for Quaternary Studies, Dublin.

Cosham, B 2012 'Appendix 13—Visual assessment of archaeometallurgical material from E4305, Ballinorig West 4, Co. Kerry', *in* S Hourihan, *N22 Tralee Bypass/Tralee to Bealagrellagh, Co. Kerry. Archaeological services contract, stage (iii)—excavation. Final excavation report for Ballinorig West 4 in the townland of Ballinorig West, Co. Kerry.* Report to Kerry County Council on behalf of Rubicon Heritage Services Ltd. TII Digital Heritage Collections, Digital Repository of Ireland (https://doi.org/10.7486/DRI.cr571k74v, accessed May 2019).

Cox, R C & Gould, M H 1998 *Civil Engineering Heritage Ireland*. Thomas Telford Publications, London.

Coyne, F 1999a *Archaeological Excavation Report of Cloghermore KCC6.5 (99E0130).* Unpublished excavation report for Kerry County Council on behalf of Aegis Archaeology.

Coyne, F 1999b *Archaeological Excavation Report of Cloghermore (99E0130ext).* Unpublished excavation report for Kerry County Council on behalf of Aegis Archaeology.

Coyne, F 2002 'Gortatlea and Flemby', *in* I Bennett (ed.), *Excavations 2000: summary accounts of archaeological excavations in Ireland*, 146. Wordwell, Bray.

Coyne, F 2003 'Western Pap, Derrynafinnia', *in* I Bennett (ed.), *Excavations 2001: summary accounts of archaeological excavations in Ireland*, 164. Wordwell, Bray.

Coyne, F 2011 'Abbey Carpark, Tralee', *in* I Bennett (ed.), *Excavations 2008: summary accounts of archaeological excavations in Ireland*, 191–2. Wordwell, Dublin.

Crane, C P 1907 *Kerry*. Methuen & Co., London.

Crew, P & Rehren, T 2002 'Appendix 1: High-temperature workshop residues from Tara: iron, bronze and glass', *in* H Roche, *Excavations at Ráith na Rig, Tara, Co. Meath, 1997*, 83–102. Discovery Programme Reports 6. Royal Irish Academy, Dublin.

Cropper, C 2012 'Appendix 11—Glass beads from Ballinorig West 4, Co. Kerry', *in* S Hourihan, *N22 Tralee Bypass/Tralee to Bealagrellagh, Co. Kerry. Archaeological services contract, stage (iii)—excavation. Final excavation report for Ballinorig West 4 in the townland of Ballinorig West, Co. Kerry.* Report to Kerry County Council on behalf of Rubicon Heritage Services Ltd. TII Digital Heritage Collections, Digital Repository of Ireland (https://doi.org/10.7486/DRI.cr571k74v, accessed May 2019).

Cuppage, J & Bennett, I 1986 *Archaeological Survey of the Dingle Peninsula: a description of the field antiquities of the barony of Corca Dhuibhne from the Mesolithic period to the 17th century AD. Suirbhé seandálaíochta Chorca Dhuibhne.* Oidhreacht Chorca Dhuibhne, Ballyferriter.

Delaney, S 2006 'Site 121, Balriggan 1, Balriggan', *in* I Bennett (ed.), *Excavations 2003: summary accounts of archaeological excavations in Ireland*, 325–8. Wordwell, Bray.

Delaney, S 2012 *N22 Tralee Bypass/Tralee to Bealagrellagh: Manor East 4 (E4328) stage IV excavation report*. Report to Kerry County Council on behalf of Irish Archaeological Consultancy Ltd. TII Digital Heritage Collections, Digital Repository of Ireland (https://doi.org/10.7486/DRI.hx12b1027, accessed May 2019).

Delaney, S, Bayley, D, Lyne, E, McNamara, S, Nunan, J & Molloy, K 2012a *Borderlands: archaeological investigations along the route of the M18 Gort to Crusheen road scheme*. NRA Scheme Monographs 9. National Roads Authority, Dublin.

Delaney, S, Lyne, E & Nunan, J 2012b 'Crops, iron and water', *in* S Delaney, D Bayley, E Lyne, S McNamara, J Nunan & K Molloy, *Borderlands: archaeological investigations along the route of the M18 Gort to Crusheen road scheme*, 139–59. NRA Scheme Monographs 9. National Roads Authority, Dublin.

Delaney, S, McKeon, J & McNamara, S 2012c 'Two Iron Age ring-ditches in Ballyboy, Co. Galway', *in* C Corlett & M Potterton (eds), *Life and Death in Iron Age Ireland*, 93–104. Wordwell, Dublin.

Dillon, M & Tierney, J 2011 'Charcoal and other plant remains', *in* F Delaney and J Tierney, *In the Lowlands of South Galway. Archaeological excavations on the N18 Oranmore to Gort National Road Scheme*, 195–200. NRA Scheme Monographs 7. National Roads Authority, Dublin.

Dodson, J R 1990 'The Holocene vegetation of a prehistorically inhabited valley, Dingle Peninsula, Co. Kerry', *Proceedings of the Royal Irish Academy*, Vol. 90B, 151–74.

Doody, M 2000 'Bronze Age houses in Ireland', *in* A Desmond, G Johnson, M McCarthy, J Sheehan & E Shee Twohig (eds), *New Agendas in Irish Prehistory: papers in commemoration of Liz Anderson*, 135–59. Wordwell, Bray.

Dowd, M 2004 'Caherweesheen, Tralee', *in* I Bennett (ed.), *Excavations 2002: summary accounts of archaeological excavations in Ireland*, 224. Wordwell, Bray.

Dowd, M & Carden, R 2016 'First evidence of a Late Upper Palaeolithic human presence in Ireland', *Quaternary Science Reviews*, Vol. 139, 158–63.

Dowd, M & Fairburn, N 2005 'Excavations at Farranastack, Co. Kerry: evidence for the use of shaft furnaces in medieval iron production', *Journal of Irish Archaeology*, Vol. 14, 115–21.

Dunne, L 1998 'Mounthawk 1, Tralee', *in* I Bennett (ed.), *Excavations 1997: summary accounts of archaeological excavations in Ireland*, 87–8. Wordwell, Bray.

Dunne, L 1999 'Late Iron Age crematoria at Ballyvelly, Tralee', *Archaeology Ireland*, Vol. 13, No. 2, 10–11.

Dunne, L 2002 'Manor West, Tralee', *in* I Bennett (ed.), *Excavations 2000: summary accounts of archaeological excavations in Ireland*, 153–5. Wordwell, Bray.

Dunne, L 2003a 'Ballybunnion', *in* I Bennett (ed.), *Excavations 2001: summary accounts of archaeological excavations in Ireland*, 160. Wordwell, Bray.

Dunne, L 2003b 'Ardagh', *in* I Bennett (ed.), *Excavations 2001: summary accounts of archaeological excavations in Ireland*, 159. Wordwell, Bray.

Dunne, L & Bartlett, T 2009 'Knockanacuig/Lohercannan', *in* I Bennett (ed.), *Excavations 2006: summary accounts of archaeological excavations in Ireland*, 226–7. Wordwell, Dublin.

Dunne, L & Buckley, K 2009 'Carrigeendaniel, Tralee', *in* I Bennett (ed.), *Excavations 2006: summary accounts of archaeological excavations in Ireland*, 231. Wordwell, Dublin.

Dunne, L & Buckley, K 2010 'Ballingowan/Ratass', *in* I Bennett (ed.), *Excavations 2007: summary accounts of archaeological excavations in Ireland*, 169–70. Wordwell, Dublin.

Dunne, L & Buckley, K 2011 'Caherleaheen', *in* I Bennett (ed.), *Excavations 2008: summary accounts of archaeological excavations in Ireland*, 181–2. Wordwell, Dublin.

Dunne, L & Kiely, J 2005 'Recent archaeological excavations in the Tralee area', *in* M Connolly (ed.), *Past Kingdoms: recent archaeological research, survey & excavation in Co. Kerry*, 39–64. The Heritage Council and Kerry County Council, Kerry.

Edwards, N 1990 *The Archaeology of Early Medieval Ireland*. Batsford, London.

Eogan, G 1964 'The Later Bronze Age in Ireland in the light of recent research', *Proceedings of the Prehistoric Society*, Vol. 30, 268–351.

Eogan, G 1974 'Report on the excavations of some passage graves, unprotected inhumation burials and a settlement site at Knowth, Co. Meath', *Proceedings of the Royal Irish Academy*, Vol. 74C, 11–113.

Eogan, G 1983 *The Hoards of the Irish Later Bronze Age*. University College Dublin, Dublin.
Eogan, J 2007 'Ring-ditch', *Seanda*, Issue 2, 56.
Eogan, J 2011 'The later prehistory of the Lower Suir Valley (2400 BC–AD 400)', *in* J Eogan & E Shee Twohig (eds), *Cois tSiúire—nine thousand years of human activity in the Lower Suir Valley*, 251–81. NRA Scheme Monographs 8. National Roads Authority, Dublin.
Eogan, J 2012 'An Iron Age penannular ring-ditch at Ballybronoge South, Co. Limerick', *in* C Corlett & M Potterton (eds), *Life and Death in Iron Age Ireland in the Light of Recent Archaeological Excavations*, 105–19. Wordwell, Dublin.
Eogan, J & Shee Twohig, E (eds) 2011 *Cois tSiúire—nine thousand years of human activity in the Lower Suir Valley.* NRA Scheme Monographs 8. National Roads Authority, Dublin.
Evans, C & Knight, M 2001 'The "community of builders": the Barleycroft post alignments', *in* J Bruck (ed.), *Bronze Age Landscapes: tradition and transformation*, 83–98. Oxbow Books, Oxford.
Fairburn, N 2003a *Assessment of the Metallurgical Residues from the Archaeological Investigations at Ballydowny, Co. Kerry*. Unpublished report for Eachtra Archaeological Projects.
Fairburn, N 2003b *Report on Industrial Residues from Shandon, Co. Waterford.* Unpublished report for Eachtra Archaeological Projects.
Fanning, T 1977 'An ogham stone and cross-slab from Ratass Church, Tralee', *Journal of the Kerry Archaeological and Historical Society*, No. 10, 14–18.
Fanning, T 1981 'Excavation of an Early Christian cemetery and settlement at Reask, County Kerry', *Proceedings of the Royal Irish Academy*, Vol. 81C, 67–172.
Feehan, J 2003 *Farming in Ireland: history, heritage and environment.* University College Dublin, Dublin.
Fenton, A 1978 *The Northern Isles: Orkney and Shetland.* John Donald, Edinburgh.
Fleming, E (ed.) 2016 *The Home Place: an inventory of traditional rural architecture in north and east Kerry*. Kerry County Council, Tralee.
Gale, R & Cutler, D 2000 *Plants in Archaeology.* Westbury and Royal Botanic Gardens, Kew.
Gibson, A 1989 'Medieval corn drying kilns at Capo, Kincardineshire, and Abercairney, Perthshire', *Proceedings of the Society of Antiquaries of Scotland*, Vol. 118, 219–29.
Gibson, A 2002 *Prehistoric Pottery in Britain and Ireland.* Tempus, Stroud.
Gillespie, R F & Kerrigan, A 2012 *Of Troughs and Tuyères: the archaeology of the N5 Charlestown Bypass*. NRA Scheme Monographs 6. National Roads Authority, Dublin.
Ginn, V and Rathbone, S 2012 *Corrstown: a coastal community. Excavations of a Bronze Age village in Northern Ireland.* Oxbow Books, Oxford.
Griffith, R 1847–64 *General Valuation of Rateable Property in Ireland, 1847–1864* (http://www.askaboutireland.ie/griffith-valuation/index.xml, accessed November 2018).
Grogan, E 1996 'Neolithic houses in Ireland', *in* T Darvill & J Thomas (eds), *Neolithic Houses in Northwest Europe and Beyond; Neolithic Studies Group Seminar Papers 1*, 41–62. Oxbow Monograph 57. Oxbow Books, Oxford.
Grogan, E 2004 'Middle Bronze Age burial traditions in Ireland', *in* H Roche, E Grogan, J

Bradley, J Coles & B Raftery (eds), *From Megaliths to Metals: essays in honour of George Eogan*, 61–71. Oxbow Books, Oxford.

Grogan, E 2005 *The North Munster Project* (2 vols). Wordwell, Bray.

Grogan, E & Eogan, G 1987 'Lough Gur excavations by Seán P. Ó Ríordáin: further Neolithic and Beaker habitations on Knockadoon', *Proceedings of the Royal Irish Academy*, Vol. 87C, 299–506.

Grogan, E & Roche, H 2009a 'An assessment of Middle Bronze Age domestic pottery in Ireland', *in* G Cooney, K Becker, J Coles, M Ryan & S Sievers (eds), *Relics of Old Decency: archaeological studies in later prehistory: festschrift for Barry Raftery*, 127–36. Wordwell, Dublin.

Grogan, E & Roche, H 2009b 'The prehistoric pottery from the N8 Cashel to Mitchelstown Scheme', *in* M McQuade, B Molloy & C Moriarty (eds), *In the Shadow of the Galtees: archaeological excavations along the N8 Cashel to Mitchelstown road scheme*, 288–314. NRA Scheme Monographs 4. National Roads Authority, Dublin.

Grogan, E & Roche, H 2010 'Clay and fire: the development and distribution of pottery traditions in prehistoric Ireland', *in* M Stanley, E Danaher & J Eogan (eds), *Creative Minds. Proceedings of a public seminar on archaeological discoveries on national road schemes, August 2009*, 27–45. Archaeology and the National Roads Authority Monograph Series No. 7. National Roads Authority, Dublin.

Grogan, E & Roche, H 2011 'The prehistoric pottery assemblage', *in* M Tierney, H Leininger & J O'Dowd, *Archaeological Excavation of AR022 Kealgorm—final report*, 183–9. Report to Kerry County Council on behalf of the Archaeology Company. TII Digital Heritage Collections, Digital Repository of Ireland (https://doi.org/10.7486/DRI.vq28c332d, accessed May 2019).

Grogan, E, O'Donnell, L & Johnston, P 2007 *The Bronze Age Landscapes of the Pipeline to the West: an integrated archaeological and environmental assessment*. Wordwell, Dublin.

Harding, J 2003 *Desk Top Assessment of the Neolithic Monument Complex of Thornborough, North Yorkshire* (http://thornborough.ncl.ac.uk/desktop_assessment/desktop_pitals.htm, accessed September 2013).

Harrison, S 2010 *The Results of Geophysical Survey along the Route of the N22 Tralee Bypass/Tralee to Bealagrellagh Road Scheme, R0277*. Report to Kerry County Council on behalf of Headland Archaeology (Ireland) Ltd. TII Digital Heritage Collections, Digital Repository of Ireland (https://doi.org/10.7486/DRI.b564j760h, accessed May 2019).

Hartwell, B 1998 'The Ballynahatty Complex', *in* A Gibson & D Simpson (eds), *Prehistoric Ritual and Religion*, 32–44. Sutton, Stroud.

Hawkes, A 2018 *The Archaeology of Prehistoric Burnt Mounds in Ireland*. Archaeopress, Oxford.

Hegarty, L & Kiely, J 2019 'Glenatlucky 1—Early Bronze Age burial', *in* P Johnston & J Kiely (eds), *Hidden Voices: the archaeology of the M8 Fermoy–Mitchelstown motorway*, 75–7. TII Heritage 7. Transport Infrastructure Ireland, Dublin.

Hegarty, L, Long, P & Price, J 2011 'Ballyduff East 43—Fulachtaí fia', *in* J Eogan & E Shee Twohig (eds), *Cois tSiúire—nine thousand years of human activity in the Lower Suir Valley*, 21–4.

NRA Scheme Monographs 8. National Roads Authority, Dublin.

Hencken, J 1950 'Lagore Crannog: an Irish royal residence of the seventh to tenth centuries AD', *Proceedings of the Royal Irish Academy*, Vol. 53C, 1–247.

Henderson, J 2000 *The Science and Archaeology of Materials—an investigation of inorganic materials.* Routledge, London.

Herity, M 1982 'Irish decorated Neolithic pottery', *Proceedings of the Royal Irish Academy*, Vol. 82C, 247–404.

Hillman, G 1981 'Reconstructing crop husbandry practices from charred remains of plants', *in* R Mercer (ed.), *Farming Practice in British Prehistory*, 123–62. Edinburgh University Press, Edinburgh.

Horner, A 2007 'Ireland's time–space revolution: improvements to pre-Famine travel', *History Ireland*, Vol. 15, No. 5, 22–7.

Hull, G, Taylor, K, Anthony, S, Comber, M, Cramp, L, Ford, S & Keys, L 2006 'Archaeological sites on the route of the N21 Castleisland to Abbeyfeale road improvement scheme, Co. Kerry', *Journal of the Kerry Archaeological and Historical Society*, Vol. 6, 5–59.

Huttman, J P 1972 'The impact of land reform on agricultural production in Ireland', *Agricultural History*, Vol. 46, No. 3, 353–68.

Jeffrey, S 1991 'Burnt mounds, fulling and early textiles?', *in* M A Hodder & L Barfield (eds), *Burnt Mounds and Hot Stone Technology: papers from the Second International Burnt Mound Conference, Sandwell, 12th–14th October 1990*, 97–108. Sandwell Metropolitan Borough Council, Sandwell.

Jessen, K 1949 'Studies in Late Quaternary deposits and flora-history of Ireland', *Proceedings of the Royal Irish Academy*, Vol. 52B, 85–290.

Johnston, P 2003 'Analysis of the plant remains', *in* R Tobin, *Corbally 2001/2002 (Licence No. 01E0299), Stratigraphic Report; kilns and associated features.* Unpublished report for Margaret Gowen and Co. Ltd.

Johnston, P 2007 'Analysis of charred plant remains', *in* E Grogan, L O'Donnell & P Johnston (eds), *The Bronze Age Landscapes of the Pipeline to the West: an integrated archaeological and environmental assessment*, 70–9. Wordwell, Dublin.

Joubert, S 2010 *N22 Tralee Bypass/Tralee to Bealagrellagh, Co. Kerry. Report on archaeological testing at Manor East and Camp, Tralee, Co. Kerry. Excavation report, under Ministerial Directions Number A056 (E4186).* Unpublished report to Kerry County Council on behalf of the National Roads Authority.

Kavanagh, R 1973 'The encrusted urn in Ireland', *Proceedings of the Royal Irish Academy*, Vol. 73C, 507–617.

Kelly, F 1997 *Early Irish Farming.* Dundalgan Press, Dundalk.

Kenny, N 2010 'Charcoal production in medieval Ireland', *in* M Stanley, E Danaher & J Eogan (eds), *Creative Minds. Proceedings of a public seminar on archaeological discoveries on national road schemes, August 2009*, 99–115. Archaeology and the National Roads Authority Monograph Series No. 7. National Roads Authority, Dublin.

Kerr, T R 2007 *Early Christian Settlement in Northwest Ulster.* British Archaeological Reports, British Series 430. Oxford.

Kiely, J 2000 'Cloghers, Tralee', *in* I Bennett (ed.), *Excavations 1998: summary accounts of archaeological excavations in Ireland*, 97. Wordwell, Bray.

Kiely, J 2002 'Cloghers, Tralee', *in* I Bennett (ed.), *Excavations 2000: summary accounts of archaeological excavations in Ireland*, 149. Wordwell, Bray.

Kiely, J 2003 'A Neolithic house at Cloghers, Co. Kerry', *in* I Armit, E Murphy, E Nelis & D Simpson (eds), *Neolithic Settlement in Ireland and Western Britain*, 182–7. Oxbow Books, Oxford.

Kiely, J 2004 'Ballydowny, Killarney', *in* I Bennett (ed.), *Excavations 2002: summary accounts of archaeological excavations in Ireland*, 218–19. Wordwell, Bray.

Kiely, J & O'Callaghan, N 2010 *Archaeological Excavation Report 02E0055—Ballydowny, Killarney, Co. Kerry: fulachta fiadh, ring-ditch, iron/copper working areas.* Unpublished report to Sundays Well Properties, Killarney, on behalf of Eachtra Archaeological Projects.

Kieran, E & Hayden, B 2010 *Report on the Results of Underwater Archaeological Survey on the N22 Tralee Bypass/Tralee to Bealagrellagh Road Scheme.* Unpublished report to Kerry County Council on behalf of Headland Archaeology (Ireland) Ltd.

Knox, H T 1907 'Notes on gig-mills and drying kilns near Ballyhaunis, County Mayo', *Proceedings of the Royal Irish Academy*, Vol. 26C, 265–74.

Linnane, S J & Kinsella, J 2009 'Military lords and defensive beginnings: a preliminary assessment of the social role of an impressive rath at Baronstown', *in* M B Deevy & D Murphy (eds), *Places Along the Way: first findings on the M3*, 101–22. NRA Scheme Monographs 5. National Roads Authority, Dublin.

Little, D J, Mitchell, F J G, von Engelbrechten, S & Farrell, E P 1996 'Assessment of the impact of past disturbance and prehistoric *Pinus sylvestris* on vegetation dynamics and soil development in Uragh Wood, SW Ireland', *The Holocene*, Vol. 6, Issue 1, 90–9.

Long, P 2010a *N22 Tralee Bypass/Tralee to Bealagrellagh, Co. Kerry. Archaeological services contract, stage (i) and stage (ii)—standard test excavation and pre-excavation services. Final test excavation report, under Ministerial Directions Number A056 (E4152).* Unpublished report to Kerry County Council on behalf of Headland Archaeology (Ireland) Ltd.

Long, P 2010b *N22 Tralee Bypass/Tralee to Bealagrellagh, Co. Kerry. Archaeological services contract, stage (i) and stage (ii)—standard test excavation and pre-excavation services. Final test excavation report, under Ministerial Directions Number A056 (E4153).* Unpublished report to Kerry County Council on behalf of Headland Archaeology (Ireland) Ltd.

Long, P 2010c *N22 Tralee Bypass/Tralee to Bealagrellagh, Co. Kerry. Archaeological services contract, stage (i) and stage (ii)—standard test excavation and pre-excavation services. Final test excavation report, under Ministerial Directions Number A056 (E4154).* Unpublished report to Kerry County Council on behalf of Headland Archaeology (Ireland) Ltd.

Long, P 2010d *N22 Tralee Bypass/Tralee to Bealagrellagh, Co. Kerry. Archaeological services contract, stage (i) and stage (ii)—standard test excavation and pre-excavation services. Final test excavation report, under Ministerial Directions Number A056 (E4155).* Unpublished report to Kerry County Council on behalf of Headland Archaeology (Ireland) Ltd.

Long, P 2010e *N22 Tralee Bypass/Tralee to Bealagrellagh, Co. Kerry. Archaeological services contract, stage (i) and stage (ii)—standard test excavation and pre-excavation services. Final test excavation report, under Ministerial Directions Number A056 (E4151).* Unpublished report to Kerry County Council on behalf of Headland Archaeology (Ireland) Ltd.

Long, P 2012 'New discoveries near Kilflynn, Co. Kerry', *Journal of the Kerry Archaeological and Historical Society*, Series 2, Vol. 12, 45–56.

Lynch, A 1981 *Man and Environment in South-West Ireland, 4000 BC–AD 800: a study of man's impact on the development of soil and vegetation.* British Archaeological Reports, British Series 85. Oxford.

Lynch, G and Roundtree, S 2009 *Bricks: a guide to the repair of historic brickwork.* The Stationery Office, Dublin.

Lynch, L 2010 'Manor West, Killierisk, Tralee', *in* I Bennett (ed.), *Excavations 2007: summary accounts of archaeological excavations in Ireland*, 184. Wordwell, Dublin.

McClatchie, M, Bogaard, A, Colledge, S, Whitehouse, N, Schulting, R J, Barratt, P & McLaughlin, T R 2014 'Neolithic farming in north-western Europe: archaeobotanical evidence from Ireland', *Journal of Archaeological Science*, Vol. 51, 206–15.

McCormick, F, Kerr, T, McClatchie, M & O'Sullivan, A 2011 *The Archaeology of Livestock and Cereal Production in Early Medieval Ireland, AD 400–100.* Early Medieval Archaeology Project (EMAP) Report 5, submitted for Irish National Strategic Archaeological Research (INSTAR) programme (http://www.emap.ie/emap_reports.html, accessed December 2013).

McCracken, E 1971 *The Irish Woods Since Tudor Times.* David and Charles, Newton Abbot.

McDonnell, J G 2001 'Pyrotechnology', *in* D R Brothwell & A M Pollard (eds), *Handbook of Archaeological Sciences*, 493–505. Wiley, Chichester.

McGarry, T 2009 'Irish late prehistoric burial ring-ditches', *in* G Cooney, K Becker, J Coles, M Ryan & S Sievers (eds), *Relics of Old Decency: archaeological studies in later prehistory: festschrift for Barry Raftery*, 413–23. Wordwell, Dublin.

McKinley, J I 1994 'Bone fragment size in British cremation burials and its implications for pyre technology and ritual', *Journal of Archaeological Science*, Vol. 21, 339–42.

McKinley, J I 1997 'Bronze Age barrows and funerary rites and rituals of cremation', *Proceedings of the Prehistoric Society*, Vol. 63, 129–45.

MacMahon, B 2017 *The Great Famine in Tralee and North Kerry.* Mercier Press, Cork.

McNamara, C 2011 'Ireland in the "age of improvement"', *History Ireland*, Vol. 19, No. 2, 28–9.

McQuade, M, Molloy, B & Moriarty, C 2009 *In the Shadow of the Galtees: archaeological excavations along the N8 Cashel to Mitchelstown road scheme.* NRA Scheme Monographs 4. National Roads Authority, Dublin.

McSparron, J C & Williams, B B 2009 'The excavation of an early medieval rath with later medieval occupation at Drumadoon, Co. Antrim', *Proceedings of the Royal Irish Academy*, Vol 109C, 105–64.

Mallory, J P 1992 'A Neolithic settlement at Bay Farm II, Carnlough, Co. Antrim', *Ulster Journal of Archaeology*, Vol. 54–5 [1991/2], 3–12.

Mannion, M 2012 'Appendix 10—Report on the glass bead E4292:018:001', *in* S Hourihan, *N22 Tralee Bypass/Tralee to Bealagrellagh, Co. Kerry. Archaeological services contract, stage (iii)—excavation. Final excavation report for Knockawaddra West 2 in the townland of Knockawaddra West, Co. Kerry*. Report to Kerry County Council on behalf of Rubicon Heritage Services Ltd. TII Digital Heritage Collections, Digital Repository of Ireland (https://doi.org/10.7486/DRI.dz01d882p, accessed May 2019).

Marguerie, D & Hunout, J Y 2007 'Charcoal analysis and dendrochronology: data from archaeological sites in north-western France', *Journal of Archaeological Science*, Vol. 34, 1417–33.

Masser, P & Bailey, E 2008 *RN105–A4 Corridor Improvements (Dungannon–Ballygawley), Phase 2. Archaeological investigations of Site 1, Grange, Co. Tyrone*. Unpublished report to the Northern Ireland Road Service on behalf of Headland Archaeology (UK) Ltd.

Mears, R & Hillman, G 2007 *Wild Food*. Hodder & Stoughton, London.

Miller, J & Ramsay, S 2009 'Botanical evidence', *in* I Banks, P R J Duffy & G MacGregor (eds), 'Archaeology of landscape change in south-west Scotland, 6000 BC–AD 1400: excavations at William Grant and Sons Distillery, Girvan', *Scottish Archaeological Internet Reports*, Vol. 32, 1–45 (http://www.sair.org.uk/sair32, accessed March 2013).

Mitchell, F J G 1988 'The vegetational history of the Killarney Oakwoods, SW Ireland: evidence from fine spatial resolution pollen analysis', *Journal of Ecology*, Vol. 76, 415–36.

Mitchell, F J G 1990 'The history and vegetation dynamics of a yew wood (*Taxus baccata* L.) in S.W. Ireland', *New Phytologist*, Vol. 115, 573–7.

Mitchell, G F 1951 'Studies in Quaternary Deposits: No. 7', *Proceedings of the Royal Irish Academy*, Vol. 53B [1950/1], 111–206.

Mitchell, [G] F & Ryan, M 1997 *Reading the Irish Landscape*. Town House, Dublin.

Moloney, C 2012 'A possible prehistoric ceremonial avenue at Ballingowan, Tralee', *Journal of the Kerry Archaeological and Historical Society*, Series 2, Vol. 12, 57–68.

Monk, M 1981 'Post-Roman drying kilns and the problem of function: preliminary statement', *in* D Ó Corráin (ed.), *Irish antiquity: essays and studies presented to Professor M.J. O'Kelly*, 216–30. Tower Books, Cork.

Monk, M 1986 'Evidence from macroscopic plant remains for crop husbandry in prehistoric and early historic Ireland: a review', *Journal of Irish Archaeology*, Vol. 3 [1985/6], 31–6.

Monk, M 2007 'A greasy subject', *Archaeology Ireland*, Vol. 21, No. 1, 22–4.

Monk, M & Kelleher, E 2005 'An assessment of the archaeological evidence for Irish corn-drying kilns in the light of results of archaeological experiments and archaeobotanical studies', *Journal of Irish Archaeology*, Vol. 14, 77–144.

Monk, M & Power, O 2012 'More than a grain of truth emerges from a rash of corn-drying kilns?', *Archaeology Ireland*, Vol. 26, No. 2, 38–41.

Monk, M & Power, O 2014 'Casting light from the fires of corn-drying kilns on the Later Irish Iron Age', *Archaeology Ireland*, Vol. 28, No. 3, 39–42.

Moore, F 2010 'The ogham stones of County Kerry', *in* G Murray (ed.), *Medieval Treasures of County Kerry*, 6–18. Kerry County Museum, Tralee.

Moriarty, C 2011 *Irish Corn-Drying Kilns, their Bronze Age Origins?* (http://irisharchaeology.ie/2011/06/corn-drying-kilns-their-bronze-age-origins, accessed March 2014).

Mount, C 2011 *The Two Burial Traditions of the Beaker Period in Ireland* (http://charles-mount.ie/wp/?p=349, accessed March 2017).

Mytum, H 1992 *The Origins of Early Christian Ireland*. Routledge, London.

Nolan, J 2006 'Excavation of a children's burial ground at Tonybaun, Ballina, County Mayo', *in* J O'Sullivan & M Stanley (eds), *Settlement, Industry and Ritual. Proceedings of a public seminar on archaeological discoveries on national road schemes, September 2005*, 89–101. Archaeology and the National Roads Authority Monograph Series No. 3. National Roads Authority, Dublin.

Noonan, D & Johnston, P 2009 'Archaeological excavation report, N25 Rathsillagh to Harristown realignment, Bricketstown, Co. Wexford. Kiln, field systems, hearth, work surface', *Eachtra*, Issue 4 (http://eachtra.ie/index.php/journal/e0476-bricketstown-co-wexford/, accessed March 2012).

O'Brien, W 2004 *Ross Island. Mining, metal and society in early Ireland*. Bronze Age Studies 6. NUI Galway, Galway.

O'Callaghan, N 2009 'Ballymakegoge, Co. Kerry', *in* I Bennett (ed.), *Excavations 2006: summary accounts of archaeological excavations in Ireland*, 221. Wordwell, Dublin.

O'Callaghan, N 2011 'Caher, Co. Kerry' (https://excavations.ie/report/2011/Kerry/0022389/, accessed May 2019).

O Carroll, E 2012 'Appendix 2.2—Report on wood remains from Manor East 4, Co. Kerry, E4328', *in* S Delaney, *N22 Tralee Bypass/Tralee to Bealagrellagh: Manor East 4 (E4328) stage IV excavation report*. Report to Kerry County Council on behalf of Irish Archaeological Consultancy Ltd. TII Digital Heritage Collections, Digital Repository of Ireland (https://doi.org/10.7486/DRI.hx12b1027, accessed May 2019).

O'Carroll, G 2009 *The History of Tralee: its charter and governance*. Gerald O'Carroll, Tralee.

O'Connell, T J 2010 *Final Report on Archaeological Excavation at the Site of a Proposed Development at the Townland of Bruff & Ardykeohane in the Parish of Bruff, Coshma Barony, Co. Limerick*. Unpublished report to Limerick County Council on behalf of Headland Archaeology (Ireland) Ltd.

Ó Corráin, D 1972 *Ireland Before the Normans*. Gill and MacMillan, Dublin.

Ó Danachair, C 1972 'Traditional forms of the dwelling house in Ireland', *Journal of the Royal Society of Antiquaries of Ireland*, Vol. 102, Part 1, 77–96.

O'Donnell, L 2007 'Environmental archaeology: identifying patterns of exploitation in the Bronze Age. Charcoal and wood', *in* E Grogan, L O'Donnell & P Johnston (eds), *The Bronze Age Landscapes of the Pipeline to the West: an integrated archaeological and environmental assessment*, 27–69. Wordwell, Dublin.

O'Donnell, L 2009 'Charcoal results', *in* M McQuade, B Molloy & C Moriarty, *In the Shadow of the Galtees. Archaeological excavations along the N8 Cashel to Mitchelstown Road Scheme*, 243–

61. NRA Scheme Monographs 7. National Roads Authority, Dublin.
Ó Drisceoil, C 2005 'Excavation of a limekiln at Danecastle, Carrick-on-Bannow', *Journal of the Wexford Historical Society*, Vol. 20 [2004/5], 203–8.
Ó Drisceoil, D 1988 'Burnt mounds: cooking or bathing?', *Antiquity*, Vol. 62, 671–80.
Ó Faoláin, S 2004 'Meadowlands Hotel, Cloonalour, Tralee', *in* I Bennett (ed.), *Excavations 2002: summary accounts of archaeological excavations in Ireland*, 224–5. Wordwell, Bray.
Ó Faoláin, S 2010 'Killeisk 1', *in* I Bennett (ed.), *Excavations 2007: summary accounts of archaeological excavations in Ireland*, 485–6. Wordwell, Dublin.
O'Flaherty, E 2009 *Eighteenth Century Ireland: the long peace*. New Gill History of Ireland 4. Gill & Macmillan, Dublin.
O'Keeffe, T 1998 'Architectural traditions of the early medieval church in Munster', *in* M Monk and J Sheehan (eds), *Early Medieval Munster: archaeology, history and society*, 112–24. Cork University Press, Cork.
O'Kelly, M J 1952 'St Gobnet's House, Ballyvourney, Co. Cork', *Journal of the Cork Historical and Archaeological Society*, Vol. 57, 18–40.
O'Kelly, M J 1954 'Excavations and experiments in ancient Irish cooking places', *Journal of the Royal Society of Antiquaries of Ireland*, Vol. 95, 105–55.
O'Kelly, M J 1961 'The ancient Irish method of smelting iron', *in* G Bersu & W Dehn (eds), *V Internationaler Kongress für Vor- und Frügeshichte*, 459–61. Hamburg.
O'Kelly, M J 1963 'Two ringforts at Garryduff, Co. Cork', *Proceedings of the Royal Irish Academy*, Vol. 63C, 17–125.
O'Kelly, M J, Cleary, R & Lehane, D 1983 *Newgrange, Co. Meath, Ireland: the Late Neolithic–Beaker Period settlement*. British Archaeological Reports, International Series 190. Oxford.
Ó Ríordáin, S P 1942 'The excavation of a large earthen ringfort at Garranes, Co. Cork', *Proceedings of the Royal Irish Academy*, Vol. 47C [1941/2], 77–150.
O'Sullivan, A 1997 'Last foragers or first farmers?', *Archaeology Ireland*, Vol. 11, No. 2, 14–16.
O'Sullivan, A 2011 'Daily life and practice in an early medieval rath: encountering early Irish society through archaeology, history and palaeoecology', *in* C Corlett & M Potterton (eds), *Settlement in Early Medieval Ireland in the Light of Recent Archaeological Excavations*, 343–53. Wordwell, Dublin.
O'Sullivan, A & Nicholl, T 2010 'Early medieval settlement enclosures in Ireland: dwellings, daily life and social identity', *Proceedings of the Royal Irish Academy*, Vol. 111C, 59–90.
O'Sullivan, A & Sheehan, J 1996 *The Iveragh Peninsula: an archaeological survey of South Kerry*. Cork University Press, Cork.
O'Sullivan, A, McCormick, F, Harney, L, Kinsella, J & Kerr, F 2010 *Early Medieval Dwellings and Settlements in Ireland, AD 400–1100* (Vol. 1: text). Early Medieval Archaeology Project (EMAP) Report 4.2, submitted for Irish National Strategic Archaeological Research (INSTAR) programme (http://www.ucd.ie/archaeology/documentstore/allreports/emap_report_4.2vol1_print.pdf, accessed December 2013).
O'Sullivan, A, McCormick, F, Kerr, T & Harney, L 2014 *Early Medieval Ireland AD 400–1100*.

The evidence from archaeological excavations. Royal Irish Academy, Dublin.

O'Sullivan, M & Downey, L 2004 'Know your monuments: *Fulachta fiadh*', *Archaeology Ireland*, Vol. 18, No. 1, 35–7.

O'Sullivan, M & Downey, L 2005 'Know your monuments: Limekilns', *Archaeology Ireland*, Vol. 19, No. 2, 18–22.

Pavia, S & Bolton, J 2000 *Stone, Brick and Mortar*. Wordwell, Bray.

Pleiner, R 2000 *Iron in Archaeology: the European bloomery smelters*. Archeologický Ústav Avčr, Praha.

Plunkett, G 2009 'Land-use patterns and cultural change in the Middle to Late Bronze Age in Ireland: inferences from pollen records', *Vegetation History and Archaeobotany*, Vol. 18, No. 4, 273–95.

Pollock, D & Halpin, E 2011 'Killaspy B—Bronze Age fulacht fia and medieval smithy', *in* J Eogan & E Shee Twohig (eds), *Cois tSiúire—nine thousand years of human activity in the Lower Suir Valley*, 156–60. NRA Scheme Monographs 8. National Roads Authority, Dublin.

Pryor, F 1999 *Farmers in Prehistoric Britain*. Tempus, Stroud.

Quinn, B & Moore, D 2007 'Ale, brewing and *fulachta fiadh*', *Archaeology Ireland*, Vol. 21, No. 3, 8–11.

Raftery, B 1994 *Pagan Celtic Ireland: the enigma of the Irish Iron Age*. Thames and Hudson, London.

Raftery, B 2005 'Iron-age Ireland', *in* D Ó Cróinín (ed.), *A New History of Ireland. Prehistoric and early Ireland*, 134–81. Oxford University Press, Oxford.

Ramsey, W G 1989 *Middle Bronze Age Weapons in Ireland*. Unpublished PhD thesis, Queen's University Belfast.

Reilly, F, Brown, T, Davis, S, O'Brien, C & O'Donnell, L 2012 'Possible evidence of textile-processing from a burnt stone mound at Coonagh West, Co. Limerick', *Journal of Irish Archaeology*, Vol. 21, 57–84.

Reimer, P J, Baillie, M G L, Bard, E, Bayliss, A, Beck, J W, Blackwell, P G, Bronk Ramsey, C, Buck, C E, Burr, G S, Edwards, R L, Friedrich, M, Grootes, P M, Guilderson, T P, Hajdas, I, Heaton, T J, Hogg, A G, Hughen, K A, Kaiser, K F, Kromer, B, McCormac, F G, Manning, S W, Reimer, R W, Richards, D A, Southon, J R, Talamo, S, Turney, C S M, van der Plicht, J & Weyhenmeyer, C E 2009 'IntCal09 and Marine09 radiocarbon age calibration curves, 0–50,000 years cal BP', *Radiocarbon*, Vol. 51, No. 4, 1111–50.

Roche, H 1998 *Mounthawk, Tralee, Co. Kerry*. Unpublished report for Eachtra Archaeological Projects.

Roche, H 1999 *Cloghers I, Tralee, Co. Kerry*. Unpublished report for Eachtra Archaeological Projects.

Roche, H 2001 *Manor West, Tralee, Co. Kerry*. Unpublished report for Eachtra Archaeological Projects.

Roche, H & Grogan, E 2007 *The prehistoric pottery from Gortonora, Dingle, Co. Kerry*. Unpublished report for Eachtra Archaeological Projects.

Roche, H & Grogan, E 2012a 'Appendix 11—The prehistoric pottery from Manor East 1, Co. Kerry (E4323)', *in* L Clark, *N22 Tralee Bypass/Tralee to Bealagrellagh, Co. Kerry. Archaeological services contract, stage (iii)—excavation. Final excavation report for Manor East 1 in the townland of Manor East, Co. Kerry*. Report to Kerry County Council on behalf of Rubicon Heritage Services Ltd. TII Digital Heritage Collections, Digital Repository of Ireland (https://doi.org/10.7486/DRI.dr27bh148, accessed May 2019).

Roche, H & Grogan, E 2012b 'Appendix 10—The prehistoric pottery from Ballinorig West 2, Co. Kerry (E4306)', *in* L Clark, *N22 Tralee Bypass/Tralee to Bealagrellagh, Co. Kerry. Archaeological services contract, stage (iii)—excavation. Final excavation report for Ballinorig West 2 in the townland of Ballinorig West, Co. Kerry*. Report to Kerry County Council on behalf of Rubicon Heritage Services Ltd. TII Digital Heritage Collections, Digital Repository of Ireland (https://doi.org/10.7486/DRI.h4162w305, accessed May 2019).

Roche, H & Grogan, E 2012c 'Appendix 10—The prehistoric pottery from Ballingowan 1, Co. Kerry (E4288)', *in* C Moloney, *N22 Tralee Bypass/Tralee to Bealagrellagh, Co. Kerry. Archaeological services contract, stage (iii)—excavation. Final excavation report for Ballingowan 1 in the townland of Ballingowan, Co. Kerry*. Report to Kerry County Council on behalf of Rubicon Heritage Services Ltd. TII Digital Heritage Collections, Digital Repository of Ireland (https://doi.org/10.7486/DRI.hm517b50w, accessed May 2019).

Roche, H & Grogan, E 2012d 'Appendix 9—The prehistoric pottery from Ballynabrennagh Lower 1, Co. Kerry (E4297)', *in* S Hourihan, *N22 Tralee Bypass/Tralee to Bealagrellagh, Co. Kerry. Archaeological services contract, stage (iii)—excavation. Final excavation report for Ballynabrennagh Lower 1 in the townland of Ballynabrennagh Lower, Co. Kerry*. Report to Kerry County Council on behalf of Rubicon Heritage Services Ltd. TII Digital Heritage Collections, Digital Repository of Ireland (https://doi.org/10.7486/DRI.k643qk947, accessed May 2019).

Roche, H & Grogan, E 2012e 'Appendix 10—The prehistoric pottery from Ballinorig West 3, Co. Kerry (E4317)', *in* L Clark and C Troy, *N22 Tralee Bypass/Tralee to Bealagrellagh, Co. Kerry. Archaeological services contract, stage (iii)—excavation. Final excavation report for Ballinorig West 3 in the townland of Ballinorig West, Co. Kerry*. Report to Kerry County Council on behalf of Rubicon Heritage Services Ltd. TII Digital Heritage Collections, Digital Repository of Ireland (https://doi.org/10.7486/DRI.hd775j82p, accessed May 2019).

Rodwell, J S (ed.) 1991 *British Plant Communities, Vol. 1. Woods and scrub.* Cambridge University Press, Cambridge.

Ruvigny et Raineval, Marquis de 1904 *Morris of Ballybeggan and Castle Morris*. Privately printed.

Rynne, C 1999 *The Industrial Archaeology of Cork City and its Environs*. The Stationery Office, Dublin.

Rynne, C 2006 *Industrial Ireland 1750–1930. An archaeology*. The Collins Press, Cork.

Sayce, R 1945 'Canoes, coffins and cooking-troughs', *Proceedings of the Society of Antiquaries of Scotland*, Vol. 79, 106–11.

Schweingruber, F H 1990 *Microscopic Wood Anatomy* (3rd edn). Zürcher, Birmensdorf.

Scott, B G 1990 *Early Irish Ironworking.* Ulster Museum, Belfast.

Seaver, M 2006 'Through the mill—excavation of an early medieval settlement at Raystown', *in* J O'Sullivan & M Stanley (eds), *Settlement, Industry and Ritual. Proceedings of a public seminar on archaeological discoveries on national road schemes, September 2005*, 73–88. Archaeology and the National Roads Authority Monograph Series No. 3. National Roads Authority, Dublin.

Seaver, M 2011 'Interchange: excavations in an early medieval landscape at Glebe and Laughanstown, Co. Dublin', *in* C Corlett & M Potterton (eds), *Settlement in Early Medieval Ireland in the Light of Recent Archaeological Excavations*, 261–87. Wordwell, Dublin.

Sheridan, A 1995 'Irish Neolithic pottery: the story in 1995', *in* I Kinnes & G Varndell (eds), *Unbaked Urns of Rudely Shape: essays on British and Irish pottery for Ian Longworth*, 3–21. Oxbow Monograph 55. Oxbow Books, Oxford.

Smyth, J (ed.) 2009 *Brú na Bóinne World Heritage Site, Research Framework.* The Heritage Council, Dublin.

Smyth, J 2011a 'The house and group identity in the Irish Neolithic', *Proceedings of the Royal Irish Academy*, Vol. 111C, 1–31.

Smyth, J 2011b 'Breaking ground: an overview of pits and pit-digging in Neolithic Ireland', *in* J Thomas & H Anderson-Whymark (eds), *Regional Perspectives on Neolithic Pit Deposition: beyond the mundane*, 13–29. Oxbow Books, Oxford.

Smyth, J 2013 'Tides of change? The house through the Irish Neolithic', *in* D Hofmann & J Smyth (eds), *Tracking the Neolithic House in Europe*, 301–26. Springer Science and Business Media, New York.

Smyth, J 2014 *Settlement in the Irish Neolithic: new discoveries on the edge of Europe.* Prehistoric Society, Oxford.

Stace, C 2007 *New Flora of the British Isles* (2nd edn). Cambridge University Press, Cambridge.

Stefanini, B 2012a 'Appendix 2.4—Pollen assessment report for Manor East 4 and 7, N22 Tralee Bypass (E4328 and E4330)', *in* S Delaney, *N22 Tralee Bypass/Tralee to Bealagrellagh: Manor East 4 (E4328) stage IV excavation report.* Report to Kerry County Council on behalf of Irish Archaeological Consultancy Ltd. TII Digital Heritage Collections, Digital Repository of Ireland (https://doi.org/10.7486/DRI.hx12b1027, accessed May 2019).

Stefanini, B 2012b 'Appendix 2.4—Pollen assessment report for Manor East 4 and 7, N22 Tralee Bypass (E4328 and E4330)', *in* S Delaney, *N22 Tralee Bypass/Tralee to Bealagrellagh: Manor East 7 (E4330) stage IV excavation report.* Report to Kerry County Council on behalf of Irish Archaeological Consultancy Ltd. TII Digital Heritage Collections, Digital Repository of Ireland (https://doi.org/10.7486/DRI.g445rz90m, accessed May 2019).

Sternke, F 2012 'Appendix 10—Stone tool finds report for Knockawaddra Middle 2, Co. Kerry (E4295)', *in* S Hourihan and L Clark, *N22 Tralee Bypass/Tralee to Bealagrellagh, Co. Kerry. Archaeological services contract, stage (iii)—excavation. Final excavation report for Knockawaddra Middle 2 in the townland of Knockawaddra Middle, Co. Kerry.* Report to Kerry

County Council on behalf of Rubicon Heritage Services Ltd. TII Digital Heritage Collections, Digital Repository of Ireland (https://doi.org/10.7486/DRI.gt550678g, accessed May 2019).

Stout, M 1997 *The Irish Ringfort*. Four Courts Press, Dublin.

Stuijts, I 2005 'Wood and charcoal identification', *in* M Gowan, J Ó Néill & M Phillips (eds), *The Lisheen Mine Archaeological Project 1996–8*, 137–85. Wordwell, Bray.

Sweetman, P D 1985 'A Late Neolithic/Early Bronze Age pit circle at Newgrange, Co Meath', *Proceedings of the Royal Irish Academy*, Vol. 85C, 195–221.

Taylor, K 2010 'Ballynahinch', *in* I Bennett (ed.), *Excavations 2007: summary accounts of archaeological excavations in Ireland*, 440–2. Wordwell, Dublin.

Thomas, A 1992 *The Walled Towns of Ireland*, Vol. 2. Irish Academic Press, Dublin.

Thomas, J 1999 *Understanding the Neolithic*. Routledge, London.

Timpany, S 2011 *The Charred Plant Remains from Site E4089, Mahanagh 3, Co. Galway*. Report to Galway County Council on behalf of Headland Archaeology (Ireland) Ltd. TII Digital Heritage Collections, Digital Repository of Ireland (https://doi.org/10.7486/DRI.5h743987q, accessed May 2019).

Timpany, S 2015 'Environmental change in prehistory', *in* T Bolger, C Moloney and D Shiels (eds), *A Journey Along the Carlow Corridor. The archaeology of the M9 Carlow Bypass*, 77–86. National Roads Scheme Monograph Series No. 16. National Roads Authority, Dublin.

Timpany, S, Power, O & Monk, M 2011 'Agricultural boom and bust in medieval Ireland: plant macrofossil evidence from kiln sites along the N9/N10 in County Kildare', *in* S Conran, E Danaher & M Stanley (eds), *Past Times, Changing Fortunes. Proceedings of a public seminar on archaeological discoveries on national road schemes, August 2010*, 73–84. Archaeology and the National Roads Authority Monograph Series No. 8. National Roads Authority, Dublin.

Toal, C 1995 *North Kerry Archaeological Survey*. Brandon, Dingle.

Tourunen, A 2008 'Fauna and fulachta fiadh: animal bones from burnt mounds on the N9/N10 Carlow Bypass', *in* J O'Sullivan & M Stanley (eds), *Roads, Rediscovery and Research. Proceedings of a public seminar on archaeological discoveries on national road schemes, August 2007*, 37–44. Archaeology and the National Roads Authority Monograph Series No. 5. National Roads Authority, Dublin.

Tralee Town Council 2003 *Tralee Town Development Plan (2003–2009)*. Tralee Town Council, Tralee.

Troy, C 2011 *The Osteological Assemblage from Ask, Co. Wexford, E3502*. Report for Valerie J. Keeley Ltd. TII Digital Heritage Collections, Digital Repository of Ireland (https://doi.org/10.7486/DRI.h1291v592, accessed May 2019).

Troy, C 2015 'Contextualising cremations: evidence from prehistoric burials', *in* T Bolger, C Moloney & D Shiels (eds), *A Journey Along the Carlow Corridor. The archaeology of the M9 Carlow Bypass*, 131–44. NRA Scheme Monographs 16. National Roads Authority, Dublin.

Troy, C & Lalonde, S 2011 'Bronze Age bling—Wessex gold in an Offaly burial', *Offaly Heritage Journal*, Vol. 6, 14–24.

Waddell, J 1990 *The Bronze Age Burials of Ireland.* Galway University Press, Galway.

Waddell, J 2010 *The Prehistoric Archaeology of Ireland* (4th edn). Wordwell, Dublin.

Waddington, C 1997 'A review of "pit-alignments" and a tentative interpretation of the Milfield complex', *Durham Archaeological Journal*, Vol. 13, 21–2.

Wallace, A & Anguilano, L 2010 'Iron-smelting and smithing: new evidence emerging on Irish road schemes', *in* M Stanley, E Danaher & J Eogan (eds), *Creative Minds. Proceedings of a public seminar on archaeological discoveries on national road schemes, August 2009*, 69–84. Archaeology and the National Roads Authority Monograph Series No. 7. National Roads Authority, Dublin.

Walsh, F 2009 *Tober 1, Tober, Co. Offaly, Final Report. N6 Kinnegad–Athlone scheme phase 2: Kilbeggan to Athlone dual carriageway on behalf of Westmeath County Council.* Report to Westmeath County Council on behalf of Irish Archaeological Consultancy Ltd. TII Digital Heritage Collections, Digital Repository of Ireland (https://doi.org/10.7486/DRI.6w92hs62j, accessed May 2019).

Whitehouse, N J, Schulting, R J, McClatchie, M, Barratt, P, Rowan McLaughlin, T, Bogaard, A, Colledge, S, Marchant, R, Gaffrey, J & Bunting, M J 2014 'Neolithic agriculture on the European western frontier: the boom and bust of early farming in Ireland', *Journal of Archaeological Science*, Vol. 51, 181–205.

Woodman, P C 1985 *Excavations at Mount Sandel 1973–77.* Northern Ireland Archaeological Monographs No. 2. HMSO, Belfast.

Woodman, P C & Anderson, E 1990 'The Irish Later Mesolithic: a partial picture', *in* M Vermeersch & P Van Peer (eds), *Contributions to the Mesolithic in Europe*, 377–87. Leuven University Press, Leuven.

Woodman, P C, Anderson, E & Finlay, N 1999 *Excavations at Ferriter's Cove, 1983–95: last foragers, first farmers in the Dingle Peninsula.* Wordwell, Bray.

Woodman, P C, Finlay, N & Anderson, E 2006 *The Archaeology of a Collection: the Keiller–Knowles Collection of the National Museum of Ireland.* National Museum of Ireland Monograph Series 2. Wordwell, Bray.

Yates, D 2010 *N22 Tralee Bypass/Tralee to Bealagrellagh, Co. Kerry. Archaeological services contract, stage (i) and stage (ii)—standard test excavation and pre-excavation services.* Unpublished report to Kerry County Council on behalf of Headland Archaeology (Ireland) Ltd.

Index

Note: Page numbers in *italics* indicate illustrations.
Tables are indicated by (table) following the page number.